2021

Constitutional Law

2021 Supplement

Constitutional Law

Eighth Edition

Geoffrey R. Stone
Edward H. Levi Distinguished Service Professor of Law
University of Chicago Law School

Louis Michael Seidman
Carmack Waterhouse Professor of Constitutional Law
Georgetown University Law Center

Cass R. Sunstein
Robert Walmsley University Professor
Harvard Law School

Mark V. Tushnet
William Nelson Cromwell Professor of Law
Harvard Law School

Pamela S. Karlan
Kenneth & Harle Montgomery Professor of Public Interest Law
Stanford Law School

Aziz Z. Huq
Frank and Bernice J. Greenberg Professor of Law
University of Chicago Law School

SUSTAINABLE FORESTRY INITIATIVE

Certified Chain of Custody
At Least 10% Certified Forest Content
www.sfiprogram.org
SFI-01028

About Wolters Kluwer Legal & Regulatory U.S.

Wolters Kluwer Legal & Regulatory U.S. delivers expert content and solutions in the areas of law, corporate compliance, health compliance, reimbursement, and legal education. Its practical solutions help customers successfully navigate the demands of a changing environment to drive their daily activities, enhance decision quality and inspire confident outcomes.

Serving customers worldwide, its legal and regulatory portfolio includes products under the Aspen Publishers, CCH Incorporated, Kluwer Law International, ftwilliam.com and MediRegs names. They are regarded as exceptional and trusted resources for general legal and practice-specific knowledge, compliance and risk management, dynamic workflow solutions, and expert commentary.

Contents

Table of Cases

Table of Authorities

Weinstein, Hate Speech Bans, Democracy, and Political Legitimacy, 32 Const. Comm. 527 (2017), 1221

Wells, Free Speech Hypocrisy: Campus Free Speech Conflicts and the Sub-Legal First Amendment, 89 U. Colo. L. Rev. 533 (2018), 1074

Werbel, A., Lust on Trial (2018), 1164

West, Favoring the Press, 106 Cal. L. Rev. 91, 94-95 (2018), 1415

Winkler, A., We the Corporations 372-373 (2018), 1385

Wright, The Heckler's Veto Today, 68 Case W. Res. L. Rev. 159 (2017), 1074

Wu, Is the First Amendment Obsolete?, in L. Bollinger & G. Stone, The Free Speech Century 272-273 (2019), 1430

Wurman, Nondelegation at the Founding, 130 Yale L.J. 1490, 1495 (2021), 437

Zick, T., The First Amendment in the Trump Era 2-4 (2019), 1401

BIOGRAPHICAL NOTES ON SELECTED U.S. SUPREME COURT JUSTICES

Page lxiv.

After the biography of Justice Alito, add the following:

AMY CONEY BARRETT (1972-): Following the death of Justice Ruth Bader Ginsburg, President Donald Trump appointed Amy Coney Barrett as her successor. Barrett's nomination was controversial because four years earlier Senate Republicans had refused even to hold hearings on President Obama's 2016 nomination of Merrick Garland, arguing that the Senate should not consider Supreme Court nominations during the last year of a president's term. In Barrett's case, though, Republican senators rushed to confirm Barrett in the final months of Trump's term of office. Barrett was confirmed by a vote of 52-48. In earlier years, Barrett attended the Notre Dame Law School, graduating first in her class in 1997. She then clerked for Judge Lawrence Silberman on the D.C. Circuit and then for Supreme Court Justice Antonin Scalia. After a few years of practice, Barrett joined the faculty at Notre Dame Law School, where she taught federal courts, evidence, constitutional law, and statutory interpretation. In 2017, President Trump nominated Barrett to the United States Court of Appeals for the Seventh Circuit. A controversial nominee in part because she made clear in her scholarship the importance of her Catholic faith to her understanding and analysis of the law, she was confirmed by a sharply divided vote of 52-43. Three years later, President Trump nominated Barrett to the Supreme Court.

After the biography of Justice Kagan, add the following:

BRETT KAVANAUGH (1965-): When Brett Kavanaugh assumed his seat on the Supreme Court, he became the first justice in American history to replace the justice for whom he clerked. Along with his fellow Justice, Neil Gorsuch, Kavanaugh had clerked for Anthony Kennedy during the 1993 Term. (Gorsuch and Kavanaugh also attended the same high school). Before his appointment to the high court, Kavanaugh worked for Ken Starr as Associate Counsel in the Office of Special Counsel that investigated President Clinton and was widely credited with being the principal author of the "Starr Report" to Congress on Clinton's alleged misconduct. In 2000, he was part of the legal team that worked for candidate George W. Bush during the dispute over the Florida election recount. He then joined the Bush administration as Associate White House Counsel, Assistant to the President, and White House Staff Secretary. After a period in private practice, he served on the United States Court of Appeals for the District of Columbia Circuit from 2006 until his appointment to the Supreme Court. Because Justice Kennedy was widely viewed as a centrist, and because Kavanaugh was expected to push the Court in a conservative direction, his nomination was bound to be controversial. The hearings became explosive when Christine Blasey Ford, a psychology professor at Palo Alto University, accused him of sexually assaulting her when they were high school students. Kavanaugh denied the charges and, in angry testimony before the Senate Judiciary Committee, characterized the charges as "a calculated and orchestrated political hit." Despite the charges, the Committee voted to send Kavanaugh's nomination to the Senate floor, where he was confirmed on a near party-line vote.

I
THE CONSTITUTION AND THE SUPREME COURT

E. *"Case or Controversy" Requirements and the Passive Virtues*

Page 114.   Before the Note, add the following:

GILL v. WHITFORD

138 S. Ct. 1916 (2018)

CHIEF JUSTICE ROBERTS delivered the opinion of the Court.

The State of Wisconsin, like most other States, entrusts to its legislature the periodic task of redrawing the boundaries of the State's legislative districts. A group of Wisconsin Democratic voters filed a complaint in the District Court, alleging that the legislature carried out this task with an eye to diminishing the ability of Wisconsin Democrats to convert Democratic votes into Democratic seats in the legislature. The plaintiffs asserted that, in so doing, the legislature had infringed their rights under the First and Fourteenth Amendments. . . .

[Certain] of the plaintiffs before us alleged that they had [a] personal stake in this case, but never followed up with the requisite proof. The District Court and this Court therefore lack the power to resolve their claims. We vacate the judgment and remand the case for further proceedings, in the course of which those plaintiffs may attempt to demonstrate standing in accord with the analysis in this opinion.

I

Wisconsin's Legislature consists of a State Assembly and a State Senate. The 99 members of the Assembly are chosen from single districts that must "consist of contiguous territory and be in as compact form as practicable." State senators are likewise chosen from single-member districts, which are laid on top of the State Assembly districts so that three Assembly districts form one Senate district.

The Wisconsin Constitution gives the legislature the responsibility to "apportion and district anew the members of the senate and assembly" at the first session following each census. In recent decades, however, that responsibility has just as often been taken up by federal courts. Following the census in 1980, 1990, and 2000, federal courts drew the State's legislative districts when the Legislature and the Governor—split on party lines—were unable to agree on new districting plans. The Legislature has broken the logjam just twice in the last 40 years. In 1983, a Democratic Legislature passed, and a Democratic Governor signed, a new districting plan that remained in effect until the 1990 census. In 2011, a Republican Legislature passed, and a Republican Governor signed, the districting plan at issue here, known as Act 43. Following the passage of Act 43, Republicans won majorities in the State Assembly in the 2012 and 2014 elections. In 2012, Republicans won 60 Assembly seats with 48.6% of the two-party statewide vote for Assembly candidates. In 2014, Republicans won 63 Assembly seats with 52% of the statewide vote.

In July 2015, twelve Wisconsin voters filed a complaint in the Western District of Wisconsin challenging Act 43. The plaintiffs identified themselves as "supporters of the public policies espoused by the Democratic Party and of Democratic Party candidates." They alleged that Act 43 is a partisan gerrymander that "unfairly favor[s] Republican voters and candidates," and that it does so by "cracking" and "packing" Democratic voters around Wisconsin.

As they explained:

Cracking means dividing a party's supporters among multiple districts so that they fall short of a majority in each one. Packing means concentrating one party's backers in a few districts that they win by overwhelming margins.

Four of the plaintiffs—Mary Lynne Donohue, Wendy Sue Johnson, Janet Mitchell, and Jerome Wallace—alleged that they lived in State Assembly districts where Democrats have been cracked or packed. All of the plaintiffs also alleged that, regardless of "whether they themselves reside in a district that has been packed or cracked," they have been "harmed by the manipulation of district boundaries" because Democrats statewide "do not have the same opportunity provided to Republicans to elect representatives of their choice to the Assembly."

The plaintiffs argued that, on a statewide level, the degree to which packing and cracking has favored one party over another can be measured by a single calculation: an "efficiency gap" that compares each party's respective "wasted" votes across all legislative districts. "Wasted" votes are those cast for a losing candidate or for a winning candidate in excess of what that candidate needs to win. The plaintiffs alleged that Act 43 resulted in an unusually large efficiency gap that favored Republicans. . . .

Over the past five decades this Court has been repeatedly asked to decide what judicially enforceable limits, if any, the Constitution sets on the gerrymandering of voters along partisan lines. Our previous attempts at an answer have left few clear landmarks for addressing the question. What our precedents have to say on the topic is, however, instructive as to the myriad

3

competing considerations that partisan gerrymandering claims involve. Our efforts to sort through those considerations have generated conflicting views both of how to conceive of the injury arising from partisan gerrymandering and of the appropriate role for the Federal Judiciary in remedying that injury. . . .

Our considerable efforts in [previous cases] leave unresolved whether such claims may be brought in cases involving allegations of partisan gerrymandering. In particular, two threshold questions remain: what is necessary to show standing in a case of this sort, and whether those claims are justiciable. Here we do not decide the latter question because the plaintiffs in this case have not shown standing under the theory upon which they based their claims for relief. . . .

We have long recognized that a person's right to vote is "individual and personal in nature." Thus, "voters who allege facts showing disadvantage to themselves as individuals have standing to sue" to remedy that disadvantage. The plaintiffs in this case alleged that they suffered such injury from partisan gerrymandering, which works through "packing" and "cracking" voters of one party to disadvantage those voters. That is, the plaintiffs claim a constitutional right not to be placed in legislative districts deliberately designed to "waste" their votes in elections where their chosen candidates will win in landslides (packing) or are destined to lose by closer margins (cracking).

To the extent the plaintiffs' alleged harm is the dilution of their votes, that injury is district specific. An individual voter in Wisconsin is placed in a single district. He votes for a single representative. [Its boundaries determine] whether and to what extent a particular voter is packed or cracked. This "disadvantage to [the voter] as [an] individual," therefore results from the boundaries of the particular district in which he resides. And a plaintiff's remedy must be "limited to the inadequacy that produced [his] injury in fact." In this case the remedy that is proper and sufficient lies in the revision of the boundaries of the individual's own district.

For similar reasons, we have held that a plaintiff who alleges that he is the object of a racial gerrymander — a drawing of district lines on the basis of race—has standing to assert only that his own district has been so gerrymandered. A plaintiff who complains of gerrymandering, but who does not live in a gerrymandered district, "assert[s] only a generalized grievance against governmental conduct of which he or she does not approve." Plaintiffs who complain of racial gerrymandering in their State cannot sue to invalidate the whole State's legislative districting map; such complaints must proceed "district-by-district." . . .

Here, the plaintiffs' partisan gerrymandering claims turn on allegations that their votes have been diluted. That harm arises from the particular composition of the voter's own district, which causes his vote—having been packed or cracked—to carry less weight than it would carry in another, hypothetical district. Remedying the individual voter's harm, therefore, does not necessarily require restructuring all of the State's legislative districts. It requires revising only such districts as are necessary to reshape the voter's district—so that the voter may be unpacked or uncracked, as the case may be. . . .

The plaintiffs argue that their legal injury is not limited to the injury that they have suffered as individual voters, but extends also to the statewide harm to their interest "in their collective representation in the legislature," and in influencing the legislature's overall "composition and policymaking." But our cases to date have not found that this presents an individual and personal injury of the kind required for Article III standing. On the facts of this case, the plaintiffs may not rely on "the kind of undifferentiated, generalized grievance about the conduct of government that we have refused to countenance in the past." A citizen's interest in the overall composition of the legislature is embodied in his right to vote for his representative. . . .

We leave for another day consideration of other possible theories of harm not presented here and whether those theories might present justiciable claims giving rise to statewide remedies. . . . The reasoning of this Court with respect to the disposition of this case is set forth in this opinion and none other. And the sum of the standing principles articulated here, as applied to this case, is that

5

the harm asserted by the plaintiffs is best understood as arising
from a burden on those plaintiffs' own votes. In this gerrymandering context that burden arises through a voter's placement in a
"cracked" or "packed" district.

II

Four of the plaintiffs in this case—Mary Lynne Donohue, Wendy
Sue Johnson, Janet Mitchell, and Jerome Wallace—pleaded a
particularized burden along such lines. They alleged that Act 43
had "dilut[ed] the influence" of their votes as a result of packing or cracking in their legislative districts. The facts necessary
to establish standing, however, must not only be alleged at the
pleading stage, but also proved at trial. As the proceedings in the
District Court progressed to trial, the plaintiffs failed to meaningfully pursue their allegations of individual harm. The plaintiffs
did not seek to show such requisite harm since, on this record, it
appears that not a single plaintiff sought to prove that he or she
lives in a cracked or packed district. They instead rested their case
at trial—and their arguments before this Court—on their theory
of statewide injury to Wisconsin Democrats, in support of which
they offered three kinds of evidence.

First, the plaintiffs presented the testimony of the lead plaintiff,
Professor Whitford. But Whitford's testimony does not support
any claim of packing or cracking of himself as a voter. Indeed,
Whitford expressly acknowledged that Act 43 did not affect the
weight of his vote. His testimony points merely to his hope of
achieving a Democratic majority in the legislature—what the
plaintiffs describe here as their shared interest in the composition
of "the legislature as a whole." Under our cases to date, that is a
collective political interest, not an individual legal interest, and
the Court must be cautious that it does not become "a forum for
generalized grievances."

Second, the plaintiffs provided evidence regarding the mapmakers' deliberations as they drew district lines. As the District Court
recounted, the plaintiffs' evidence showed that the mapmakers

"test[ed] the partisan makeup and performance of districts as they might be configured in different ways." Each of the map-makers' alternative configurations came with a table that listed the number of "Safe" and "Lean" seats for each party, as well as "Swing" seats. The mapmakers also labeled certain districts as ones in which "GOP seats [would be] strengthened a lot," or which would result in "Statistical Pick Ups" for Republicans. And they identified still other districts in which "GOP seats [would be] strengthened a little," "weakened a little," or were "likely lost."

[That] evidence may well be pertinent with respect to any ultimate determination whether the plaintiffs may prevail in their claims against the defendants, assuming such claims present a jus-ticiable controversy. But the question at this point is whether the plaintiffs have established injury in fact. That turns on effect, not intent, and requires a showing of a burden on the plaintiffs' votes that is "actual or imminent, not 'conjectural' or 'hypothetical.' "

Third, the plaintiffs offered evidence concerning the impact that Act 43 had in skewing Wisconsin's statewide political map in favor of Republicans. This evidence, which made up the heart of the plaintiffs' case, was derived from partisan-asymmetry studies. . . . The plaintiffs contend that these studies measure de-viations from "partisan symmetry," which they describe as the "social scientific tenet that [districting] maps should treat parties symmetrically." In the District Court, the plaintiffs' case rested largely on a particular measure of partisan asymmetry — the "ef-ficiency gap" of wasted votes. That measure was first developed in two academic articles published shortly before the initiation of this lawsuit. . . .

The plaintiffs and their *amici curiae* promise us that the effi-ciency gap and similar measures of partisan asymmetry will allow the federal courts — armed with just "a pencil and paper or a hand calculator" — to finally solve the problem of partisan gerryman-dering that has confounded the Court for decades. We need not doubt the plaintiffs' math. The difficulty for standing purposes is that these calculations are an average measure. They do not address the effect that a gerrymander has on the votes of particular citizens. Partisan-asymmetry metrics such as the efficiency gap measure something else entirely: the effect that a gerrymander has on the fortunes of political parties.

Consider the situation of Professor Whitford, who lives in District 76, where, defendants contend, Democrats are "naturally" packed due to their geographic concentration, with that of plaintiff Mary Lynne Donohue, who lives in Assembly District 26 in Sheboygan, where Democrats like her have allegedly been deliberately cracked. By all accounts, Act 43 has not affected Whitford's individual vote for his Assembly representative—even plaintiffs' own demonstration map resulted in a virtually identical district for him. Donohue, on the other hand, alleges that Act 43 burdened her individual vote. Yet neither the efficiency gap nor the other measures of partisan asymmetry offered by the plaintiffs are capable of telling the difference between what Act 43 did to Whitford and what it did to Donohue. The single statewide measure of partisan advantage delivered by the efficiency gap treats Whitford and Donohue as indistinguishable, even though their individual situations are quite different.

That shortcoming confirms the fundamental problem with the plaintiffs' case as presented on this record. It is a case about group political interests, not individual legal rights. But this Court is not responsible for vindicating generalized partisan preferences. The Court's constitutionally prescribed role is to vindicate the individual rights of the people appearing before it.

In cases where a plaintiff fails to demonstrate Article III standing, we usually direct the dismissal of the plaintiff's claims. This is not the usual case. It concerns an unsettled kind of claim this Court has not agreed upon, the contours and justiciability of which are unresolved. Under the circumstances, and in light of the plaintiffs' allegations that Donohue, Johnson, Mitchell, and Wallace live in districts where Democrats like them have been packed or cracked, we decline to direct dismissal.

We therefore remand the case to the District Court so that the plaintiffs may have an opportunity to prove concrete and particularized injuries using evidence—unlike the bulk of the evidence presented thus far—that would tend to demonstrate a burden on their individual votes. We express no view on the merits of the plaintiffs' case. We caution, however, that "standing is not dispensed in gross": A plaintiff's remedy must be tailored to redress the plaintiff's particular injury.

The judgment of the District Court is vacated, and the case is remanded for further proceedings consistent with this opinion.

It is so ordered.

JUSTICE KAGAN, with whom JUSTICE GINSBURG, JUSTICE BREYER, and JUSTICE SOTOMAYOR join, concurring. . . .

I write to address in more detail what kind of evidence the present plaintiffs (or any additional ones) must offer to support that allegation. And I write to make some observations about what would happen if they succeed in proving standing—that is, about how their vote dilution case could then proceed on the merits. The key point is that the case could go forward in much the same way it did below: Given the charges of statewide packing and cracking, affecting a slew of districts and residents, the challengers could make use of statewide evidence and seek a statewide remedy.

I also write separately because I think the plaintiffs may have wanted to do more than present a vote dilution theory. Partisan gerrymandering no doubt burdens individual votes, but it also causes other harms. And at some points in this litigation, the plaintiffs complained of a different injury—an infringement of their First Amendment right of association. The Court rightly does not address that alternative argument: The plaintiffs did not advance it with sufficient clarity or concreteness to make it a real part of the case. But because on remand they may well develop the associational theory, I address the standing requirement that would then apply. As I'll explain, a plaintiff presenting such a theory would not need to show that her particular voting district was packed or cracked for standing purposes because that fact would bear no connection to her substantive claim. Indeed, everything about the litigation of that claim—from standing on down to remedy—would be statewide in nature.

Partisan gerrymandering, as this Court has recognized, is "incompatible with democratic principles." More effectively every day, that practice enables politicians to entrench themselves in power against the people's will. And only the courts can do anything to remedy the problem, because gerrymanders benefit those who control the political branches. None of those facts gives judges any excuse to disregard Article III's demands. The Court is right to say they were not met here. But partisan gerrymandering injures enough individuals and organizations in enough concrete ways to ensure that standing requirements, properly applied, will not often or long prevent courts from reaching the merits of cases like this one. Or from insisting, when they do, that partisan officials stop degrading the nation's democracy.

I . . .

The harm of vote dilution, as this Court has long stated, is "individual and personal in nature." It arises when an election practice — most commonly, the drawing of district lines — devalues one citizen's vote as compared to others. Of course, such practices invariably affect more than one citizen at a time. [But] we understood the injury as giving diminished weight to each particular vote, even if millions were so touched. In such cases, a voter living in an overpopulated district suffered "disadvantage to [herself] as [an] individual [ ]": Her vote counted for less than the votes of other citizens in her State. And that kind of disadvantage is what a plaintiff asserting a vote dilution claim — in the one-person, one-vote context or any other — always alleges.

To have standing to bring a partisan gerrymandering claim based on vote dilution, then, a plaintiff must prove that the value of her own vote has been "contract[ed]." And that entails showing, as the Court holds, that she lives in a district that has been either packed or cracked, for packing and cracking are the ways in which a partisan gerrymander dilutes votes. Consider the perfect form of each variety. When a voter resides in a packed district, her preferred candidate will win no matter what; when a voter

10

lives in a cracked district, her chosen candidate stands no chance of prevailing. But either way, such a citizen's vote carries less weight—has less consequence—than it would under a neutrally drawn map. So when she shows that her district has been packed or cracked, she proves, as she must to establish standing, that she is "among the injured."

In many partisan gerrymandering cases, that threshold showing will not be hard to make. Among other ways of proving packing or cracking, a plaintiff could produce an alternative map (or set of alternative maps)—comparably consistent with traditional districting principles—under which her vote would carry more weight. For example, a Democratic plaintiff living in a 75%-Democratic district could prove she was packed by presenting a different map, drawn without a focus on partisan advantage, that would place her in a 60%-Democratic district. Or conversely, a Democratic plaintiff residing in a 35%-Democratic district could prove she was cracked by offering an alternative, neutrally drawn map putting her in a 50-50 district. The precise numbers are of no import. The point is that the plaintiff can show, through drawing alternative district lines, that partisan-based packing or cracking diluted her vote.

Here, the Court is right that the plaintiffs have so far failed to make such a showing. William Whitford was the only plaintiff to testify at trial about the alleged gerrymander's effects. He expressly acknowledged that his district would be materially identical under any conceivable map, whether or not drawn to achieve partisan advantage. That means Wisconsin's plan could not have diluted Whitford's own vote. . . . Four other plaintiffs differed from Whitford by alleging in the complaint that they lived in packed or cracked districts. But for whatever reason, they failed to back up those allegations with evidence as the suit proceeded. So they too did not show the injury—a less valuable vote—central to their vote dilution theory.

That problem, however, may be readily fixable. The Court properly remands this case to the District Court "so that the plaintiffs may have an opportunity" to "demonstrate a burden on their individual votes." That means the plaintiffs—both the four who initially made those assertions and any others (current or newly joined)—now can introduce evidence that their individual districts were packed or cracked. And if the plaintiffs' more general charges have a basis in fact, that evidence may well be at hand. Recall that the plaintiffs here alleged—and the District Court found—that a unified Republican government set out to ensure that Republicans would control as many State Assembly seats as possible over a decade (five consecutive election cycles). To that end, the government allegedly packed and cracked Democrats throughout the State, not just in a particular district or region. Assuming that is true, the plaintiffs should have a mass of packing and cracking proof, which they can now also present in district-by-district form to support their standing. In other words, a plaintiff residing in each affected district can show, through an alternative map or other evidence, that packing or cracking indeed occurred there. And if (or to the extent) that test is met, the court can proceed to decide all distinctive merits issues and award appropriate remedies.

When the court addresses those merits questions, it can consider statewide (as well as local) evidence. Of course, the court below and others like it are currently debating, without guidance from this Court, what elements make up a vote dilution claim in the partisan gerrymandering context. But assume that the plaintiffs must prove illicit partisan intent—a purpose to dilute Democrats' votes in drawing district lines. The plaintiffs could then offer evidence about the mapmakers' goals in formulating the entire statewide map (which would predictably carry down to individual districting decisions). So, for example, the plaintiffs here introduced proof that the mapmakers looked to partisan voting data when drawing districts throughout the State—and that they graded draft maps according to the amount of advantage those maps conferred on Republicans. . . .

Similarly, cases like this one might warrant a statewide remedy. Suppose that mapmakers pack or crack a critical mass of State

Assembly districts all across the State to elect as many Republican politicians as possible. And suppose plaintiffs residing in those districts prevail in a suit challenging that gerrymander on a vote dilution theory. The plaintiffs might then receive exactly the relief sought in this case. [The] Court recognizes as much. It states that a proper remedy in a vote dilution case "does not *necessarily* require restructuring all of the State's legislative districts." Not necessarily — but possibly. It all depends on how much redistricting is needed to cure all the packing and cracking that the mapmakers have done.

II

Everything said so far relates only to suits alleging that a partisan gerrymander dilutes individual votes. [But] partisan gerrymanders inflict other kinds of constitutional harm as well. Among those injuries, partisan gerrymanders may infringe the First Amendment rights of association held by parties, other political organizations, and their members. The plaintiffs here have sometimes pointed to that kind of harm. To the extent they meant to do so, and choose to do so on remand, their associational claim would occasion a different standing inquiry than the one in the Court's opinion. . . .

Standing, we have long held, "turns on the nature and source of the claim asserted." Indeed, that idea lies at the root of today's opinion. It is because the Court views the harm alleged as vote dilution that it (rightly) insists that each plaintiff show packing or cracking in her own district to establish her standing. But when the harm alleged is not district specific, the proof needed for standing should not be district specific either. And the associational injury flowing from a statewide partisan gerrymander, whether alleged by a party member or the party itself, has nothing to do with the packing or cracking of any single district's lines. The complaint in such a case is instead that the gerrymander has burdened the ability of like-minded people across the State to affiliate in a political party and carry out that organization's activities and objects.

Because a plaintiff can have that complaint without living in a packed or cracked district, she need not show what the Court demands today for a vote dilution claim. Or said otherwise: Because on this alternative theory, the valued association and the injury to it are statewide, so too is the relevant standing requirement.

On occasion, the plaintiffs here have indicated that they have an associational claim in mind. In addition to repeatedly alleging vote dilution, their complaint asserted in general terms that Wisconsin's districting plan infringes their "First Amendment right to freely associate with each other without discrimination by the State based on that association." Similarly, the plaintiffs noted before this Court that "[b]eyond diluting votes, partisan gerrymandering offends First Amendment values by penalizing citizens because of . . . their association with a political party." And finally, the plaintiffs' evidence of partisan asymmetry well fits a suit alleging associational injury. . . .

In the end, though, I think the plaintiffs did not sufficiently advance a First Amendment associational theory to avoid the Court's holding on standing. Despite referring to that theory in their complaint, the plaintiffs tried this case as though it were about vote dilution alone. . . .

But nothing in the Court's opinion prevents the plaintiffs on remand from pursuing an associational claim, or from satisfying the different standing requirement that theory would entail. [Nothing] about that injury is "generalized" or "abstract," as the Court says is true of the plaintiffs' dissatisfaction with the "overall composition of the legislature." A suit raising an associational theory complains of concrete "burdens on a disfavored party" and its members as they pursue their political interests and goals. And when the suit alleges that a gerrymander has imposed those burdens on a statewide basis, then its litigation should be statewide too — as to standing, liability, and remedy alike. . . .

[An opinion by Justice Thomas, joined by Justice Gorsuch, concurring in part and concurring in the judgment has been omitted.]

Page 118.   Before section b of the Note, add the following:

In Trump v. Hawaii, 138 S. Ct. 2392 (2018), the Court upheld a presidential proclamation that imposed a "travel ban" on nationals from certain countries. (The case is discussed in greater detail in the supplement to page 1487 of the Main Volume). Before resolving the merits, the Court explored the question of standing. It bracketed the question whether plaintiffs might have standing on the ground that the proclamation violated their right to be free from federal establishments of religion. Instead it noted that the "three individual plaintiffs assert another, more concrete injury: the alleged real-world effect that the Proclamation has had in keeping them separated from certain relatives who seek to enter the country." The Court agreed "that a person's interest in being united with his relatives is sufficiently concrete and particularized to form the basis of an Article III injury in fact."

Page 121.   At the end of section c of this Note, add the following:

In Virginia House of Delegates v. Bethune-Hill, 139 S. Ct. 1945 (2019), the Court held that the Virginia House of Delegates lacked standing to object to a judicial ruling that districts had been racially gerrymandered in violation of the Equal Protection Clause. The House claimed to represent the state of Virginia, but the Court could find no legal basis for that claimed authority. Under Virginia law, the Attorney General represents the state. The Court added: "This Court has never held that a judicial decision invalidating a state law as unconstitutional inflicts a discrete, cognizable injury on each organ of government that participated in the law's passage. The Court's precedent thus lends no support for the notion that one House of a bicameral legislature, resting solely on its role in the legislative process, may appeal on its own behalf a judgment invalidating a state enactment." True, the House helps to draw up the redistricting plan, but under the Virginia Constitution, redistricting authority is allocated to the "General Assembly," of which the House is only a part.

Page 127.   Add the following at the end of the first full paragraph:

In *Carney v. Adams*, 141 S. Ct. 493 (2020), the Court applied the "ready and able" standard to hold that a plaintiff could not challenge Deleware's rules for judicial eligibility when he had failed to apply for open judicial positions when able, and when he had changed his partisan affiliation so as to make himself ineligible for a judicial nomination, and thus in a position to file a constitutional challenge.

Page 128.   At the end of Note 4, add the following:

In *Uzuegbunam v. Preczewski*, 141 S. Ct. 792 (2021), two university students sued officials at their university over the institution's free speech policy. After the university discontinued the challenged policy, one of the plaintiffs sought nominal damages for its past enforcement. The Court held that nominal damages can redress the completed constitutional violation that allegedly occurred when campus officials enforced the speech policies against him. Looking to English and American common law, the Court found a rule allowing nominal damages for a violation of any legal right. "A contrary rule would have meant, in many cases, that there was no remedy at all for those rights, such as due process or voting rights, that were not readily reducible to monetary valuation."

Contrast *Uzuegbunam* with *California v. Texas*, ___ S. Ct. ___ (2021), where the Court rejected a challenge to the Patient

Protection and Affordable Care Act (ACA) for the third time. As enacted in 2010, ACA required most Americans to obtain minimum health insurance coverage. It imposed a monetary penalty on those who failed to do so. In 2017, Congress reset this penalty to zero dollars. The Court held that neither individual nor state plaintiffs had standing to challenge the constitutionality of the zero-dollar-penalty insurance mandate under the Taxing Power. The individual plaintiffs could not satisfy the traceability requirement because "there is no possible Government action that is causally connected to the plaintiffs' injury — the costs of purchasing health insurance." The Court explained that their request for a declaratory judgment did not create standing because such relief can only be issued if the underlying dispute could *otherwise* be heard in federal court, i.e., in an action for damages or an injunction. The plaintiffs could not, however, seek damages or an injunction given the absence of government action against them.

The state plaintiffs, for similar reasons, "failed to show that the challenged minimum essential coverage provision, without any prospect of penalty, will harm them by leading more individuals to enroll" in other state-run healthcare programs and hence impose financial costs on the states. The Court also rejected a theory of standing based on other provisions beyond the mandate:

> The state plaintiffs add that § 5000A(a)'s minimum essential coverage provision also causes them to incur additional costs directly. They point to the costs of providing beneficiaries of state health plans with information about their health insurance coverage, as well as the cost of furnishing the IRS with that related information. The problem with these claims, however, is that other provisions of Act, not the minimum essential coverage provision, impose these other requirements. Nothing in the text of these form provisions suggests that they would not operate without § 5000A(a). To show that the minimum essential coverage requirement is unconstitutional would not show that enforcement of any of these other provisions violates the Constitution. The

state plaintiffs do not claim the contrary. The Government's conduct in question is therefore not "fairly traceable" to enforcement of the "allegedly unlawful" provision of which the plaintiffs complain. . . .

Page 132.   At the end of section 6 of the Note, add the following:

The Court resolved a complicated standing question in Department of Commerce v. New York, 588 U.S. ___ (2019). At issue was the Department's reinstatement of a question about citizenship on the 2020 census questionnaire. The states that brought suit referred to "a number of injuries—diminishment of political representation, loss of federal funds, degradation of census data, and diversion of resources—all of which turn on their expectation that reinstating a citizenship question will depress the census response rate and lead to an inaccurate population count." They emphasized that they might lose a seat in Congress or qualify for less in the way of federal funding.

The Court found standing. "Several state respondents here have shown that if noncitizen households are undercounted by as little as 2%—lower than the District Court's 5.8% prediction—they will lose out on federal funds that are distributed on the basis of state population. That is a sufficiently concrete and imminent injury to satisfy Article III, and there is no dispute that a ruling in favor of respondents would redress that harm." The Court acknowledged the government's argument "that any harm to respondents is not fairly traceable to the Secretary's decision, because such harm depends on the independent action of third parties choosing to violate their legal duty to respond to the census." But it noted that "the evidence at trial established that noncitizen households have historically responded to the census at lower rates than other groups, and the District Court did not clearly err in crediting the Census Bureau's theory that the discrepancy is likely attributable at least in part to noncitizens' reluctance to answer a citizenship question." Standing was adequately premised "on the predictable effect of Government action on the decisions of third parties." No member of the Court disagreed with this conclusion.

Page 135.   Before section 2 of the Note, add the following:

In June Medical Services v. Russo, 591 U.S. ___ (2020), the Court ruled on a third-party standing issue in the context of a challenge to a state abortion law. (The Court's decision regarding the substance of the challenge is discussed at the Supplement to page 887 of the Main Volume). In 2014, Louisiana enacted Act 620, which established an admitting privileges requirement for abortion providers, similar to the one that the Supreme Court found unconstitutional in Whole Woman's Health v. Hellerstedt, Main Volume at 879 (2016). A group of abortion clinics and providers challenged the law in federal court on the ground that it infringed on their patients' access right to an abortion, asking for a preliminary injunction to stay the law from taking effect. During these proceedings, the State acknowledged there was "no question that the physicians had standing to contest the law" and requested the district court to rule on the merits as soon as possible. After the district court declared Act 620 unconstitutional, the Fifth Circuit reversed the decision and the Supreme Court remanded the case after its decision in *Whole Woman's Health.* The district court found the law unconstitutional a second time in 2017, a decision that was once again reversed by the Fifth Court, before the plaintiffs filed a petition for certiorari to the Supreme Court. In a cross-petition, the State asserted that the proper parties to challenge the law were the patients themselves, and that the plaintiffs did not meet the requirements for third-party standing to bring suit on their behalf.

The Court rejected the argument and ruled 5-4 in favor of the plaintiffs on the standing issue, with Chief Justice Roberts joining the plurality opinion in concurrence. Writing for the Court, Justice Breyer concluded that the State had "waived [the standing] argument" by its "unmistakable concession of standing as part of its effort to obtain a quick decision from the District Court." Critically, the majority made clear that the Court's standard rule against resting claims on the legal rights of third parties is "prudential" rather than constitutional, and therefore objections could be "forfeited or waived" if parties did not assert them earlier in the proceedings. Refusing to rule on the merits after five years of legal action would "foster repetitive and time-consuming litigation under the guise of caution and prudence" (quoting *Craig v. Boren,* 429 U.S. 390, 193-194 (1976)).

Aside from the issue of waiver, the Court also found that the plaintiffs would have third-party standing under the Courts own precedents. Citing to a long line of abortion-related cases, Justice Breyer stated that the rule against third-party standing "is hardly absolute." In his words, "[the Court] has long permitted abortion providers to invoke the rights of their actual or potential patients in challenges to abortion-related regulations." A second line of Court precedents have "generally permitted plaintiffs to assert third-party rights in cases where the 'enforcement of the challenged restriction *against the litigant* would result indirectly in the violation of third parties' rights'" (quoting Kowalski v. Tesmer, 543 U.S. 125, 130 (2004)). The Court opinion placed the case at the "intersection of these two lines of precedents," as "[t]he plaintiffs are abortion providers challenging a law that regulates their conduct." Because abortion providers are "better positioned than their patients to address the burdens of compliance," they are "'the least awkward' and most 'obvious' claimants" (quoting *Craig*, 420 U.S., at 197).

Justice Breyer also contended that none of the traditional concerns against third-party standing were present in the case. The threat of sanctions to the abortion providers "eliminates any risk that their claims are abstract or hypothetical" and gives abortion providers "every incentive" to contest the lawsuit. He rejected the dissenters' view that abortion providers challenging a law enacted to protect patients by invoking their patients' rights would lead to an unacceptable conflict of interest: "[That] is a common feature of [third-party] standing." Chief Justice Roberts in concurrence fully endorsed the plurality's standing analysis.

Justice Thomas dissented, as did Justice Alito, who was joined by Justice Gorsuch and joined in part by Justices Thomas and Kavanaugh. Justice Gorsuch and Justice Kavanaugh (whose opinion did not address standing) also filed separate dissents.

Justice Thomas's opinion rejected the majority's "prudential" categorization of the rule against third-party standing as "inconsistent with our more recent standing precedents," stating that "'the proper place' for that rule is in Article III's case-or-controversy requirement." He further added that third-party standing is at odds with Article III, as plaintiffs have "no private right of [their] own genuinely at stake." Justice Thomas concluded that because "[abortion] is an individual right that is inherently personal," the abortion providers "cannot establish a personal legal injury" and therefore no waiver "however explicit" gives the Court jurisdiction to decide the case.

Justice Alito charged the majority with "a misreading of the record," asserting that the State's waiver was "simply an accurate statement of circuit precedent." Justice Alito's dissent identified a "blatant conflict of interest between an abortion provider and its patients," because the provider has an incentive to avoid "burdensome regulation" that aims to protect its patients' health. As "any other party unhappy with [regulation], the provider should be limited to its own rights." As a second reason, Justice Alito also found that abortion providers did not qualify for the limited exception to the rule against third-party standing, because abortion patients neither have "a close relationship with the [provider]" nor are they "hindered from bringing suit" themselves. According to Justice Alito, the third-party standing precedents relied on by the majority pronounce an "abortion-only rule" that "cannot be reconciled with other established precedents" and therefore should be overruled.

Justice Gorsuch's dissent agreed with Justice Alito's reasoning, stating that the "narrow circumstances" that justify third-party standing were not present in this case, because abortion providers had made no showing that patients were hindered from defending their own rights and providers also lacked anything but a "hypothetical" relationship with their future clients. Utilizing the same rationale as Justice Alito, Justice Gorsuch found a potential conflict of interest "hard to ignore."

June Medical's holding regarding third-party standing can be considered a clear victory for abortion advocates, as providers often act as plaintiffs in lawsuits that challenge abortion-restricting laws. The case also strongly endorses the view of third-party standing as a prudential, and not a constitutional concern, giving more flexibility to Courts in ruling on the issue going forward.

Page 142.   Before Note, add the following:

RUCHO v. COMMON CAUSE

588 U.S. ___ (2019)

CHIEF JUSTICE ROBERTS delivered the opinion of the Court.

Chief Justice Marshall famously wrote that it is "the province and duty of the judicial department to say what the law is." Marbury v. Madison, 1 Cranch 137, 177 (1803). Sometimes, however, "the law is that the judicial department has no business entertaining the claim of unlawfulness—because the question is entrusted to one of the political branches or involves no judicially enforceable rights." Vieth v. Jubelirer, 541 U.S. 267, 277 (2004) (plurality opinion). In such a case the claim is said to present a "political question" and to be nonjusticiable—outside the courts' competence and therefore beyond the courts' jurisdiction. Baker v. Carr, 369 U.S. 186, 217 (1962). Among the political question cases the Court has identified are those that lack "judicially discoverable and manageable standards for resolving [them]." Ibid. . . .

The question here is whether there is an "appropriate role for the Federal Judiciary" in remedying the problem of partisan gerrymandering—whether such claims are claims of legal right, resolvable according to legal principles, or political questions that must find their resolution elsewhere. . . .

In the leading case of Baker v. Carr, voters in Tennessee complained that the State's districting plan for state representatives "debase[d]" their votes, because the plan was predicated on a 60-year-old census that no longer reflected the distribution of population in the State. . . . The Court concluded that the claim of population inequality among districts did . . . could be decided under basic equal protection principles. In Wesberry v. Sanders, the Court extended its ruling to malapportionment of congressional districts, holding that Article I, § 2, required that "one man's vote in a congressional election is to be worth as much as another's."

Another line of challenges to districting plans has focused on race. Laws that explicitly discriminate on the basis of race, as well as those that are race neutral on their face but are unexplainable on grounds other than race, are of course presumptively invalid. . . .

Partisan gerrymandering claims have proved far more difficult to adjudicate. The basic reason is that, while it is illegal for a jurisdiction to depart from the one-person, one-vote rule, or to engage in racial discrimination in districting, "a jurisdiction may engage in constitutional political gerrymandering." . . . To hold that legislators cannot take partisan interests into account when drawing district lines would essentially countermand the Framers' decision to entrust districting to political entities. The "central problem" is not determining whether a jurisdiction has engaged in partisan gerrymandering. It is "determining when political gerrymandering has gone too far." *Vieth*, 541 U.S., at 296 (plurality opinion). . . .

A

In considering whether partisan gerrymandering claims are justiciable, we are mindful of Justice Kennedy's counsel in Vieth:

Any standard for resolving such claims must be grounded in a "limited and precise rationale" and be "clear, manageable, and politically neutral." 541 U.S., at 306-308 (opinion concurring in judgment). An important reason for those careful constraints is that, as a Justice with extensive experience in state and local politics put it, "[t]he opportunity to control the drawing of electoral boundaries through the legislative process of apportionment is a critical and traditional part of politics in the United States." *Bandemer*, 478 U.S., at 145 (opinion of O'Connor, J.)

As noted, the question is one of degree: How to "provid[e] a standard for deciding how much partisan dominance is too much." *LULAC*, 548 U.S., at 420 (opinion of Kennedy, J.). And it is vital in such circumstances that the Court act only in accord with especially clear standards: "With uncertain limits, intervening courts—even when proceeding with best intentions—would risk assuming political, not legal, responsibility for a process that often produces ill will and distrust." *Vieth*, 541 U.S., at 307 (opinion of Kennedy, J.). If federal courts are to "inject [themselves] into the most heated partisan issues" by adjudicating partisan gerrymandering claims, *Bandemer*, 478 U.S., at 145 (opinion of O'Connor, J.), they must be armed with a standard that can reliably differentiate unconstitutional from "constitutional political gerrymandering."

B

Partisan gerrymandering claims rest on an instinct that groups with a certain level of political support should enjoy a commensurate level of political power and influence. Explicitly or implicitly, a districting map is alleged to be unconstitutional because it makes it too difficult for one party to translate statewide support into seats in the legislature. But such a claim is based on a "norm that does not exist" in our electoral system—"statewide elections for representatives along party lines." *Bandemer*, 478 U.S., at 159 (opinion of O'Connor, J.).

Partisan gerrymandering claims invariably sound in a desire for proportional representation. As Justice O'Connor put it, such claims are based on "a conviction that the greater the departure from proportionality, the more suspect an apportionment plan becomes." Ibid. "Our cases, however, clearly foreclose any claim that the Constitution requires proportional representation or that legislatures in reapportioning must draw district lines to come as near as possible to allocating seats to the contending parties in proportion to what their anticipated statewide vote will be." Id., at 130 (plurality opinion).

The Founders certainly did not think proportional representation was required. For more than 50 years after ratification of the Constitution, many States elected their congressional representatives through at-large or "general ticket" elections. Such States typically sent single-party delegations to Congress. See E. Engstrom, Partisan Gerrymandering and the Construction of American Democracy 43-51 (2013). That meant that a party could garner nearly half of the vote statewide and wind up without any seats in the congressional delegation. The Whigs in Alabama suffered that fate in 1840: "their party garnered 43 percent of the statewide vote, yet did not receive a single seat." Id., at 48. When Congress required single-member districts in the Apportionment Act of 1842, it was not out of a general sense of fairness, but instead a (mis)calculation by the Whigs that such a change would improve their electoral prospects. Id., at 43-44.

Unable to claim that the Constitution requires proportional representation outright, plaintiffs inevitably ask the courts to make their own political judgment about how much representation particular political parties deserve—based on the votes of their supporters—and to rearrange the challenged districts to achieve that end. But federal courts are not equipped to apportion political power as a matter of fairness, nor is there any basis for concluding that they were authorized to do so. As Justice Scalia put it for the plurality in *Vieth*:

" 'Fairness' does not seem to us a judicially manageable standard. . . . Some criterion more solid and more demonstrably met than that seems to us necessary to enable the state legislatures to discern the limits of their districting discretion, to meaningfully constrain the discretion of the courts, and to win public acceptance for the courts' intrusion into a process that is the very foundation of democratic decisionmaking."

541 U.S., at 291.

The initial difficulty in settling on a "clear, manageable and politically neutral" test for fairness is that it is not even clear what fairness looks like in this context. There is a large measure of "unfairness" in any winner-take-all system. Fairness may mean a greater number of competitive districts. Such a claim seeks to undo packing and cracking so that supporters of the disadvantaged party have a better shot at electing their preferred candidates. But making as many districts as possible more competitive could be a recipe for disaster for the disadvantaged party. . . .

On the other hand, perhaps the ultimate objective of a "fairer" share of seats in the congressional delegation is most readily achieved by yielding to the gravitational pull of proportionality and engaging in cracking and packing, to ensure each party its "appropriate" share of "safe" seats. . . . Such an approach, however, comes at the expense of competitive districts and of individuals in districts allocated to the opposing party.

Or perhaps fairness should be measured by adherence to "traditional" districting criteria, such as maintaining political subdivisions, keeping communities of interest together, and protecting incumbents. But protecting incumbents, for example, enshrines a particular partisan distribution. And the "natural political geography" of a State—such as the fact that urban electoral districts are often dominated by one political party—can itself lead to inherently packed districts. As Justice Kennedy has explained, traditional criteria such as compactness and contiguity "cannot promise political neutrality when used as the basis for relief. Instead, it seems, a decision under these standards would unavoidably have significant political effect, whether intended or not." *Vieth*, 541 U.S., at 308-309 (opinion concurring in judgment).

Deciding among just these different visions of fairness (you can imagine many others) poses basic questions that are political, not legal. There are no legal standards discernible in the Constitution for making such judgments, let alone limited and precise standards that are clear, manageable, and politically neutral. Any judicial decision on what is "fair" in this context would be an "unmoored determination" of the sort characteristic of a political question beyond the competence of the federal courts. Zivotofsky v. Clinton, 566 U.S. 189, 196 (2012).

And it is only after determining how to define fairness that you can even begin to answer the determinative question: "How much is too much?" At what point does permissible partisanship become unconstitutional? If compliance with traditional districting criteria is the fairness touchstone, for example, how much deviation from those criteria is constitutionally acceptable and how should mapdrawers prioritize competing criteria? Should a court "reverse gerrymander" other parts of a State to counteract "natural" gerrymandering caused, for example, by the urban concentration of one party? If a districting plan protected half of the incumbents but redistricted the rest into head to head races, would that be constitutional? A court would have to rank the relative importance of those traditional criteria and weigh how much deviation from each to allow.

If a court instead focused on the respective number of seats in the legislature, it would have to decide the ideal number of seats for each party and determine at what point deviation from that balance went too far. If a 5-3 allocation corresponds most closely to statewide vote totals, is a 6-2 allocation permissible, given that legislatures have the authority to engage in a certain degree of partisan gerrymandering? Which seats should be packed and which cracked? Or if the goal is as many competitive districts as possible, how close does the split need to be for the district to be considered competitive? Presumably not all districts could qualify, so how to choose? Even assuming the court knew which version of fairness to be looking for, there are no discernible and manageable standards for deciding whether there has been a violation. The questions are "unguided and ill suited to the development of judicial standards," *Vieth*, 541 U.S., at 296 (plurality opinion), and "results from one gerrymandering case to the next would likely be disparate and inconsistent," id., at 308 (opinion of Kennedy, J.).

Appellees contend that if we can adjudicate one-person, one-vote claims, we can also assess partisan gerrymandering claims. But the one-person, one-vote rule is relatively easy to administer as a matter of math. The same cannot be said of partisan gerrymandering claims, because the Constitution supplies no objective measure for assessing whether a districting map treats a political party fairly. It hardly follows from the principle that each person must have an equal say in the election of representatives that a person is entitled to have his political party achieve representation in some way commensurate to its share of statewide support.

More fundamentally, "vote dilution" in the one-person, one-vote cases refers to the idea that each vote must carry equal weight. In other words, each representative must be accountable to (approximately) the same number of constituents. That requirement does not extend to political parties. It does not mean that each party must be influential in proportion to its number of supporters. As we stated unanimously in *Gill*, "this Court is not responsible for vindicating generalized partisan preferences. The Court's constitutionally prescribed role is to vindicate the individual rights of the people appearing before it."

Nor do our racial gerrymandering cases provide an appropriate standard for assessing partisan gerrymandering. "[N]othing in our case law compels the conclusion that racial and political gerrymanders are subject to precisely the same constitutional scrutiny. In fact, our country's long and persistent history of racial discrimination in voting — as well as our Fourteenth Amendment jurisprudence, which always has reserved the strictest scrutiny for discrimination on the basis of race — would seem to compel the opposite conclusion." *Shaw I*, 509 U.S., at 650 (citation omitted). Unlike partisan gerrymandering claims, a racial gerrymandering claim does not ask for a fair share of political power and influence, with all the justiciability conundrums that entails. It asks instead for the elimination of a racial classification. A partisan gerrymandering claim cannot ask for the elimination of partisanship.

IV

Appellees and the dissent propose a number of "tests" for evaluating partisan gerrymandering claims, but none meets the need for a limited and precise standard that is judicially discernible and manageable. And none provides a solid grounding for judges to take the extraordinary step of reallocating power and influence between political parties.

A

The Common Cause District Court concluded that all but one of the districts in North Carolina's 2016 Plan violated the Equal Protection Clause by intentionally diluting the voting strength of Democrats. In reaching that result the court first required the plaintiffs to prove "that a legislative mapdrawer's predominant purpose in drawing the lines of a particular district was to 'subordinate adherents of one political party and entrench a rival party in power.'" The District Court next required a showing "that the dilution of the votes of supporters of a disfavored party in a particular district—by virtue of cracking or packing—is likely to persist in subsequent elections such that an elected representative from the favored party in the district will not feel a need to be responsive to constituents who support the disfavored party." 318 F. Supp. 3d, at 867. Finally, after a prima facie showing of partisan vote dilution, the District Court shifted the burden to the defendants to prove that the discriminatory effects are "attributable to a legitimate state interest or other neutral explanation." Id., at 868.

The District Court's "predominant intent" prong is borrowed from the racial gerrymandering context. In racial gerrymandering cases, we rely on a "predominant intent" inquiry to determine whether race was, in fact, the reason particular district boundaries were drawn the way they were. If district lines were drawn for the purpose of separating racial groups, then they are subject to strict scrutiny because "race-based decisionmaking is inherently suspect." *Miller*, 515 U.S., at 915. But determining that lines were drawn on the basis of partisanship does not indicate that the districting was improper. A permissible intent—securing partisan advantage—does not become constitutionally impermissible, like racial discrimination, when that permissible intent "predominates."

The District Court tried to limit the reach of its test by requiring plaintiffs to show, in addition to predominant partisan intent, that vote dilution "is likely to persist" to such a degree that the elected representative will feel free to ignore the concerns of the supporters of the minority party. 318 F. Supp. 3d, at 867. But "[t]o allow district courts to strike down apportionment plans on the basis of their prognostications as to the outcome of future elections . . . invites 'findings' on matters as to which neither judges nor anyone else can have any confidence." *Bandemer*, 478 U.S., at 160 (opinion of O'Connor, J.). See *LULAC*, 548 U.S., at 420 (opinion of Kennedy, J.) ("[W]e are wary of adopting a constitutional standard that invalidates a map based on unfair results that would occur in a hypothetical state of affairs."). And the test adopted by the Common Cause court requires a far more nuanced prediction than simply who would prevail in future political contests. Judges must forecast with unspecified certainty whether a prospective winner will have a margin of victory sufficient to permit him to ignore the supporters of his defeated opponent (whoever that may turn out to be). Judges not only have to pick the winner—they have to beat the point spread.

The appellees assure us that "the persistence of a party's advantage may be shown through sensitivity testing: probing how a plan would perform under other plausible electoral conditions." Brief for Appellees League of Women Voters of North Carolina et al. in No. 18-422, p. 55. See also 318 F. Supp. 3d, at 885. Experience proves that accurately predicting electoral outcomes is not so simple, either because the plans are based on flawed assumptions about voter preferences and behavior or because demographics

and priorities change over time. In our two leading partisan gerrymandering cases themselves, the predictions of durability proved
to be dramatically wrong. In 1981, Republicans controlled both
houses of the Indiana Legislature as well as the governorship.
Democrats challenged the state legislature districting map enacted by the Republicans. This Court in Bandemer rejected that
challenge, and just months later the Democrats increased their
share of House seats in the 1986 elections. Two years later the
House was split 50-50 between Democrats and Republicans, and
the Democrats took control of the chamber in 1990. Democrats
also challenged the Pennsylvania congressional districting plan at
issue in *Vieth*. Two years after that challenge failed, they gained
four seats in the delegation, going from a 12-7 minority to an 11-8
majority. At the next election, they flipped another Republican
seat.

Even the most sophisticated districting maps cannot reliably
account for some of the reasons voters prefer one candidate over
another, or why their preferences may change. Voters elect individual candidates in individual districts, and their selections
depend on the issues that matter to them, the quality of the candidates, the tone of the candidates' campaigns, the performance
of an incumbent, national events or local issues that drive voter
turnout, and other considerations. Many voters split their tickets.
Others never register with a political party, and vote for candidates from both major parties at different points during their life-
times. For all of those reasons, asking judges to predict how a
particular districting map will perform in future elections risks
basing constitutional holdings on unstable ground outside judicial
expertise.

It is hard to see what the District Court's third prong — providing the defendant an opportunity to show that the discriminatory
effects were due to a "legitimate redistricting objective" — adds
to the inquiry. 318 F. Supp. 3d, at 861. The first prong already requires the plaintiff to prove that partisan advantage predominates.
Asking whether a legitimate purpose other than partisanship was

the motivation for a particular districting map just restates the question.

B

The District Courts also found partisan gerrymandering claims justiciable under the First Amendment, coalescing around a basic three-part test: proof of intent to burden individuals based on their voting history or party affiliation; an actual burden on political speech or associational rights; and a causal link between the invidious intent and actual burden. Both District Courts concluded that the districting plans at issue violated the plaintiffs' First Amendment right to association. The District Court in North Carolina relied on testimony that, after the 2016 Plan was put in place, the plaintiffs faced "difficulty raising money, attracting candidates, and mobilizing voters to support the political causes and issues such Plaintiffs sought to advance." 318 F. Supp. 3d, at 932. Similarly, the District Court in Maryland examined testimony that "revealed a lack of enthusiasm, indifference to voting, a sense of disenfranchisement, a sense of disconnection, and confusion," and concluded that Republicans in the Sixth District "were burdened in fundraising, attracting volunteers, campaigning, and generating interest in voting." 348 F. Supp. 3d, at 523-524.

To begin, there are no restrictions on speech, association, or any other First Amendment activities in the districting plans at issue. The plaintiffs are free to engage in those activities no matter what the effect of a plan may be on their district.

The plaintiffs' argument is that partisanship in districting should be regarded as simple discrimination against supporters of the opposing party on the basis of political viewpoint. Under that theory, any level of partisanship in districting would constitute an infringement of their First Amendment rights. But as the Court has explained, "[i]t would be idle . . . to contend that any political consideration taken into account in fashioning a reapportionment plan is sufficient to invalidate it." *Gaffney*, 412 U.S., at 752. The

First Amendment test simply describes the act of districting for partisan advantage. It provides no standard for determining when partisan activity goes too far.

As for actual burden, the slight anecdotal evidence found sufficient by the District Courts in these cases shows that this too is not a serious standard for separating constitutional from unconstitutional partisan gerrymandering. The District Courts relied on testimony about difficulty drumming up volunteers and enthusiasm. How much of a decline in voter engagement is enough to constitute a First Amendment burden? How many door knocks must go unanswered? How many petitions unsigned? How many calls for volunteers unheeded? The Common Cause District Court held that a partisan gerrymander places an unconstitutional burden on speech if it has more than a "de minimis" "chilling effect or adverse impact" on any First Amendment activity. 318 F. Supp. 3d, at 930. The court went on to rule that there would be an adverse effect "even if the speech of [the plaintiffs] was not in fact chilled"; it was enough that the districting plan "makes it easier for supporters of Republican candidates to translate their votes into seats," thereby "enhanc[ing] the[ir] relative voice." Id., at 933 (internal quotation marks omitted).

These cases involve blatant examples of partisanship driving districting decisions. But the First Amendment analysis below offers no "clear" and "manageable" way of distinguishing permissible from impermissible partisan motivation. The Common Cause court embraced that conclusion, observing that "a judicially manageable framework for evaluating partisan gerrymandering claims need not distinguish an 'acceptable' level of partisan gerrymandering from 'excessive' partisan gerrymandering" because "the Constitution does not authorize state redistricting bodies to engage in such partisan gerrymandering." Id., at 851. The decisions below prove the prediction of the *Vieth* plurality that "a First Amendment claim, if it were sustained, would render unlawful all consideration of political affiliation in districting," 541 U.S., at 294, contrary to our established precedent.

C

The dissent proposes using a State's own districting criteria as a neutral baseline from which to measure how extreme a partisan gerrymander is. The dissent would have us line up all the possible maps drawn using those criteria according to the partisan distribution they would produce. Distance from the "median" map would indicate whether a particular districting plan harms supporters of one party to an unconstitutional extent.

As an initial matter, it does not make sense to use criteria that will vary from State to State and year to year as the baseline for determining whether a gerrymander violates the Federal Constitution. The degree of partisan advantage that the Constitution tolerates should not turn on criteria offered by the gerrymanderers themselves. It is easy to imagine how different criteria could move the median map toward different partisan distributions. As a result, the same map could be constitutional or not depending solely on what the mapmakers said they set out to do. That possibility illustrates that the dissent's proposed constitutional test is indeterminate and arbitrary.

Even if we were to accept the dissent's proposed baseline, it would return us to "the original unanswerable question (How much political motivation and effect is too much?)." *Vieth*, 541 U.S., at 296-297 (plurality opinion). Would twenty percent away from the median map be okay? Forty percent? Sixty percent? Why or why not? (We appreciate that the dissent finds all the unanswerable questions annoying, see *Post*, at 22, but it seems a useful way to make the point.) The dissent's answer says it all: "This much is too much." *Post*, at 25-26. That is not even trying to articulate a standard or rule.

The dissent argues that there are other instances in law where matters of degree are left to the courts. True enough. But those instances typically involve constitutional or statutory provisions or common law confining and guiding the exercise of judicial discretion. For example, the dissent cites the need to determine "substantial anticompetitive effect[s]" in antitrust law. *Post*, at 27 (citing Ohio v. American Express Co., 585 U.S. ___ (2018)). That language, however, grew out of the Sherman Act, understood from the beginning to have its "origin in the common law" and to be "familiar in the l0aw of this country prior to and at the time of the adoption of the [A]ct." Standard Oil Co. of N.J. v. United States, 221 U.S. 1, 51 (1911). Judges began with a significant body of law about what constituted a legal violation. In other cases, the pertinent statutory terms draw meaning from related provisions or statutory context. Here, on the other hand, the Constitution provides no basis whatever to guide the exercise of judicial discretion. Common experience gives content to terms such as "substantial risk" or "substantial harm," but the same cannot be said of substantial deviation from a median map. There is no way to tell whether the prohibited deviation from that map should kick in at 25 percent or 75 percent or some other point. The only provision in the Constitution that specifically addresses the matter assigns it to the political branches. See Art. I, § 4, cl. 1.

D

. . . What the appellees and dissent seek is an unprecedented expansion of judicial power. We have never struck down a partisan gerrymander as unconstitutional—despite various requests over the past 45 years. The expansion of judicial authority would not be into just any area of controversy, but into one of the most intensely partisan aspects of American political life. That intervention would be unlimited in scope and duration—it would recur over and over again around the country with each new round of districting, for state as well as federal representatives. Consideration of the impact of today's ruling on democratic principles cannot ignore the effect of the unelected and politically unaccountable branch of the Federal Government assuming such an extraordinary and unprecedented role.

* * *

No one can accuse this Court of having a crabbed view of the reach of its competence. But we have no commission to allocate

35

political power and influence in the absence of a constitutional directive or legal standards to guide us in the exercise of such authority. "It is emphatically the province and duty of the judicial department to say what the law is." Marbury v. Madison, 1 Cranch, at 177. In this rare circumstance, that means our duty is to say "this is not law."

The judgments of the United States District Court for the Middle District of North Carolina and the United States District Court for the District of Maryland are vacated, and the cases are remanded with instructions to dismiss for lack of jurisdiction.

It is so ordered.

JUSTICE KAGAN, with whom JUSTICE GINSBURG, JUSTICE BREYER, and JUSTICE SOTOMAYOR join, dissenting.

For the first time ever, this Court refuses to remedy a constitutional violation because it thinks the task beyond judicial capabilities.

And not just any constitutional violation. The partisan gerrymanders in these cases deprived citizens of the most fundamental of their constitutional rights: the rights to participate equally in the political process, to join with others to advance political beliefs, and to choose their political representatives. In so doing, the partisan gerrymanders here debased and dishonored our democracy, turning upside-down the core American idea that all governmental power derives from the people. These gerrymanders enabled politicians to entrench themselves in office as against voters' preferences. They promoted partisanship above respect for the popular will. They encouraged a politics of polarization and dysfunction. If left unchecked, gerrymanders like the ones here may irreparably damage our system of government.

And checking them is not beyond the courts. The majority's abdication comes just when courts across the country, including those below, have coalesced around manageable judicial standards to resolve partisan gerrymandering claims. Those standards satisfy the majority's own benchmarks. They do not require—indeed, they do not permit—courts to rely on their own ideas of electoral fairness, whether proportional representation or any other. And they limit courts to correcting only egregious gerrymanders, so judges do not become omnipresent players in the political process. But yes, the standards used here do allow—as well they should—judicial intervention in the worst-of-the-worst cases of democratic subversion, causing blatant constitutional harms. In other words, they allow courts to undo partisan gerrymanders of the kind we face today from North Carolina and Maryland. In giving such gerrymanders a pass from judicial review, the majority goes tragically wrong. . . .

The people get to choose their representatives. And then they get to decide, at regular intervals, whether to keep them. Madison again: "[R]epublican liberty" demands "not only, that all power should be derived from the people; but that those entrusted with it should be kept in dependence on the people." 2 The Federalist No. 37, p. 4 (J. & A. McLean eds. 1788). Members of the House of Representatives, in particular, are supposed to "recollect[ ] [that] dependence" every day. To retain an "intimate sympathy with the people," they must be "compelled to anticipate the moment" when their "exercise of [power] is to be reviewed." Id., Nos. 52, 57, at 124, 155. Election day—next year, and two years later, and two years after that—is what links the people to their representatives, and gives the people their sovereign power. That day is the foundation of democratic governance.

And partisan gerrymandering can make it meaningless. At its most extreme—as in North Carolina and Maryland—the practice amounts to "rigging elections." Vieth v. Jubelirer, 541 U.S. 267, 317 (2004) (Kennedy, J., concurring in judgment) (internal quotation marks omitted). By drawing districts to maximize the power of some voters and minimize the power of others, a party in office at the right time can entrench itself there for a decade or more, no matter what the voters would prefer. Just ask the people of North Carolina and Maryland. The "core principle of republican government," this Court has recognized, is "that the voters should choose their representatives, not the other way around." Arizona State Legislature v. Arizona Independent Redistricting Comm'n,

576 U.S. ___, ___ (2015) (slip op., at 35) (internal quotation marks omitted). Partisan gerrymandering turns it the other way around. By that mechanism, politicians can cherry-pick voters to ensure their reelection. And the power becomes, as Madison put it, "in the Government over the people." 4 Annals of Cong. 934.

The majority disputes none of this. I think it important to underscore that fact: The majority disputes none of what I have said (or will say) about how gerrymanders undermine democracy. Indeed, the majority concedes (really, how could it not?) that gerrymandering is "incompatible with democratic principles." Ante, at 30 (quoting *Arizona State Legislature*, 576 U.S., at ___ (slip op., at 1)). And therefore what? That recognition would seem to demand a response. The majority offers two ideas that might qualify as such. One is that the political process can deal with the problem—a proposition so dubious on its face that I feel secure in delaying my answer for some time. The other is that political gerrymanders have always been with us. To its credit, the majority does not frame that point as an originalist constitutional argument. After all (as the majority rightly notes), racial and residential gerrymanders were also once with us, but the Court has done something about that fact. The majority's idea instead seems to be that if we have lived with partisan gerrymanders so long, we will survive.

That complacency has no cause. Yes, partisan gerrymandering goes back to the Republic's earliest days. (As does vociferous opposition to it.) But big data and modern technology—of just the kind that the mapmakers in North Carolina and Maryland used—make today's gerrymandering altogether different from the crude linedrawing of the past. Old-time efforts, based on little more than guesses, sometimes led to so-called dummymanders—gerrymanders that went spectacularly wrong. Not likely in today's world. Mapmakers now have access to more granular data about party preference and voting behavior than ever before. County-level voting data has given way to precinct-level or city-block-level data; and increasingly, mapmakers avail themselves of data sets providing wide-ranging information about even individual voters. See Brief for Political Science Professors as Amici Curiae 20-22. Just as important, advancements in computing technology have enabled mapmakers to put that information to use with unprecedented efficiency and precision. While bygone mapmakers may have drafted three or four alternative districting plans, today's mapmakers can generate thousands of possibilities at the touch of a key — and then choose the one giving their party maximum advantage (usually while still meeting traditional districting requirements). The effect is to make gerrymanders far more effective and durable than before, insulating politicians against all but the most titanic shifts in the political tides. These are not your grandfather's — let alone the Framers' — gerrymanders. . . .

Partisan gerrymandering of the kind before us not only subverts democracy (as if that weren't bad enough). It violates individuals' constitutional rights as well. That statement is not the lonesome cry of a dissenting Justice. This Court has recognized extreme partisan gerrymandering as such a violation for many years.

Partisan gerrymandering operates through vote dilution — the devaluation of one citizen's vote as compared to others. A mapmaker draws district lines to "pack" and "crack" voters likely to support the disfavored party. See generally Gill v. Whitford, 585 U.S. ___, ___-___ (2018) (slip op., at 14-16). He packs supermajorities of those voters into a relatively few districts, in numbers far greater than needed for their preferred candidates to prevail. Then he cracks the rest across many more districts, spreading them so thin that their candidates will not be able to win. Whether the person is packed or cracked, his vote carries less weight — has less consequence — than it would under a neutrally drawn (non-partisan) map. In short, the mapmaker has made some votes count for less, because they are likely to go for the other party.

That practice implicates the Fourteenth Amendment's Equal Protection Clause. The Fourteenth Amendment, we long ago recognized, "guarantees the opportunity for equal participation by all voters in the election" of legislators. Reynolds v. Sims, 377 U.S. 533, 566 (1964). And that opportunity "can be denied by a debasement or dilution of the weight of a citizen's vote just as effectively

39

as by wholly prohibiting the free exercise of the franchise." Id., at 555. Based on that principle, this Court in its one-person-one-vote decisions prohibited creating districts with significantly different populations. A State could not, we explained, thus "dilut[e] the weight of votes because of place of residence." Id., at 566. The constitutional injury in a partisan gerrymandering case is much the same, except that the dilution is based on party affiliation. In such a case, too, the districters have set out to reduce the weight of certain citizens' votes, and thereby deprive them of their capacity to "full[y] and effective[ly] participat[e] in the political process[ ]." Id., at 565. As Justice Kennedy (in a controlling opinion) once hypothesized: If districters declared that they were drawing a map "so as most to burden [the votes of] Party X's" supporters, it would violate the Equal Protection Clause. *Vieth*, 541 U.S., at 312. For (in the language of the one-person-one-vote decisions) it would infringe those voters' rights to "equal [electoral] participation." *Reynolds*, 377 U.S., at 566; see Gray v. Sanders, 372 U.S. 368, 379-380 (1963) ("The concept of 'we the people' under the Constitution visualizes no preferred class of voters but equality among those who meet the basic qualifications").

And partisan gerrymandering implicates the First Amendment too. That Amendment gives its greatest protection to political beliefs, speech, and association. Yet partisan gerrymanders subject certain voters to "disfavored treatment"—again, counting their votes for less—precisely because of "their voting history [and] their expression of political views." *Vieth*, 541 U.S., at 314 (opinion of Kennedy, J.). And added to that strictly personal harm is an associational one. Representative democracy is "unimaginable without the ability of citizens to band together in [support of] candidates who espouse their political views." California Democratic Party v. Jones, 530 U.S. 567, 574 (2000). By diluting the votes of certain citizens, the State frustrates their efforts to translate those affiliations into political effectiveness. See *Gill*, 585 U.S., at ___ (Kagan, J., concurring) (slip op., at 9) ("Members of the disfavored party[,] deprived of their natural political strength[,] may face difficulties fundraising, registering voters, [and] eventually accomplishing their policy objectives"). In both those ways, partisan gerrymanders of the kind we confront here undermine the protections of "democracy embodied in the First Amendment." Elrod v. Burns, 427 U.S. 347, 357 (1976) (internal quotation marks omitted). . . .

II

So the only way to understand the majority's opinion is as follows: In the face of grievous harm to democratic governance and flagrant infringements on individuals' rights—in the face of escalating partisan manipulation whose compatibility with this Nation's values and law no one defends—the majority declines to provide any remedy. For the first time in this Nation's history, the majority declares that it can do nothing about an acknowledged constitutional violation because it has searched high and low and cannot find a workable legal standard to apply.

The majority gives two reasons for thinking that the adjudication of partisan gerrymandering claims is beyond judicial capabilities. First and foremost, the majority says, it cannot find a neutral baseline—one not based on contestable notions of political fairness—from which to measure injury. According to the majority, "[p]artisan gerrymandering claims invariably sound in a desire for proportional representation." But the Constitution does not mandate proportional representation. So, the majority contends, resolving those claims "inevitably" would require courts to decide what is "fair" in the context of districting. They would have "to make their own political judgment about how much representation particular political parties deserve" and "to rearrange the challenged districts to achieve that end." And second, the majority argues that even after establishing a baseline, a court would have no way to answer "the determinative question: 'How much is too much?' " No "discernible and manageable" standard is available, the majority claims—and so courts could willy-nilly become embroiled in fixing every districting plan. Ante, at 20; see ante, at 15-16.

I'll give the majority this one—and important—thing: It identifies some dangers everyone should want to avoid. Judges should not be apportioning political power based on their own vision of electoral fairness, whether proportional representation or any other. And judges should not be striking down maps left, right, and center, on the view that every smidgen of politics is a smidgen too much. Respect for state legislative processes—and restraint in the exercise of judicial authority—counsels intervention in only egregious cases.

But in throwing up its hands, the majority misses something under its nose: What it says can't be done has been done. Over the past several years, federal courts across the country—including, but not exclusively, in the decisions below—have largely converged on a standard for adjudicating partisan gerrymandering claims (striking down both Democratic and Republican districting plans in the process). See also *Ohio A. Philip Randolph Inst.*, 373 F. Supp. 3d 978; League of Women Voters of Michigan v. Benson, 373 F. Supp. 3d 867 (ED Mich. 2019). And that standard does what the majority says is impossible. The standard does not use any judge-made conception of electoral fairness—either proportional representation or any other; instead, it takes as its baseline a State's own criteria of fairness, apart from partisan gain. And by requiring plaintiffs to make difficult showings relating to both purpose and effects, the standard invalidates the most extreme, but only the most extreme, partisan gerrymanders.

Below, I first explain the framework courts have developed, and describe its application in these two cases. Doing so reveals in even starker detail than before how much these partisan gerrymanders deviated from democratic norms. As I lay out the lower courts' analyses, I consider two specific criticisms the majority levels—each of which reveals a saddening nonchalance about the threat such districting poses to self-governance. All of that lays the groundwork for then assessing the majority's more general view, described above, that judicial policing in this area cannot be either neutral or restrained. The lower courts' reasoning, as I'll show, proves the opposite.

A

Start with the standard the lower courts used. The majority disaggregates the opinions below, distinguishing the one from the other and then chopping up each into "a number of 'tests.'" But in doing so, it fails to convey the decisions' most significant—and common—features. Both courts focused on the harm of vote dilution, though the North Carolina court mostly grounded its analysis in the Fourteenth Amendment and the Maryland court in the First. And both courts (like others around the country) used basically the same three-part test to decide whether the plaintiffs had made out a vote dilution claim. As many legal standards do, that test has three parts: (1) intent; (2) effects; and (3) causation. First, the plaintiffs challenging a districting plan must prove that state officials' "predominant purpose" in drawing a district's lines was to "entrench [their party] in power" by diluting the votes of citizens favoring its rival. *Rucho*, 318 F. Supp. 3d, at 864 (quoting *Arizona State Legislature*, 576 U.S., at ___ (slip op., at 1)). Second, the plaintiffs must establish that the lines drawn in fact have the intended effect by "substantially" diluting their votes. *Lamone*, 348 F. Supp. 3d, at 498. And third, if the plaintiffs make those showings, the State must come up with a legitimate, non-partisan justification to save its map. See *Rucho*, 318 F. Supp. 3d, at 867. If you are a lawyer, you know that this test looks utterly ordinary. It is the sort of thing courts work with every day.

Turn now to the test's application. First, did the North Carolina and Maryland districters have the predominant purpose of entrenching their own party in power? Here, the two District Courts catalogued the overwhelming direct evidence that they did. To remind you of some highlights: North Carolina's redistricting committee used "Partisan Advantage" as an official criterion for drawing district lines. And from the first to the last, that committee's chair (along with his mapmaker) acted to ensure a 10-3 partisan split, whatever the statewide vote, because he thought that "electing Republicans is better than electing Democrats." For their part, Maryland's Democrats—the Governor, senior Congressman, and State Senate President alike—openly admitted to a single driving purpose: flip the Sixth District from Republican to Democratic. They did not blanch from moving some 700,000 voters into new districts (when one-person-one-vote rules required relocating just 10,000) for that reason and that reason alone.

The majority's response to the District Courts' purpose analysis is discomfiting. The majority does not contest the lower courts' findings; how could it? Instead, the majority says that state officials' intent to entrench their party in power is perfectly "permissible," even when it is the predominant factor in drawing district lines. Ante, at 23. But that is wrong. True enough, that the intent to inject "political considerations" into districting may not raise any constitutional concerns. In Gaffney v. Cummings, 412 U.S. 735 (1973), for example, we thought it non-problematic when state officials used political data to ensure rough proportional representation between the two parties. And true enough that even the naked purpose to gain partisan advantage may not rise to the level of constitutional notice when it is not the driving force in mapmaking or when the intended gain is slight. But when political actors have a specific and predominant intent to entrench themselves in power by manipulating district lines, that goes too far. Consider again Justice Kennedy's hypothetical of mapmakers who set out to maximally burden (i.e., make count for as little as possible) the votes going to a rival party. Does the majority really think that goal is permissible? But why even bother with hypotheticals? Just consider the purposes here. It cannot be permissible and thus irrelevant, as the majority claims, that state officials have as their purpose the kind of grotesquely gerrymandered map that, according to all this Court has ever said, violates the Constitution.

On to the second step of the analysis, where the plaintiffs must prove that the districting plan substantially dilutes their votes. The majority fails to discuss most of the evidence the District Courts relied on to find that the plaintiffs had done so. But that evidence—particularly from North Carolina—is the key to understanding both the problem these cases present and the solution to it they offer. The evidence reveals just how bad the two gerrymanders were (in case you had any doubts). And it shows how the same technologies and data that today facilitate extreme partisan gerrymanders also enable courts to discover them, by exposing just how much they dilute votes. See *Vieth*, 541 U.S., at 312-313 (opinion of Kennedy, J.) (predicting that development).

Consider the sort of evidence used in North Carolina first. There, the plaintiffs demonstrated the districting plan's effects mostly by relying on what might be called the "extreme outlier approach." (Here's a spoiler: the State's plan was one.) The approach—which also has recently been used in Michigan and Ohio litigation—begins by using advanced computing technology to randomly generate a large collection of districting plans that incorporate the State's physical and political geography and meet its declared districting criteria, except for partisan gain. For each of those maps, the method then uses actual precinct-level votes from past elections to determine a partisan outcome (i.e., the number of Democratic and Republican seats that map produces). Suppose we now have 1,000 maps, each with a partisan outcome attached to it. We can line up those maps on a continuum—the most favorable to Republicans on one end, the most favorable to Democrats on the other. We can then find the median outcome—that is, the outcome smack dab in the center—in a world with no partisan manipulation. And we can see where the State's actual plan falls on the spectrum—at or near the median or way out on one of the tails? The further out on the tail, the more extreme the partisan distortion and the more significant the vote dilution.

Using that approach, the North Carolina plaintiffs offered a boatload of alternative districting plans—all showing that the State's map was an out-out-out-outlier. One expert produced 3,000 maps, adhering in the way described above to the districting criteria that the North Carolina redistricting committee had used, other than partisan advantage. To calculate the partisan outcome of those maps, the expert also used the same election data (a composite of seven elections) that Hofeller had employed when devising the North Carolina plan in the first instance. The results were, shall we say, striking. Every single one of the 3,000 maps would have produced at least one more Democratic House

Member than the State's actual map, and 77% would have elected three or four more. See *Rucho*, 318 F. Supp. 3d, at 875-876, 894; App. 276. A second expert obtained essentially the same results with maps conforming to more generic districting criteria (e.g., compactness and contiguity of districts). Over 99% of that expert's 24,518 simulations would have led to the election of at least one more Democrat, and over 70% would have led to two or three more. See *Rucho*, 318 F. Supp. 3d, at 893-894. Based on those and other findings, the District Court determined that the North Carolina plan substantially dilutes the plaintiffs' votes.

Because the Maryland gerrymander involved just one district, the evidence in that case was far simpler—but no less powerful for that. . . . The 2010 census required only a minimal change in the Sixth District's population—the subtraction of about 10,000 residents from more than 700,000. But instead of making a correspondingly minimal adjustment, Democratic officials reconfigured the entire district. They moved 360,000 residents out and another 350,000 in, while splitting some counties for the first time in almost two centuries. The upshot was a district with 66,000 fewer Republican voters and 24,000 more Democratic ones. In the old Sixth, 47% of registered voters were Republicans and only 36% Democrats. But in the new Sixth, 44% of registered voters were Democrats and only 33% Republicans. That reversal of the district's partisan composition translated into four consecutive Democratic victories, including in a wave election year for Republicans (2014). In what was once a party stronghold, Republicans now have little or no chance to elect their preferred candidate. The District Court thus found that the gerrymandered Maryland map substantially dilutes Republicans' votes.

The majority claims all these findings are mere "prognostications" about the future, in which no one "can have any confidence." But the courts below did not gaze into crystal balls, as the majority tries to suggest. Their findings about these gerrymanders' effects on voters—both in the past and predictably in the future—were evidence-based, data-based, statistics-based.

Knowledge-based, one might say. The courts did what anyone would want a decisionmaker to do when so much hangs in the balance. They looked hard at the facts, and they went where the facts led them. They availed themselves of all the information that mapmakers (like Hofeller and Hawkins) and politicians (like Lewis and O'Malley) work so hard to amass and then use to make every districting decision. They refused to content themselves with unsupported and out-of-date musings about the unpredictability of the American voter. They did not bet America's future — as today the majority does — on the idea that maps constructed with so much expertise and care to make electoral outcomes impervious to voting would somehow or other come apart. They looked at the evidence — at the facts about how these districts operated — and they could reach only one conclusion. By substantially diluting the votes of citizens favoring their rivals, the politicians of one party had succeeded in entrenching themselves in office. They had beat democracy.

B

The majority's broadest claim, as I've noted, is that this is a price we must pay because judicial oversight of partisan gerrymandering cannot be "politically neutral" or "manageable." Courts, the majority argues, will have to choose among contested notions of electoral fairness. (Should they take as the ideal mode of districting proportional representation, many competitive seats, adherence to traditional districting criteria, or so forth?). And even once courts have chosen, the majority continues, they will have to decide "[h]ow much is too much?" — that is, how much deviation from the chosen "touchstone" to allow? In answering that question, the majority surmises, they will likely go far too far. So the whole thing is impossible, the majority concludes. To prove its point, the majority throws a bevy of question marks on the page. (I count nine in just two paragraphs.) But it never tries to analyze the serious question presented here — whether the kind of standard developed below falls prey to those objections, or instead allows for neutral and manageable oversight. The answer, as you've already heard enough to know, is the latter. That kind of oversight is not only possible; it's been done.

Consider neutrality first. Contrary to the majority's suggestion, the District Courts did not have to—and in fact did not—choose among competing visions of electoral fairness. That is because they did not try to compare the State's actual map to an "ideally fair" one (whether based on proportional representation or some other criterion). Instead, they looked at the difference between what the State did and what the State would have done if politicians hadn't been intent on partisan gain. Or put differently, the comparator (or baseline or touchstone) is the result not of a judge's philosophizing but of the State's own characteristics and judgments. The effects evidence in these cases accepted as a given the State's physical geography (e.g., where does the Chesapeake run?) and political geography (e.g., where do the Democrats live on top of each other?). So the courts did not, in the majority's words, try to "counteract 'natural' gerrymandering caused, for example, by the urban concentration of one party." Ante, at 19. Still more, the courts' analyses used the State's own criteria for electoral fairness—except for naked partisan gain. Under their approach, in other words, the State selected its own fairness baseline in the form of its other districting criteria. All the courts did was determine how far the State had gone off that track because of its politicians' effort to entrench themselves in office.

The North Carolina litigation well illustrates the point. The thousands of randomly generated maps I've mentioned formed the core of the plaintiffs' case that the North Carolina plan was an "extreme[ ] outlier." *Rucho*, 318 F. Supp. 3d, at 852 (internal quotation marks omitted); see supra, at 18-20. Those maps took the State's political landscape as a given. In North Carolina, for example, Democratic voters are highly concentrated in cities. That fact was built into all the maps; it became part of the baseline. See *Rucho*, 318 F. Supp. 3d, at 896-897. On top of that, the maps took the State's legal landscape as a given. They incorporated the State's districting priorities, excluding partisanship. So in North

Carolina, for example, all the maps adhered to the traditional criteria of contiguity and compactness. See supra, at 19-20. But the comparator maps in another State would have incorporated different objectives—say, the emphasis Arizona places on competitive districts or the requirement Iowa imposes that counties remain whole. See Brief for Mathematicians et al. as Amici Curiae 19-20. The point is that the assemblage of maps, reflecting the characteristics and judgments of the State itself, creates a neutral baseline from which to assess whether partisanship has run amok. Extreme outlier as to what? As to the other maps the State could have produced given its unique political geography and its chosen districting criteria. Not as to the maps a judge, with his own view of electoral fairness, could have dreamed up.

The Maryland court lacked North Carolina's fancy evidence, but analyzed the gerrymander's effects in much the same way—not as against an ideal goal, but as against an ex ante baseline. To see the difference, shift gears for a moment and compare Maryland and Massachusetts—both of which (aside from Maryland's partisan gerrymander) use traditional districting criteria. In those two States alike, Republicans receive about 35% of the vote in statewide elections. See Almanac of American Politics 2016, at 836, 880. But the political geography of the States differs. In Massachusetts, the Republican vote is spread evenly across the State; because that is so, districting plans (using traditional criteria of contiguity and compactness) consistently lead to an all-Democratic congressional delegation. By contrast, in Maryland, Republicans are clumped—into the Eastern Shore (the First District) and the Northwest Corner (the old Sixth). Claims of partisan gerrymandering in those two States could come out the same way if judges, à la the majority, used their own visions of fairness to police districting plans; a judge in each State could then insist, in line with proportional representation, that 35% of the vote share entitles citizens to around that much of the delegation. But those suits would not come out the same if courts instead asked: What would have happened, given the State's natural political geography and chosen districting criteria, had officials not indulged in partisan manipulation? And that is what the District Court in Maryland inquired into. The court did not strike down the new Sixth District because a judicial ideal of proportional representation commanded another Republican seat. It invalidated that district because the quest for partisan gain made the State override its own political geography and districting criteria. So much, then, for the impossibility of neutrality.

The majority's sole response misses the point. According to the majority, "it does not make sense to use" a State's own (non-partisan) districting criteria as the baseline from which to measure partisan gerrymandering because those criteria "will vary from State to State and year to year." But that is a virtue, not a vice—a feature, not a bug. Using the criteria the State itself has chosen at the relevant time prevents any judicial predilections from affecting the analysis—exactly what the majority claims it wants. At the same time, using those criteria enables a court to measure just what it should: the extent to which the pursuit of partisan advantage—by these legislators at this moment—has distorted the State's districting decisions. Sure, different non-partisan criteria could result, as the majority notes, in different partisan distributions to serve as the baseline. But that in itself raises no issue: Everyone agrees that state officials using non-partisan criteria (e.g., must counties be kept together? should districts be compact?) have wide latitude in districting. The problem arises only when legislators or mapmakers substantially deviate from the baseline distribution by manipulating district lines for partisan gain. So once again, the majority's analysis falters because it equates the demand to eliminate partisan gerrymandering with a demand for a single partisan distribution—the one reflecting proportional representation. But those two demands are different, and only the former is at issue here.

The majority's "how much is too much" critique fares no better than its neutrality argument. How about the following for a first-cut answer: This much is too much. By any measure, a map that produces a greater partisan skew than any of 3,000 randomly generated maps (all with the State's political geography and districting criteria built in) reflects "too much" partisanship. Think about what I just said: The absolute worst of 3,001 possible maps. The only one that could produce a 10-3 partisan split even as Republicans got a bare majority of the statewide vote. And again: How much is too much? This much is too much: A map that without any evident non-partisan districting reason (to the contrary) shifted the composition of a district from 47% Republicans and 36% Democrats to 33% Republicans and 42% Democrats. A map that in 2011 was responsible for the largest partisan swing of a congressional district in the country. Even the majority acknowledges that "[t]hese cases involve blatant examples of partisanship driving districting decisions." If the majority had done nothing else, it could have set the line here. How much is too much? At the least, any gerrymanders as bad as these.

And if the majority thought that approach too case-specific, it could have used the lower courts' general standard—focusing on "predominant" purpose and "substantial" effects—without fear of indeterminacy. I do not take even the majority to claim that courts are incapable of investigating whether legislators mainly intended to seek partisan advantage. That is for good reason. Although purpose inquiries carry certain hazards (which courts must attend to), they are a common form of analysis in constitutional cases. Those inquiries would be no harder here than in other contexts.

Nor is there any reason to doubt, as the majority does, the competence of courts to determine whether a district map "substantially" dilutes the votes of a rival party's supporters from the everything-but-partisanship baseline described above. (Most of the majority's difficulties here really come from its idea that ideal visions set the baseline. But that is double-counting—and, as already shown, wrong to boot.) As this Court recently noted, "the law is full of instances" where a judge's decision rests on "estimating rightly . . . some matter of degree"—including the "substantial[ity]" of risk or harm. . . . To the extent additional guidance has developed over the years (as under the Sherman Act), courts themselves have been its author—as they could be in this context too. And contrary to the majority's suggestion, courts all the time make judgments about the substantiality of harm without reducing them to particular percentages. If courts are no longer competent to do so, they will have to relinquish, well, substantial portions of their docket.

And the combined inquiry used in these cases set the bar high, so that courts could intervene in the worst partisan gerrymanders, but no others. Or to say the same thing, so that courts could intervene in the kind of extreme gerrymanders that nearly every Justice for decades has thought to violate the Constitution. Illicit purpose was simple to show here only because politicians and mapmakers thought their actions could not be attacked in court. They therefore felt free to openly proclaim their intent to entrench their party in office. But if the Court today had declared that behavior justiciable, such smoking guns would all but disappear. Even assuming some officials continued to try implementing extreme partisan gerrymanders, they would not brag about their efforts. So plaintiffs would have to prove the intent to entrench through circumstantial evidence—essentially showing that no other explanation (no geographic feature or non-partisan districting objective) could explain the districting plan's vote dilutive effects. And that would be impossible unless those effects were even more than substantial—unless mapmakers had packed and cracked with abandon in unprecedented ways. As again, they did here. That the two courts below found constitutional violations does not mean their tests were unrigorous; it means that the conduct they confronted was constitutionally appalling—by even the strictest measure, inordinately partisan.

The majority, in the end, fails to understand both the plaintiffs' claims and the decisions below. Everything in today's opinion assumes that these cases grew out of a "desire for proportional representation" or, more generally phrased, a "fair share of political power." And everything in it assumes that the courts below had to (and did) decide what that fair share would be. But that is not so. The plaintiffs objected to one specific practice—the extreme manipulation of district lines for partisan gain. Elimination of that practice could have led to proportional representation. Or it could have led to nothing close. What was left after the practice's removal could have been fair, or could have been unfair, by any number of measures. That was not the crux of this suit. The plaintiffs asked only that the courts bar politicians from entrenching themselves in power by diluting the votes of their rivals' supporters. And the courts, using neutral and manageable—and eminently legal—standards, provided that (and only that) relief. This Court should have cheered, not overturned, that restoration of the people's power to vote. . . .

The gerrymanders here—and they are typical of many—violated the constitutional rights of many hundreds of thousands of American citizens. Those voters (Republicans in the one case, Democrats in the other) did not have an equal opportunity to participate in the political process. Their votes counted for far less than they should have because of their partisan affiliation. When faced with such constitutional wrongs, courts must intervene: "It is emphatically the province and duty of the judicial department to say what the law is." Marbury v. Madison, 1 Cranch 137, 177 (1803). That is what the courts below did. Their decisions are worth a read. They (and others that have recently remedied similar violations) are detailed, thorough, painstaking. They evaluated with immense care the factual evidence and legal arguments the parties presented. They used neutral and manageable and strict standards. They had not a shred of politics about them. Contra the majority, see ante, at 34, this was law.

That is not to deny, of course, that these cases have great political consequence. They do. Among the amicus briefs here is one from a bipartisan group of current and former Members of the House of Representatives. They describe all the ways partisan gerrymandering harms our political system—what they call "a cascade of negative results." Brief as Amicus Curiae 5. These artificially drawn districts shift influence from swing voters to party-base voters who participate in primaries; make bipartisanship and pragmatic compromise politically difficult or impossible;

and drive voters away from an ever more dysfunctional political process. Last year, we heard much the same from current and former state legislators. In their view, partisan gerrymandering has "sounded the death-knell of bipartisanship," creating a legislative environment that is "toxic" and "tribal." Gerrymandering, in short, helps create the polarized political system so many Americans loathe.

And gerrymandering is, as so many Justices have emphasized before, anti-democratic in the most profound sense. In our government, "all political power flows from the people." *Arizona State Legislature*, 576 U.S., at (slip op., at 35). And that means, as Alexander Hamilton once said, "that the people should choose whom they please to govern them." 2 Debates on the Constitution 257 (J. Elliot ed. 1891). But in Maryland and North Carolina they cannot do so. In Maryland, election in and election out, there are 7 Democrats and 1 Republican in the congressional delegation. In North Carolina, however the political winds blow, there are 10 Republicans and 3 Democrats. Is it conceivable that someday voters will be able to break out of that prefabricated box? Sure. But everything possible has been done to make that hard. To create a world in which power does not flow from the people because they do not choose their governors.

Of all times to abandon the Court's duty to declare the law, this was not the one. The practices challenged in these cases imperil our system of government. Part of the Court's role in that system is to defend its foundations. None is more important than free and fair elections. With respect but deep sadness, I dissent.

II
FEDERALISM AT WORK: CONGRESS AND THE NATIONAL ECONOMY

A. The Values of Federalism and Some Techniques for Implementing Them

Page 180. At the end of Note 6, add the following:

5a. *Federalism and the COVID pandemic in the United States.* Substantial aspects of the response to the COVID pandemic were left to state and local governments: mask mandates, school closings, shut-downs of economic activity. The national government engaged in some modest efforts to coordinate these local responses and provided substantial financial guarantees to pharmaceutical companies developing vaccines. Did federalism aid or hinder the overall response?

Consider these possibilities: (1) Federalism aided the response by preventing or discouraging the national government from imposing a uniformly lax system of regulation—a national ban on mask mandates, for example. State and local governments could and did impose more stringent regulations than the national government would have. (2) Federalism hindered the response by preventing or discouraging the national government from imposing a uniformly stringent system of regulation—a national mask mandate, for example. State and local governments could and did regulate more laxly than was socially desirable.

How strongly should the evaluation of those possibilities be influenced by the facts (1) that the incumbent president favored relatively lax regulation (and his successor favored more stringent regulation) and (2) that at the time Congress was under divided partisan control, making it unlikely or impossible for it to develop a regulatory response different from the president's?

Page 185.   At the end of Note 3, add the following:

Conrad Weiler, Jr., *How "Commerce Among the Several States" Became "Interstate Commerce," and Why It Matters*, 34 Const. Comment. 329 (2019), examines the use of the two formulations in Supreme Court opinions and argues that "interstate commerce" was used typically to narrow the scope of "commerce among the several states."

D.   State Regulation of Interstate Commerce

Page 292.   At the end of Note 1, add the following:

See Tennessee Wine & Spirits Assn. v. Thomas, 139 S. Ct. 2449 (2019) (after observing that "it would be strange if the Constitution contained no provision curbing state protectionism," Justice Alito writing for seven members of the Court "reiterate[d] that the Commerce Clause by its own force restricts state protectionism."); Virginia Uranium Ltd. v. Warren, 139 S. Ct. 1894 (2019).

Page 296. At the end of the Note, add the following:

The Court overruled *Quill* in South Dakota v. Wayfair, Inc., 138 S. Ct. 2080 (2018). South Dakota had attempted to impose its sales tax on large internet retailers who had no physical presence in the state but shipped substantial amounts of goods into it. (Formally, local purchasers are supposed to pay a use tax themselves, but, according to the Court, "compliance rates are notoriously low.") "Each year," Justice Kennedy's opinion for the majority observed, "the physical presence rule becomes further removed from economic reality and results in significant revenue losses to the States." The Court therefore held that the rule that a state can tax only activities with a "substantial nexus" to it did not require that the retailer have a physical presence in the state. It was clear that the retailer had sufficient "economic and virtual contacts" with South Dakota to satisfy the general "substantial nexus" requirement. The state sought to impose its taxes only on sellers who did more than $100,000 worth of business in the state. "This quantity of business could not have occurred unless the seller availed itself of the substantial privilege of carrying on business in South Dakota. And [Wayfair and other sellers] are large, national companies that undoubtedly maintain an extensive virtual presence."

On the question of Congress's role, Chief Justice Roberts, dissenting (joined by Justices Breyer, Sotomayor, and Kagan), wrote that, though he agreed that *Quill* was "wrongly decided," "[any] alteration of [the] rules with the potential to disrupt the development of [a] critical segment of the economy should be undertaken by Congress." He noted that "Congress has been considering whether to alter the rule established in *Bellas Hess* for some time. [By] suddenly changing the ground rules, the Court may have waylaid Congress's consideration of the issue. [State] officials can be expected to redirect their attention from working with Congress on a national solution." Observing that "[over] 10,000 jurisdictions levy sales taxes," with different rates, exemptions, and product category definitions, the Chief Justice argued that compliance with these varying rules would impose large costs, particularly on small businesses. "People starting a business selling their embroidered pillowcases or carved decoys can offer their wares throughout the country — but probably not if they have to figure out the tax due on every sale." (Might the requirement of a "substantial nexus" protect such businesses?) For the Chief Justice, "A good reason to leave these matters to Congress is that legislators may more directly consider the competing interests at stake. [Congress] might elect to accommodate these competing interests, by, for example, allowing States to tax Internet sales by remote retailers only if revenue from such sales exceeds some set amount per year."

Justice Kennedy responded, "While it can be conceded that Congress has the authority to change the physical presence rule, Congress cannot change the constitutional default rule. It is inconsistent with the Court's proper role to ask Congress to address a false constitutional premise of this Court's own creation."

Note that the "constitutional default rule" allocates the burden of securing congressional action. The "physical presence" rule allocates that burden to the states, who must secure congressional legislation authorizing them to tax retailers who lack a physical presence. Despite efforts such as those described by the Chief Justice, the states had been unable to secure such legislation over several decades of effort. *Wayfair* allocates the burden to internet retailers, who must (if they want) secure legislation setting national standards for taxation of their sales. The Chief Justice observed that states collected between 87 and 96 percent of the sales taxes associated with sales by the 100 largest internet retailers, and that "[some] companies, including the online behemoth Amazon, now voluntarily collect and remit sales tax in every State that assesses one — even those in which they have no physical presence." Should these considerations affect the Court's choice of default rule (and if so, how)?

E. Preemption

Page 302. At the end of Note 2 in Notes: Preemption, add the following:

Field preemption requires an inquiry into whether state legislation interferes with accomplishing the "full purposes and objectives of Congress." In a context where the parties discussed whether field preemption applied to state legislation with specific purposes, Justice Gorsuch questioned the possibility (and utility) of such an inquiry:

> State legislatures are composed of individuals who often pursue legislation for multiple and unexpressed purposes, so what legal rules should determine when and how to ascribe a particular intention to a particular legislator? What if an impermissible intention existed but wasn't necessary to her vote? And what percentage of the legislature must harbor the impermissible intention before we can impute it to the collective institution? Putting all that aside, how are courts supposed to conduct a reasonable inquiry into these questions when recorded state legislative history materials are often not as readily available or complete as their federal counterparts? And if trying to peer inside legislators' skulls is too fraught an enterprise, shouldn't we limit ourselves to trying to glean legislative purposes from the statutory text where we began?

Virginia Uranium Ltd. v. Warren, 139 S. Ct. 1894 (2019) (joined by Justices Thomas and Kavanaugh). Justice Ginsburg, Justices Sotomayor and Kagan, wrote that these observations "sweep[] well beyond the confines of this case, and therefore seem[] to me inappropriate in an opinion speaking for the Court, rather than for individual members of the Court." Note that Justice Gorsuch's concerns appear to apply equally to attempts to discern congressional purposes in field preemption inquiries. Chief Justice Roberts and Justices Breyer and Alito dissented.

III
THE SCOPE OF CONGRESS'S POWERS: TAXING AND SPENDING, WAR POWERS, INDIVIDUAL RIGHTS, AND STATE AUTONOMY

D. *The Tenth Amendment as a Federalism-Based Limitation on Congressional Power*

Page 369.   At the end of section 2 of the Note, add the following:

2a. *What counts as commandeering?* In *New York*, the Supreme Court dealt with a federal statute that essentially required states to enact legislation. Can federal statutes that prohibit states from enacting legislation violate the anticommandeering principle? In this light, consider Murphy v. National Collegiate Athletic Ass'n, 138 S. Ct. 1461 (2018).

In 1992, Congress enacted the Professional and Amateur Sports Protection Act (PASPA). PASPA did not make sports betting a violation of federal law, but it did prohibit states from "authoriz[ing]" betting on sporting events.

At the time PASPA was enacted, New Jersey prohibited betting on sports, but the state enacted legislation that would have legalized sports betting in Atlantic City and at horseracing tracks. When the NCAA and three major professional sports leagues brought an action to enjoin New Jersey's sports betting law, New Jersey responded that PASPA violated the anticommandeering principle because it prevented the State from modifying or repealing its laws prohibiting sports gambling.

In an opinion by Justice Alito, the Supreme Court agreed. The Court declared that the repeal of existing laws banning gambling was an "authoriz[ation]" of gambling. PASPA's provision forbidding states from authorizing sports gambling "violates the anticommandeering rule. That provision unequivocally dictates what a state legislature may and may not do. . . . [S]tate legislatures are put under the direct control of Congress. It is as if federal officers were installed in state legislative chambers and were armed with the authority to stop legislators from voting on any offending proposals. A more direct affront to state sovereignty is not easy to imagine." PASPA's defenders had argued that commandeering occurs only when Congress commands a state or local government to do something, and not when Congress prohibits them from acting. The Court disagreed: "This distinction is empty. It was a matter of happenstance that the laws challenged in *New York* and *Printz* commanded 'affirmative' action as opposed to imposing a prohibition. The basic principle — that Congress cannot issue direct orders to state legislatures — applies in either event.

"Here is an illustration. PASPA includes an exemption for States that permitted sports betting at the time of enactment, . . . but suppose Congress did not adopt such an exemption. Suppose Congress ordered States with legalized sports betting to take the affirmative step of criminalizing that activity and ordered the remaining States to retain their laws prohibiting sports betting. There is no good reason why the former would intrude more deeply on state sovereignty than the latter."

Is the action/inaction distinction really meaningless with respect to commandeering? Does *Murphy* significantly expand the doctrine?

IV
THE DISTRIBUTION OF NATIONAL POWERS

A. *Introduction*

Page 379.   At the end of section 2 of the Note, add the following:

Many modern critics of separation of powers claim that Madison's theory has not worked as he intended because he failed to anticipate the growth of political parties. Today, these critics claim, politicians are loyal to their fellow party members rather than to the branch where they sit.

Compare Fontana and Huq, Institutional Loyalties in Constitutional Law, 85 U. Chi. L. Rev. 1, 10, 11 (2018). The authors argue that "[The] behavior of federal officials cannot always be explained simply by partisan or ideological motives. The current working of our constitutional system evinces the lingering influence of institutional loyalty of the kind Madison anticipated, particularly in the executive and judicial contexts."

As a normative matter, they claim that institutional loyalties are not "intrinsically desirable ends," but instead should be valued only when they "motivate constitutional compliance, counteract disabling partisan polarization, and dampen the agency costs of representative democracy."

Applying these criteria, they conclude that it would be desirable to "[increase] institutional loyalty within the legislature while diminishing it within the judiciary. The executive branch presents a subtler question. In some contexts, the executive is powerfully motivated by institutional loyalty in ways that redound to the public good. This may be especially so when elected actors press agendas that are directly disruptive of longstanding democratic or institutional practice. But in other regards, there is a case for diluting their effects in ways that protect the rule of law from potentially corrupting and distorting influences."

B.   Case Study: Presidential Seizure

Page 390.   Before the Note, add the following:

3. *Emergency power and the wall.* During the 2016 presidential campaign, candidate Donald Trump promised repeatedly to build a wall, paid for by Mexico, across the southern border of the United States. In December 2018, the Trump administration demanded $5.6 billion to begin construction of the wall. Congress refused to appropriate the money, and the impasse led to a thirty-five-day partial government shutdown — the longest in American history.

The shutdown ended when Congress passed and the President signed an appropriations measure that did not contain the $5.6 billion but, instead, designated $1.35 billion for "the construction of primary pedestrian fencing, including levee pedestrian fencing in the Rio Grande Valley Sector" of the border.

Dissatisfied with this outcome, the President thereupon announced that he would transfer funds appropriated for other purposes to construct the wall. In order to accomplish this objective, he declared a national emergency, relying upon "the Constitution and laws of the United States, including [the National Emergency Act, 50 U.S.C. § 1601 et seq]."

The National Emergency Act does not, itself, create any emergency power. Instead, it provides that "[with] respect to Acts of Congress authorizing the exercise during the period of a national emergency of any special or extraordinary power, the President is authorized to declare such a national emergency." 16 U.S.C. § 1621. The Act further provides that a national emergency declared pursuant to the Act shall terminate if Congress enacts a joint resolution so declaring, 16 U.S.C. § 1622(a), and that within six months of the declaration of an emergency, "each House of Congress shall meet to consider a vote on a joint resolution to determine whether that emergency shall be terminated." 16 U.S.C. § 1622(b).

For his substantive authority to expend the funds, the President relied in part on 10 U.S.C. § 2808(a), which authorized the President upon a declaration of national emergency to "undertake military construction projects, not otherwise authorized by law, that are necessary to support [use] of the armed forces." Congress promptly responded to these actions by enacting a Joint Resolution pursuant to the National Emergency Act terminating the emergency. The President thereupon vetoed the resolution, and proponents of the resolution lacked the votes to override his veto. Various parties then brought suit to enjoin the use of the funds.

Consider the following possibilities:

1. The President's actions are within Justice Jackson's category one, where the President acts "pursuant to an express or implied authorization of Congress, [and] his authority is at its maximum." Congress clearly authorized the expenditure of funds to "undertake military construction projects" upon a declaration of a national emergency, and that is exactly what the President did. There might be a statutory construction issue about whether the funds are "necessary to support [use] of the armed forces," but the President's actions raise no serious constitutional question.

2. The President's actions are within Justice Jackson's category two, where Congress has remained silent. True, Congress did not appropriate the money that the President plans to expend to build

the wall, but neither did it disapprove of the expenditure. The National Emergency Act provides the mechanism for congressional termination of a national emergency, and proponents of the termination lacked the votes to accomplish their objective. Since Congress has not taken a clear position on whether a national emergency exists, the case turns on "the imperatives of events and contemporary imponderables rather than on abstract theories of law." If the case is in this category, how should a court resolve it?

3. The President's actions are within Justice Jackson's category three, where the measures he has taken are "incompatible with the expressed or implied will of Congress," and his power is therefore "at its lowest ebb." Like the congressional refusal to grant the President power to seize private property at the time of the steel seizure controversy, Congress' refusal to appropriate funds to construct the wall and its termination of the emergency declaration make clear that it did not think that an emergency existed. The President is therefore acting in the teeth of congressional disapproval.

Page 391.   After subsection c of the Note, add the following:

c1. "As a logical matter, the notion that discretion increases as sources increase is incorrect without more. Sometimes the opposite is true. Indeed adding sources tends to drive down the probability that all sources will cancel out into uncertainty and yield discretion, according to a simple model of interpretation. . . .

"As an empirical matter, the effect of additional sources seems equally contingent. . . .

"[Analyzing] a new set of appellate decisions casts doubt on an earlier finding that increasing the stock of precedents ultimately increases judicial discretion. [New] data from appellate briefs reinforces an earlier finding that increasing brief length can reduce judicial preferences for affirmance; but the new data also indicate that more issues may increase affirmance rates, and the data fail to show a relationship between the number of sources cited and affirmance. [An] expanded set of district court decisions supports an earlier finding that a large number of doctrinal factors may prompt judges to prioritize law's core factors, without evidence of conventional ideological influence. But the data do not show that more spinning takes place when judges are asked to consider more factors. If anything, the opposite might be true." Samaha, Looking over a Crowd—Do More Interpretive Sources Mean More Discretion?, 92 N.Y.U. L. Rev. 554, 558-560 (2017).

C. Foreign Affairs

Page 410. Before the Note, add the following:

Note: The Status of Individual Rights in the National Security Context.

In her plurality opinion in *Hamdi*, Justice O'Connor asserts that even in times of armed conflict, the Court should "not give short shrift to the values that the country holds dear," and that "a state of war is not a blank check for the President when it comes to the rights of the Nation's citizens."

Compare Trump v. Hawaii, 138 S. Ct. 2392 (2018), where the Court rejected an establishment clause claim relating to a presidential order placing entry restrictions on nationals of eight foreign states, six of which were predominantly Muslim. (The opinion is considered at greater length in the supplement to page 1487 of the Main Volume). The order came in the context of repeated statements by President Trump, which the plaintiffs alleged revealed anti-Muslim bias. The plaintiffs claimed that under ordinary establishment clause principles, this bias was sufficient to make the order unconstitutional, but the Court, in an opinion by Chief Justice Roberts, declined to follow these principles in the context of presidential decisions regarding national security and entry of foreign nationals into the country.

The Court cited prior cases holding that the admission and exclusion of foreign nationals is a "fundamental sovereign attribute exercised by the Government's political departments largely immune from judicial control" and that even when entry decisions affected the constitutional rights of American citizens, it had "limited [its] review to whether the Executive gave a 'facially legitimate and bona fide' reason for its action." According to the Court,

> [a] conventional application of [these principles], asking only whether the policy is facially legitimate and bona fide, would put an end to our review. But the Government has suggested that it may be appropriate here for the inquiry to extend beyond the facial neutrality of the order. For our purposes today, we assume that we may look behind the face of the Proclamation to the extent of applying rational basis review. That standard of review considers whether the entry policy is plausibly related to the Government's stated objective to protect the country and improve vetting processes.

Applying this standard, the Court found that there was a rational basis for the order and that it was therefore constitutionally permissible.

Can Trump v. Hawaii be reconciled with *Hamdi*?

In Korematsu v. United States, the Court upheld the constitutionality of a presidential order issued pursuant to the President's war power excluding Japanese-American citizens from certain parts of the United States. (*Korematsu* is discussed at page 532 of the Main Volume.) It did so, however, only after determining that the order satisfied strict scrutiny. Is the Court's use of rational basis review in Trump v. Hawaii consistent with *Korematsu*? Responding to Justice Sotomayor's invocation of *Korematsu* in her dissenting opinion, the Court wrote the following:

Korematsu has nothing to do with this case. The forcible relocation of U.S. citizens to concentration camps, solely and explicitly on the basis of race, is objectively unlawful and outside the scope of Presidential authority. But it is wholly inapt to liken that morally repugnant order to a facially neutral policy denying certain foreign nationals the privilege of admission. The entry suspension is an act that is well within executive authority and could have been taken by any other President—the only question is evaluating the actions of this particular President in promulgating an otherwise valid Proclamation. The dissent's reference to *Korematsu*, however, affords this Court the opportunity to make express what is already obvious: *Korematsu* was gravely wrong the day it was decided, has been overruled in the court of history, and—to be clear—"has no place in law under the Constitution."

Page 419. Before section 4 of the Note, add the following:

3b. *Yemen.* Since 2015, the United States has been providing military support to a Saudi-led coalition fighting Houthi forces in Yemen. Although no American troops were directly involved in the fighting, the United States provided logistical support, shared military intelligence, and established a "Joint Planning Cell" with Saudi Arabia to coordinate military and intelligence assistance. Until November 2018, the United States also provided mid-air refueling support to Saudi aircraft.

In April 2019, Congress, purporting to utilize its authority under the War Powers Resolution, passed a joint resolution directing the President to remove U.S. Armed Forces from hostilities in or affecting Yemen within 30 days. See S.J. Res. 7, 116th Cong. (2019). President Trump then vetoed the resolution, claiming that U.S. involvement in Yemen did not constitute "hostilities" within the meaning of the War Powers Resolution. (In the wake of INS v. Chadha, page 438 of the Main Volume, Congress had enacted legislation that had the effect of subjecting War Powers resolutions to presidential veto). An effort to override the veto failed.

In his veto message, President Trump emphasized that "there are no United States military personnel in Yemen commanding, participating in, or accompanying" the Saudi coalition. Is the United States engaged in "hostilities" in Yemen within the meaning of the War Powers Resolution? In the wake of the President's veto, are methods available to Congress to end U.S. participation? Does the existence of the War Powers Resolution in any way change the balance of power between the President and Congress with regard to this dispute?

Page 420.   After the first paragraph of section 2 of the Note, add the following:

As pointed out in Bradley and Goldsmith, Presidential Control over International Law, 131 Harv. L. Rev. 1201, 1210 (2018), executive agreements have become the dominant mode of United States agreement-making. Between 1990 and 2012, the United States entered 5,491 executive agreements, but only 366 treaties.

Is the growing use of the executive agreement technique constitutionally troubling? Most commentators agree that it is not if the President is acting pursuant to a congressional delegation or pursuant to relatively clear Article II authority such as the President's power to recognize foreign governments. Suppose, though, that there is neither a clear delegation nor a clear source of Article II authority? Consider in this regard the implications of Dames & Moore v. Regan, page 394 of the Main Volume, where the Court upheld the agreement ending the Iran Hostage Crisis by interpreting prior congressional silence as acquiescence. Compare Koh, Triptych's End: A Better Framework To Evaluate 21st Century International Lawmaking, 121 Yale L.J. Online (2017) (*"Dames & Moore* seems to have recognized a modern truth: that Congress cannot and does not pass judgment on each and every act undertaken by the Executive that has external effects") with Bradley and Goldsmith, supra, at 1262 ("The considerations that were important [in *Dames & Moore*]—historical practice and independent presidential authority—do not hold for executive regulation of many other subjects, such as intellectual property or the environment").

D. Domestic Affairs

Page 429.   Before the Note, add the following:

Note: The Trump Impeachment

In August 2019, an anonymous whistleblower reported concerns about President Trump's efforts to secure the assistance of the Ukraine to discredit Joe Biden, his likely opponent in the 2020 presidential election. After the allegations became public, the White House released a summary of a conversation between President Trump and Ukrainian President Zelenski that seemed to corroborate the allegations. Evidence also emerged that President Trump had ordered the withholding of $391 million in military aid from Ukraine.

On September 24, 2019, House Speaker Nancy Pelosi inaugurated a congressional inquiry into whether the President should be impeached. In conjunction with the inquiry, the House committees issued subpoenas for testimony and documents to various administration officials. In response, the White House Counsel wrote that the inquiry "[violated] the Constitution, the rule of law, and every past precedent" and that "The President cannot allow your constitutionally illegitimate proceedings to distract him and those in the Executive Branch. [To] fulfill his duties to the American people, the Constitution, the Executive Branch, and all future occupants of the Office of the Presidency, President Trump and his

Administration cannot participate in your partisan and unconstitutional inquiry under these circumstances." Accordingly, the administration instructed officials not to comply with the subpoenas.

Following investigation by the House Intelligence Committee, the House Judiciary Committee began drafting articles of impeachment. On December 13, 2019, the Judiciary Committee adopted two articles of impeachment in a straight party-line vote. The first article, alleging abuse of power, stated that

> Using the powers of his high office, President Trump solicited the interference of a foreign government, Ukraine, in the 2020 United States Presidential election. He did so through a scheme or course of conduct that included soliciting the Government of Ukraine to publicly announce investigations that would benefit his reelection, harm the election prospects of a political opponent, and influence the 2020 United States Presidential election to his advantage. President Trump also sought to pressure the Government of Ukraine to take these steps by conditioning official United States Government acts of significant value to Ukraine on its public announcement of the investigations. President Trump engaged in this scheme or course of conduct for corrupt purposes in pursuit of personal political benefit. In so doing, President Trump used the powers of the Presidency in a manner that compromised the national security of the United States and undermined the integrity of the United States democratic process. He thus ignored and injured the interests of the Nation.

The second article, alleging obstruction of Congress, stated that

> [Without] lawful cause or excuse, President Trump directed Executive Branch agencies, offices, and officials not to comply with [subpoenas issued by Congress]. President Trump thus interposed the powers of the Presidency against the lawful subpoenas of the House of Representatives, and

assumed to himself functions and judgments necessary to the exercise of the "sole Power of Impeachment" vested by the Constitution in the House of Representatives.

On December 19, 2019, the House approved both articles by a vote of 230-197 with all but two Democrats voting in favor and all Republicans voting against.

In January, 2020, the Senate conducted a trial of the articles. Although Senators heard from representatives of both sides, the Senate voted along party lines not to permit the testimony of witnesses. On February 5, 2020, the Senate voted to acquit on both counts. The vote on the abuse of power count was 52 for acquittal and 48 for conviction. The vote on the obstruction of Congress count was 53 for acquittal and 47 for conviction. All Democrats voted for conviction on both counts. One Republican voted for conviction on the abuse of power count.

If the facts alleged in the Articles of Impeachment were true, did they constitute high crimes or misdemeanors? Assuming they did, should the House have proceeded in the absence of bipartisan support? Should the House have attempted to enforce its subpoenas in court? Should it have used self-help to enforce the subpoenas by exercising its inherent contempt power or threatening to withhold appropriations if witnesses did not testify?

TRUMP v. VANCE

___U.S. ___ (2020)

CHIEF JUSTICE ROBERTS delivered the opinion of the Court.

In our judicial system, "the public has a right to every man's evidence." Since the earliest days of the Republic, "every man" has included the President of the United States. Beginning with Jefferson and carrying on through Clinton, Presidents have uniformly testified or produced documents in criminal proceedings when called upon by federal courts. This case involves—so far as we and the parties can tell—the first *state* criminal subpoena directed to a President. The President contends that the subpoena is unenforceable. We granted certiorari to decide whether Article II and the Supremacy Clause categorically preclude, or require a heightened standard for, the issuance of a state criminal subpoena to a sitting President.

I . . .

[In 2018, the New York County District Attorney's Office began an investigation into activity involving President Trump. A year later, a grand jury served a subpoena on Mazars USA, Trump's personal accounting firm, requiring Mazars to produce financial records relating to the President and business organizations affiliated with him including tax returns and related schedules. The President then sued the District Attorney and Mazars in federal court to enjoin enforcement of the subpoena. He argued that under Article II and the Supremacy Clause, a sitting president enjoys absolute immunity from state criminal process and that the subpoena was therefore unenforceable while he was in office. The District Court refused to issue the injunction, and the Court of Appeals affirmed.]

II . . .

[The Court recounts events surrounding former Vice President Aaron Burr's trial for treason in 1807. In the runup to the trial, Burr subpoenaed certain documents from President Thomas Jefferson. Jefferson objected, but Chief Justice John Marshall, who was presiding at the trial in his capacity of Circuit Justice for Virginia, rejected Jefferson's arguments.]

The President, Marshall declared, does not "stand exempt from the general provisions of the constitution" or, in particular, the Sixth Amendment's guarantee that those accused have compulsory process for obtaining witnesses for their defense. At common law the "single reservation" to the duty to testify in response to a subpoena was "the case of the king," whose "dignity" was seen as "incompatible" with appearing "under the process of the court." But, as Marshall explained, a king is born to power and can "do no wrong." The President, by contrast, is "of the people" and subject to the law. According to Marshall, the sole argument for exempting the President from testimonial obligations was that his "duties as chief magistrate demand his whole time for national objects." But, in Marshall's assessment, those demands were "not unremitting." And should the President's duties preclude his attendance at a particular time and place, a court could work that out upon return of the subpoena.

Marshall also rejected the prosecution's argument that the President was immune from a subpoena duces tecum because executive papers might contain state secrets. "A subpoena duces tecum," he said, "may issue to any person to whom an ordinary subpoena may issue." As he explained, no "fair construction" of the Constitution supported the conclusion that the right "to compel the attendance of witnesses[ ] does not extend" to requiring those witnesses to "bring[ ] with them such papers as may be material in the defence." And, as a matter of basic fairness, permitting such information to be withheld would "tarnish the reputation of the court." As for "the propriety of introducing any papers," that would "depend on the character of the paper, not on the character of the person who holds it." Marshall acknowledged that the papers sought by Burr could contain information "the disclosure of which would endanger the public safety," but stated that, again, such concerns would have "due consideration" upon the return of the subpoena. . . .

Before Burr received the subpoenaed documents, Marshall rejected the prosecution's core legal theory for treason and Burr was accordingly acquitted. . . .

In the two centuries since the Burr trial, successive Presidents have accepted Marshall's ruling that the Chief Executive is subject to subpoena. In 1818, President Monroe received a subpoena to testify in a court-martial against one of his appointees. His Attorney General, William Wirt—who had served as a prosecutor during Burr's trial—advised Monroe that, per Marshall's ruling, a subpoena to testify may "be properly awarded to the President."

Monroe offered to sit for a deposition and ultimately submitted answers to written interrogatories.

Following Monroe's lead, his successors have uniformly agreed to testify when called in criminal proceedings, provided they could do so at a time and place of their choosing. [The Court recounts instances in which Presidents Grant, Ford, Carter, and Clinton testified in conjunction with criminal proceedings.]

The bookend to Marshall's ruling came in 1974 when the question he never had to decide—whether to compel the disclosure of official communications over the objection of the President—came to a head. [The Court summarizes the facts surrounding United States v. Nixon and the Court's holding in that case.]

III

The history surveyed above all involved *federal* criminal proceedings. Here we are confronted for the first time with a subpoena issued to the President by a local grand jury operating under the supervision of a *state* court.

In the President's view, that distinction makes all the difference. He argues that the Supremacy Clause gives a sitting President absolute immunity from state criminal subpoenas because compliance with those subpoenas would categorically impair a President's performance of his Article II functions. The Solicitor General, arguing on behalf of the United States, agrees with much of the President's reasoning but does not commit to his bottom line. Instead, the Solicitor General urges us to resolve this case by holding that a state grand jury subpoena for a sitting President's personal records must, at the very least, "satisfy a heightened standard of need," which the Solicitor General contends was not met here.

A

We begin with the question of absolute immunity. No one doubts that Article II guarantees the independence of the

Executive Branch. As the head of that branch, the President "occupies a unique position in the constitutional scheme." His duties,
which range from faithfully executing the laws to commanding
the Armed Forces, are of unrivaled gravity and breadth. Quite appropriately, those duties come with protections that safeguard the
President's ability to perform his vital functions.

In addition, the Constitution guarantees "the entire independence of the General Government from any control by the respective States." As we have often repeated, "States have no power . . .
to retard, impede, burden, or in any manner control the operations
of the constitutional laws enacted by Congress." [*McCulloch*] It
follows that States also lack the power to impede the President's
execution of those laws.

Marshall's ruling in *Burr*, entrenched by 200 years of practice and our decision in *Nixon*, confirms that *federal* criminal
subpoenas do not "rise to the level of constitutionally forbidden
impairment of the Executive's ability to perform its constitutionally mandated functions." [*Clinton*] But the President, joined in
part by the Solicitor General, argues that *state* criminal subpoenas
pose a unique threat of impairment and thus demand greater protection. To be clear, the President does not contend here that *this*
subpoena, in particular, is impermissibly burdensome. Instead he
makes a *categorical* argument about the burdens generally associated with state criminal subpoenas, focusing on three: diversion,
stigma, and harassment. We address each in turn.

1

The President's primary contention, which the Solicitor
General supports, is that complying with state criminal subpoenas
would necessarily divert the Chief Executive from his duties. He
grounds that concern in *Nixon v. Fitzgerald*, which recognized a
President's "absolute immunity from damages liability predicated
on his official acts." In explaining the basis for that immunity, this
Court observed that the prospect of such liability could "distract a
President from his public duties, to the detriment of not only the
President and his office but also the Nation that the Presidency

was designed to serve." The President contends that the diversion occasioned by a state criminal subpoena imposes an equally intolerable burden on a President's ability to perform his Article II functions.

But *Fitzgerald* did not hold that distraction was sufficient to confer absolute immunity. We instead drew a careful analogy to the common law absolute immunity of judges and prosecutors, concluding that a President, like those officials, must "deal fearlessly and impartially with the duties of his office"—not be made "unduly cautious in the discharge of [those] duties" by the prospect of civil liability for official acts. Indeed, we expressly rejected immunity based on distraction alone 15 years later in *Clinton v. Jones. . . .*

The same is true of criminal subpoenas. Just as a "properly managed" civil suit is generally "unlikely to occupy any substantial amount of " a President's time or attention, two centuries of experience confirm that a properly tailored criminal subpoena will not normally hamper the performance of the President's constitutional duties. If anything, we expect that in the mine run of cases, where a President is subpoenaed during a proceeding targeting someone else, as Jefferson was, the burden on a President will ordinarily be lighter than the burden of defending against a civil suit.

The President, however, believes the district attorney is investigating him and his businesses. In such a situation, he contends, the "toll that criminal process . . . exacts from the President is even heavier" than the distraction at issue in *Fitzgerald* and *Clinton*, because "criminal litigation" poses unique burdens on the President's time and will generate a "considerable if not overwhelming degree of mental preoccupation."

But the President is not seeking immunity from the diversion occasioned by the prospect of future criminal *liability*. Instead he concedes—consistent with the position of the Department of Justice—that state grand juries are free to investigate a sitting President with an eye toward charging him after the completion of his term. The President's objection therefore must be limited to the *additional* distraction caused by the subpoena itself. But that argument runs up against the 200 years of precedent establishing that Presidents, and their official communications, are subject to judicial process.

2

The President next claims that the stigma of being subpoenaed will undermine his leadership at home and abroad. [But] even if a tarnished reputation were a cognizable impairment, there is nothing inherently stigmatizing about a President performing "the citizen's normal duty of . . . furnishing information relevant" to a criminal investigation. Nor can we accept that the risk of association with persons or activities under criminal investigation can absolve a President of such an important public duty. Prior Presidents have weathered these associations in federal cases, and there is no reason to think any attendant notoriety is necessarily greater in state court proceedings.

To be sure, the consequences for a President's public standing will likely increase if he is the one under investigation. But, again, the President concedes that such investigations are permitted under Article II and the Supremacy Clause, and receipt of a subpoena would not seem to categorically magnify the harm to the President's reputation.

Additionally, while the current suit has cast the Mazars subpoena into the spotlight, longstanding rules of grand jury secrecy aim to prevent the very stigma the President anticipates. Of course, disclosure restrictions are not perfect. But those who make unauthorized disclosures regarding a grand jury subpoena do so at their peril.

3

Finally, the President and the Solicitor General warn that subjecting Presidents to state criminal subpoenas will make them "easily identifiable target[s]" for harassment. But we rejected a nearly identical argument in *Clinton*, where then-President Clinton argued that permitting civil liability for unofficial acts would "generate a large volume of politically motivated harassing and frivolous litigation." The President and the Solicitor General nevertheless argue that state criminal subpoenas pose a heightened risk and could undermine the President's ability to "deal fearlessly and impartially" with the States. They caution that, while federal prosecutors are accountable to and removable by the President, the 2,300 district attorneys in this country are responsive to local constituencies, local interests, and local prejudices, and might "use criminal process to register their dissatisfaction with" the President. What is more, we are told, the state courts supervising local grand juries may not exhibit the same respect that federal courts show to the President as a coordinate branch of Government.

We recognize, as does the district attorney, that harassing subpoenas could, under certain circumstances, threaten the independence or effectiveness of the Executive. Even so, in *Clinton* we found that the risk of harassment was not "serious" because federal courts have the tools to deter and, where necessary, dismiss vexatious civil suits. And, while we cannot ignore the possibility that state prosecutors may have political motivations, here again the law already seeks to protect against the predicted abuse.

First, grand juries are prohibited from engaging in "arbitrary fishing expeditions" and initiating investigations "out of malice or an intent to harass." These protections, as the district attorney himself puts it, "apply with special force to a President, in light of the office's unique position as the head of the Executive Branch." And, in the event of such harassment, a President would be entitled to the protection of federal courts. The policy against federal interference in state criminal proceedings, while strong, allows "intervention in those cases where the District Court properly finds that the state proceeding is motivated by a desire to harass or is conducted in bad faith."

Second, contrary to JUSTICE ALITO's characterization, our holding does not allow States to "run roughshod over the functioning of [the Executive B]ranch." The Supremacy Clause prohibits state judges and prosecutors from interfering with a President's official duties. Any effort to manipulate a President's policy decisions or to "retaliat[e]" against a President for official acts through issuance of a subpoena, would thus be an unconstitutional attempt to "influence" a superior sovereign "exempt" from such obstacles, see *McCulloch*. We generally "assume[] that state courts and prosecutors will observe constitutional limitations." Failing that, federal law allows a President to challenge any allegedly unconstitutional influence in a federal forum, as the President has done here.

Given these safeguards and the Court's precedents, we cannot conclude that absolute immunity is necessary or appropriate under Article II or the Supremacy Clause. Our dissenting colleagues agree. JUSTICE THOMAS reaches the same conclusion based on the original understanding of the Constitution reflected in Marshall's decision in *Burr*. And JUSTICE ALITO, also persuaded by *Burr*, "agree[s]" that "not all" state criminal subpoenas for a President's records "should be barred." On that point the Court is unanimous.

B

We next consider whether a state grand jury subpoena seeking a President's private papers must satisfy a heightened need standard. The Solicitor General would require a threshold showing that the evidence sought is "critical" for "specific charging decisions" and that the subpoena is a "last resort," meaning the evidence is "not available from any other source" and is needed "now, rather than at the end of the President's term." . . .

We disagree, for three reasons. First, such a heightened standard would extend protection designed for official documents to the President's private papers. As the Solicitor General and JUSTICE ALITO acknowledge, their proposed test is derived from executive privilege cases that trace back to *Burr*. There, Marshall explained that if Jefferson invoked presidential privilege over executive communications, the court would not "proceed against the president as against an ordinary individual" but would instead require an affidavit from the defense that "would clearly show the paper to be essential to the justice of the case." The Solicitor General and JUSTICE ALITO would have us apply a similar standard to a President's personal papers. But this argument does not account for the relevant passage from *Burr*: "If there be a paper in the possession of the executive, which is *not of an official nature*, he must stand, as respects that paper, in nearly the same situation with any other individual." And it is only "nearly" — and not "entirely" — because the President retains the right to assert privilege over documents that, while ostensibly private, "partake of the character of an official paper."

Second, neither the Solicitor General nor JUSTICE ALITO has established that heightened protection against state subpoenas is necessary for the Executive to fulfill his Article II functions. Beyond the risk of harassment, which we addressed above, the only justification they offer for the heightened standard is protecting Presidents from "unwarranted burdens." In effect, they argue that even if federal subpoenas to a President are warranted whenever evidence is material, state subpoenas are warranted "only when [the] evidence is essential." But that double standard has no basis in law. For if the state subpoena is not issued to manipulate, the documents themselves are not protected, and the Executive is not impaired, then nothing in Article II or the Supremacy Clause supports holding state subpoenas to a higher standard than their federal counterparts.

Finally, in the absence of a need to protect the Executive, the public interest in fair and effective law enforcement cuts in favor of comprehensive access to evidence. Requiring a state grand jury to meet a heightened standard of need would hobble the grand jury's ability to acquire "all information that might possibly bear on its investigation." And, even assuming the evidence withheld under that standard were preserved until the conclusion of a President's term, in the interim the State would be deprived of investigative leads that the evidence might yield, allowing memories to fade and documents to disappear. This could frustrate the identification, investigation, and indictment of third parties (for whom applicable statutes of limitations might lapse). More troubling, it could prejudice the innocent by depriving the grand jury of *exculpatory* evidence.

Rejecting a heightened need standard does not leave Presidents with "no real protection." To start, a President may avail himself of the same protections available to every other citizen. These include the right to challenge the subpoena on any grounds permitted by state law, which usually include bad faith and undue burden or breadth. And, as in federal court, "[t]he high respect that is owed to the office of the Chief Executive . . . should inform the conduct of the entire proceeding, including the timing and scope of discovery." [*Clinton*].

Furthermore, although the Constitution does not entitle the Executive to absolute immunity or a heightened standard, he is not "relegate[d]" only to the challenges available to private citizens. A President can raise subpoena-specific constitutional challenges, in either a state or federal forum. As previously noted, he can challenge the subpoena as an attempt to influence the performance of his official duties, in violation of the Supremacy Clause. This avenue protects against local political machinations "interposed as an obstacle to the effective operation of a federal constitutional power."

In addition, the Executive can—as the district attorney concedes—argue that compliance with a particular subpoena would impede his constitutional duties. Incidental to the functions confided in Article II is "the power to perform them, without obstruction or impediment." As a result, "once the President sets forth and explains a conflict between judicial proceeding and public duties," or shows that an order or subpoena would "significantly interfere with his efforts to carry out" those duties, "the matter changes." [*Clinton*] At that point, a court should use its inherent authority to quash or modify the subpoena, if necessary to ensure that such "interference with the President's duties would not occur."

* * *

Two hundred years ago, a great jurist of our Court established that no citizen, not even the President, is categorically above the common duty to produce evidence when called upon in a criminal proceeding. We reaffirm that principle today and hold that the President is neither absolutely immune from state criminal subpoenas seeking his private papers nor entitled to a heightened standard of need. The "guard[ ] furnished to this high officer" lies where it always has—in "the conduct of a court" applying established legal and constitutional principles to individual subpoenas in a manner that preserves both the independence of the Executive and the integrity of the criminal justice system.

The arguments presented here and in the Court of Appeals were limited to absolute immunity and heightened need. The Court of Appeals, however, has directed that the case be returned to the District Court, where the President may raise further arguments as appropriate.

JUSTICE KAVANAUGH, with whom JUSTICE GORSUCH joins, concurring in the judgment.

The Court today unanimously concludes that a President does not possess absolute immunity from a state criminal subpoena, but also unanimously agrees that this case should be remanded to the District Court, where the President may raise constitutional and legal objections to the subpoena as appropriate. I agree with those two conclusions. . . .

In our system of government, as this Court has often stated, no one is above the law. That principle applies, of course, to a President. At the same time, in light of Article II of the Constitution, this Court has repeatedly declared—and the Court indicates again today—that a court may not proceed against a President as it would against an ordinary litigant.

The question here, then, is how to balance the State's interests and the Article II interests. The longstanding precedent that has applied to federal criminal subpoenas for official, privileged Executive Branch information is *United States v. Nixon.* That landmark case requires that a prosecutor establish a "demonstrated, specific need" for the President's information.

The *Nixon* "demonstrated, specific need" standard is a tried-and-true test that accommodates both the interests of the criminal process and the Article II interests of the Presidency. The *Nixon* standard ensures that a prosecutor's interest in subpoenaed information is sufficiently important to justify an intrusion on the Article II interests of the Presidency. The *Nixon* standard also reduces the risk of subjecting a President to unwarranted burdens, because it provides that a prosecutor may obtain a President's information only in certain defined circumstances.

Although the Court adopted the *Nixon* standard in a different Article II context—there, involving the confidentiality of official, privileged information—the majority opinion today recognizes that there are also important Article II (and Supremacy Clause) interests at stake here. A state criminal subpoena to a President raises Article II and Supremacy Clause issues because of the potential for a state prosecutor to use the criminal process and issue subpoenas in a way that interferes with the President's duties, through harassment or diversion.

Because this case again entails a clash between the interests of the criminal process and the Article II interests of the Presidency, I would apply the longstanding *Nixon* "demonstrated, specific need" standard to this case. The majority opinion does not apply the *Nixon* standard in this distinct Article II context, as I would have done. That said, the majority opinion appropriately takes account of some important concerns that also animate *Nixon* and the Constitution's balance of powers. The majority opinion explains that a state prosecutor may not issue a subpoena for a President's personal information out of bad faith, malice, or an intent to harass a President; as a result of prosecutorial impropriety; to seek information that is not relevant to an investigation; that is overly broad or unduly burdensome; to manipulate, influence, or retaliate against a President's official acts or policy decisions; or in a way that would impede, conflict with, or interfere with a President's official duties. All nine Members of the Court agree, moreover, that a President may raise objections to a state criminal subpoena not just in state court but also in federal court. And the majority opinion indicates that, in light of the "high respect that is owed to the office of the Chief Executive," courts "should be particularly meticulous" in assessing a subpoena for a President's personal records.

In the end, much may depend on how the majority opinion's various standards are applied in future years and decades. It will take future cases to determine precisely how much difference exists between (i) the various standards articulated by the majority opinion, (ii) the overarching *Nixon* "demonstrated, specific need" standard that I would adopt, and (iii) JUSTICE THOMAS's and JUSTICE ALITO's other proposed standards. In any event, in my view, lower courts in cases of this sort involving a President will almost invariably have to begin by delving into why the State wants the information; why and how much the State needs the information, including whether the State could obtain the information elsewhere; and whether compliance with the subpoena would unduly burden or interfere with a President's official duties.

* * *

I agree that the case should be remanded to the District Court for further proceedings, where the President may raise constitutional and legal objections to the state grand jury subpoena as appropriate.

JUSTICE THOMAS, dissenting. . . .

I agree with the majority that the President does not have absolute immunity from the issuance of a grand jury subpoena. Unlike the majority, however, I do not reach this conclusion based on a primarily functionalist analysis. Instead, I reach it based on the text of the Constitution, which, as understood by the ratifying public and incorporated into an early circuit opinion by Chief Justice Marshall, does not support the President's claim of absolute immunity.

[Justice Thomas discusses the Constitution's text, the original understanding of the text, and prior precedent].

In addition to contesting the issuance of the subpoena, the President also seeks injunctive and declaratory relief against its enforcement. The majority recognizes that the President can seek relief from enforcement, but it does not vacate and remand for the lower courts to address this question. I would do so and instruct them to apply the standard articulated by Chief Justice Marshall in *Burr*: If the President is unable to comply because of his official duties, then he is entitled to injunctive and declaratory relief. . . .

The *Burr* standard places the burden on the President but also requires courts to take pains to respect the demands on the President's time. The Constitution vests the President with extensive powers and responsibilities, and courts are poorly situated to conduct a searching review of the President's assertion that he is unable to comply. . . .

In sum, the demands on the President's time and the importance of his tasks are extraordinary, and the office of the President cannot be delegated to subordinates. A subpoena imposes both demands on the President's limited time and a mental burden, even when the President is not directly engaged in complying. This understanding of the Presidency should guide courts in deciding whether to enforce a subpoena for the President's documents. . . .

Courts must also recognize their own limitations. When the President asserts that matters of foreign affairs or national defense preclude his compliance with a subpoena, the Judiciary will rarely have a basis for rejecting that assertion. Judges "simply lack the relevant information and expertise to second-guess determinations made by the President based on information properly withheld." . . .

* * *

I agree with the majority that the President has no absolute immunity from the issuance of this subpoena. The President also sought relief from enforcement of the subpoena, however, and he asked this Court to allow further proceedings on that question if we rejected his claim of absolute immunity. The Court inexplicably fails to address this request, although its decision leaves the President free to renew his request for an injunction against enforcement immediately on remand.

I would vacate and remand to allow the District Court to determine whether enforcement of this subpoena should be enjoined because the President's "duties as chief magistrate demand his whole time for national objects." Accordingly, I respectfully dissent.

JUSTICE ALITO, dissenting.

This case is almost certain to be portrayed as a case about the current President and the current political situation, but the case has a much deeper significance. While the decision will of course have a direct effect on President Trump, what the Court holds today will also affect all future Presidents—which is to say, it will affect the Presidency, and that is a matter of great and lasting importance to the Nation.

The event that precipitated this case is unprecedented. Respondent Vance, an elected state prosecutor, launched a criminal investigation of a sitting President and obtained a grand jury subpoena for his records. The specific question before us—whether the subpoena may be enforced—cannot be answered adequately without considering the broader question that frames it: whether the Constitution imposes restrictions on a State's deployment of its criminal law enforcement powers against a sitting President. If the Constitution sets no such limits, then a local prosecutor may prosecute a sitting President. And if that is allowed, it follows *a fortiori* that the subpoena at issue can be enforced. On the other hand, if the Constitution does not permit a State to prosecute a sitting President, the next logical question is whether the Constitution restrains any other prosecutorial or investigative weapons.

These are important questions that go to the very structure of the Government created by the Constitution. In evaluating these questions, two important structural features must be taken into account. . . .

The first is the nature and role of the Presidency. The Presidency, like Congress and the Supreme Court, is a permanent institution created by the Constitution. All three of these institutions are distinct from the human beings who serve in them at any point in time. In the case of Congress or the Supreme Court, the distinction is easy to perceive, since they have multiple Members. But because "[t]he President is the only person who alone composes a branch of government . . . , there is not always a clear line between his personal and official affairs." As a result, the law's treatment of the person who serves as President can have an important effect on the institution, and the institution of the Presidency plays an indispensable role in our constitutional system. . . .

The second structural feature is the relationship between the Federal Government and the States. Just as our Constitution balances power against power among the branches of the Federal Government, it also divides power between the Federal Government and the States. The Constitution permitted the States to retain many of the sovereign powers that they previously possessed, but it gave the Federal Government powers that were deemed essential for the Nation's well-being and, indeed, its survival. And it provided for the Federal Government to be independent of and, within its allotted sphere, supreme over the States. Art. VI, cl. 2. Accordingly, a State may not block or interfere with the lawful work of the National Government. . . .

[A] State's sovereign power to enforce its criminal laws must accommodate the indispensable role that the Constitution assigns to the Presidency. This must be the rule with respect to a state prosecution of a sitting President. Both the structure of the Government established by the Constitution and the Constitution's provisions on the impeachment and removal of a President make it clear that the prosecution of a sitting President is out of the question. . . .

In the proceedings below, neither respondent, nor the District Court, nor the Second Circuit was willing to concede the fundamental point that a sitting President may not be prosecuted by a local district attorney. Respondent has said that he is investigating the President and, until oral argument in this Court, he never foreswore an intention to charge the President while he is still in office. The District Court conceded only that "perhaps" a sitting President could not be prosecuted for an offense punishable by "lengthy imprisonment" but that an offense requiring only a short trial would be another matter.

The scenario apparently contemplated by the District Court is striking. If a sitting President were charged in New York County, would he be arrested and fingerprinted? He would presumably be required to appear for arraignment in criminal court, where the judge would set the conditions for his release. Could he be sent to Rikers Island or be required to post bail? Could the judge impose restrictions on his travel? If the President were scheduled to travel abroad — perhaps to attend a G–7 meeting — would he have to get judicial approval? If the President were charged with a complicated offense requiring a long trial, would he have to put his Presidential responsibilities aside for weeks on end while sitting in a Manhattan courtroom? While the trial was in progress, would aides be able to approach him and whisper in his ear about pressing matters? Would he be able to obtain a recess whenever he needed to speak with an aide at greater length or attend to an urgent matter, such as speaking with a foreign leader? Could he effectively carry out all his essential Presidential responsibilities after the trial day ended and at the same time adequately confer with his trial attorneys regarding his defense? Or should he be expected to give up the right to attend his own trial and be tried in absentia? And if he were convicted, could he be imprisoned? Would aides be installed in a nearby cell?

This entire imagined scene is farcical. . . .

While the prosecution of a sitting President provides the most dramatic example of a clash between the indispensable work of the Presidency and a State's exercise of its criminal law enforcement powers, other examples are easy to imagine. Suppose state officers obtained and sought to execute a search warrant for a sitting President's private quarters in the White House. Suppose a state court authorized surveillance of a telephone that a sitting President was known to use. Or suppose that a sitting President was subpoenaed to testify before a state grand jury and, as is generally the rule, no Presidential aides, even those carrying the so-called "nuclear football," were permitted to enter the grand jury room. What these examples illustrate is a principle that this Court has recognized: legal proceedings involving a sitting President must take the responsibilities and demands of the office into account.

It is not enough to recite sayings like "no man is above the law" and "the public has a right to every man's evidence." These sayings are true — and important — but they beg the question. The law applies equally to all persons, including a person who happens for a period of time to occupy the Presidency. But there is no question that the nature of the office demands in some instances that the application of laws be adjusted at least until the person's term in office ends. . . .

I now come to the specific investigative weapon at issue in the case before us — a subpoena for a sitting President's records. This weapon is less intrusive in an immediate sense than those mentioned above. Since the records are held by, and the subpoena was issued to, a third party, compliance would not require much work on the President's part. And after all, this is just one subpoena.

But we should heed the "great jurist," who rejected a similar argument in *McCulloch*. If we say that a subpoena to a third party is insufficient to undermine a President's performance of his duties, what about a subpoena served on the President himself? Surely in that case, the President could turn over the work of gathering the requested documents to attorneys or others recruited to perform the task. And if one subpoena is permitted, what about two? Or three? Or ten? Drawing a line based on such factors would involve the same sort of "perplexing inquiry, so unfit for the judicial department" that Marshall rejected in *McCulloch*.

The Court faced a similar issue when it considered whether a President can be sued for an allegedly unlawful act committed in the performance of official duties. See *Nixon v. Fitzgerald*. We did not ask whether the particular suit before us would have interfered with the carrying out of Presidential duties. (It could not have had that effect because President Nixon had already left office.)

Instead, we adopted a rule for all such suits, and we should take a similar approach here. The rule should take into account both the effect of subpoenas on the functioning of the Presidency and the risk that they will be used for harassment. . . .

In light of the above, a subpoena like the one now before us should not be enforced unless it meets a test that takes into account the need to prevent interference with a President's discharge of the responsibilities of the office. I agree with the Court that not all such subpoenas should be barred. There may be situations in which there is an urgent and critical need for the subpoenaed information. The situation in the Burr trial, where the documents at issue were sought by a criminal defendant to defend against a charge of treason, is a good example. But in a case like the one at hand, a subpoena should not be allowed unless a heightened standard is met. . . .

[We] should not treat this subpoena like an ordinary grand jury subpoena and should not relegate a President to the meager defenses that are available when an ordinary grand jury subpoena is challenged. But that, at bottom, is the effect of the Court's decision.

The Presidency deserves greater protection. Thus, in a case like this one, a prosecutor should be required (1) to provide at least a general description of the possible offenses that are under investigation, (2) to outline how the subpoenaed records relate to those offenses, and (3) to explain why it is important that the records be produced and why it is necessary for production to occur while the President is still in office. . . .

Unlike this rule, which would not undermine any legitimate state interests, the opinion of the Court provides no real protection for the Presidency. . . .

For all practical purposes, the Court's decision places a sitting President in the same unenviable position as any other person whose records are subpoenaed by a grand jury. . . .

* * *

The subpoena at issue here is unprecedented. Never before has a local prosecutor subpoenaed the records of a sitting President. The Court's decision threatens to impair the functioning of the Presidency and provides no real protection against the use of the subpoena power by the Nation's 2,300+ local prosecutors. Respect for the structure of Government created by the Constitution demands greater protection for an institution that is vital to the Nation's safety and well-being.

I therefore respectfully dissent.

TRUMP v. MAZARS, USA

___ U.S. ___ (2020)

CHIEF JUSTICE ROBERTS delivered the opinion of the Court.

Over the course of five days in April 2019, three committees of the U. S. House of Representatives issued four subpoenas seeking information about the finances of President Donald J. Trump, his children, and affiliated businesses. We have held that the House has authority under the Constitution to issue subpoenas to assist it in carrying out its legislative responsibilities. The House asserts that the financial information sought here—encompassing a decade's worth of transactions by the President and his family—will help guide legislative reform in areas ranging from money laundering and terrorism to foreign involvement in U. S. elections. The President contends that the House lacked a valid legislative aim and instead sought these records to harass him, expose personal matters, and conduct law enforcement activities beyond its authority. The question presented is whether the subpoenas exceed the authority of the House under the Constitution.

We have never addressed a congressional subpoena for the President's information. Two hundred years ago, it was established that Presidents may be subpoenaed during a federal criminal proceeding, [Burr] and earlier today we extended that ruling to state criminal proceedings, Trump v. Vance. Nearly fifty years ago, we held that a federal prosecutor could obtain information from a President despite assertions of executive privilege, United States v. Nixon and more recently we ruled that a private litigant could subject a President to a damages suit and appropriate discovery obligations in federal court, Clinton v. Jones.

This case is different. Here the President's information is sought not by prosecutors or private parties in connection with a particular judicial proceeding, but by committees of Congress that have set forth broad legislative objectives. Congress and the President—the two political branches established by the Constitution—have an ongoing relationship that the Framers intended to feature both rivalry and reciprocity. See The Federalist No. 51); [*Youngstown*, Jackson, J., concurring] That distinctive aspect necessarily informs our analysis of the question before us.

I

A

Each of the three committees sought overlapping sets of financial documents, but each supplied different justifications for the requests.

[The House Committee on Financial Services issued two subpoenas, one to Deutsche Bank and one to Capital One, seeking financial information of the President, his children, immediate family members, and several affiliated businesses. The subpoenas were issued pursuant to House Resolution 206, which called for "efforts to close loopholes that allow corruption, terrorism, and money laundering to infiltrate our country's financial system." The Permanent Select Committee on Intelligence issued an identical subpoena to Deutsche Bank. The House claimed that this subpoena was part of an investigation into foreign efforts to undermine the U. S. political process. Finally the House Committee on Oversight and Reform issued a subpoena, this time to the President's personal accounting firm, Mazars USA. The subpoena demanded financial information related to the President and several affiliated business entities from 2011 through 2018. The Chair of the Committee based the subpoena on then recent testimony by the President's former personal attorney, Michael Cohen, along with several documents prepared by Mazars and supplied by Cohen, which raised questions about whether the President had accurately represented his financial affairs. Chairman Cummings asserted that the Committee had "full authority to investigate" whether the President: (1) "may have engaged in illegal conduct before and during his tenure in office," (2) "has undisclosed conflicts of interest that may impair his ability to make impartial policy decisions," (3) "is complying with the Emoluments Clauses of the Constitution," and (4) "has accurately reported his finances to the Office of Government Ethics and other federal entities." "The Committee's interest in these matters," the Chair concluded, "informs its review of multiple laws and legislative proposals under our jurisdiction."]

B....

[The President, his children, and affiliated businesses filed two suits challenging the subpoenas in federal court. They claimed that the subpoenas lacked a legitimate legislative purpose and violated the separation of powers, but not that the subpoenaed material was protected by executive privilege. Both trial courts rejected the challenge, and both courts of appeals affirmed].

II

A

The question presented is whether the subpoenas exceed the authority of the House under the Constitution. Historically, disputes over congressional demands for presidential documents have not ended up in court. Instead, they have been hashed out in the "hurly-burly, the give-and-take of the political process between the legislative and the executive."

That practice began with George Washington and the early Congress. In 1792, a House committee requested Executive Branch documents pertaining to General St. Clair's campaign against the Indians in the Northwest Territory, which had concluded in an utter rout of federal forces when they were caught by surprise near the present-day border between Ohio and Indiana. Since this was the first such request from Congress, President Washington called a Cabinet meeting, wishing to take care that his response "be rightly conducted" because it could "become a precedent."

The meeting, attended by the likes of Alexander Hamilton, Thomas Jefferson, Edmund Randolph, and Henry Knox, ended with the Cabinet of "one mind": The House had authority to "institute inquiries" and "call for papers" but the President could "exercise a discretion" over disclosures, "communicat[ing] such papers as the public good would permit" and "refus[ing]" the rest. President Washington then dispatched Jefferson to speak to individual congressmen and "bring them by persuasion into the right channel." The discussions were apparently fruitful, as the House later narrowed its request and the documents were supplied without recourse to the courts.

Jefferson, once he became President, followed Washington's precedent. In early 1807, after Jefferson had disclosed that "sundry persons" were conspiring to invade Spanish territory in North America with a private army, the House requested that the President produce any information in his possession touching on the conspiracy (except for information that would harm the public interest). Jefferson chose not to divulge the entire "voluminous" correspondence on the subject, explaining that much of it was "private" or mere "rumors" and "neither safety nor justice" permitted him to "expos[e] names" apart from identifying the conspiracy's "principal actor": Aaron Burr. Instead of the entire correspondence, Jefferson sent Congress particular documents and a special message summarizing the conspiracy.

Ever since, congressional demands for the President's information have been resolved by the political branches without involving this Court. [The Court discusses examples drawn from the Reagan and Clinton presidencies.]

This dispute [represents] a significant departure from historical practice. Although the parties agree that this particular controversy is justiciable, we recognize that it is the first of its kind
to reach this Court; that disputes of this sort can raise important
issues concerning relations between the branches; that related disputes involving congressional efforts to seek official Executive
Branch information recur on a regular basis, including in the context of deeply partisan controversy; and that Congress and the
Executive have nonetheless managed for over two centuries to
resolve such disputes among themselves without the benefit of
guidance from us. Such longstanding practice " 'is a consideration of great weight' " in cases concerning "the allocation of
power between [the] two elected branches of Government," and
it imposes on us a duty of care to ensure that we not needlessly
disturb "the compromises and working arrangements that [those]
branches . . . themselves have reached." With that in mind, we
turn to the question presented.

B

Congress has no enumerated constitutional power to conduct
investigations or issue subpoenas, but we have held that each
House has power "to secure needed information" in order to legislate. This "power of inquiry—with process to enforce it—is
an essential and appropriate auxiliary to the legislative function."
Without information, Congress would be shooting in the dark, unable to legislate "wisely or effectively." The congressional power
to obtain information is "broad" and "indispensable." It encom-
passes inquiries into the administration of existing laws, studies
of proposed laws, and "surveys of defects in our social, economic
or political system for the purpose of enabling the Congress to
remedy them." . . .

Because this power is "justified solely as an adjunct to the
legislative process," it is subject to several limitations. Most importantly, a congressional subpoena is valid only if it is "related
to, and in furtherance of, a legitimate task of the Congress." The

subpoena must serve a "valid legislative purpose,"; it must "concern[ ] a subject on which legislation 'could be had,' " . . . .

Furthermore, Congress may not issue a subpoena for the purpose of "law enforcement," because "those powers are assigned under our Constitution to the Executive and the Judiciary." Thus Congress may not use subpoenas to "try" someone "before [a] committee for any crime or wrongdoing.". Congress has no "'general' power to inquire into private affairs and compel disclosures," and "there is no congressional power to expose for the sake of exposure. "Investigations conducted solely for the personal aggrandizement of the investigators or to 'punish' those investigated are indefensible."

Finally, recipients of legislative subpoenas retain their constitutional rights throughout the course of an investigation.. And recipients have long been understood to retain common law and constitutional privileges with respect to certain materials, such as attorney-client communications and governmental communications protected by executive privilege.

C

The President contends, as does the Solicitor General appearing on behalf of the United States, that the usual rules for congressional subpoenas do not govern here because the President's papers are at issue. They argue for a more demanding standard based in large part on cases involving the Nixon tapes — recordings of conversations between President Nixon and close advisers discussing the break-in at the Democratic National Committee's headquarters at the Watergate complex. The tapes were subpoenaed by a Senate committee and the Special Prosecutor investigating the break-in, prompting President Nixon to invoke executive privilege and leading to two cases addressing the showing necessary to require the President to comply with the subpoenas.

Those cases, the President and the Solicitor General now contend, establish the standard that should govern the House subpoenas here. Quoting *Nixon*, the President asserts that the House must establish a "demonstrated, specific need" for the financial information, just as the Watergate special prosecutor was required to do in order to obtain the tapes. And drawing on [a] D. C. Circuit case refusing to enforce the Senate subpoena for the tapes — the President and the Solicitor General argue that the House must show that the financial information is "demonstrably critical" to its legislative purpose.

We disagree that these demanding standards apply here. Unlike the cases before us, [the prior cases] involved Oval Office communications over which the President asserted executive privilege. [We] decline to transplant that protection root and branch to cases involving nonprivileged, private information, which by definition does not implicate sensitive Executive Branch deliberations. . . .

Such a categorical approach would represent a significant departure from the longstanding way of doing business between the branches, giving short shrift to Congress's important interests in conducting inquiries to obtain the information it needs to legislate effectively. . . .

D

The House meanwhile would have us ignore that these suits involve the President. Invoking our precedents concerning investigations that did not target the President's papers, the House urges us to uphold its subpoenas because they "relate[ ] to a valid legislative purpose" or "concern[ ] a subject on which legislation could be had." . . .

Largely following the House's lead, the courts below treated these cases much like any other, applying precedents that do not involve the President's papers. . . .

The House's approach fails to take adequate account of the significant separation of powers issues raised by congressional subpoenas for the President's information. Congress and the President have an ongoing institutional relationship as the "opposite and rival" political branches established by the Constitution. The

Federalist No. 51. As a result, congressional subpoenas directed at the President differ markedly from congressional subpoenas we have previously reviewed, and they bear little resemblance to criminal subpoenas issued to the President in the course of a specific investigation, see *Vance*; *Nixon*. Unlike those subpoenas, congressional subpoenas for the President's information unavoidably pit the political branches against one another.

Far from accounting for separation of powers concerns, the House's approach aggravates them by leaving essentially no limits on the congressional power to subpoena the President's personal records. Any personal paper possessed by a President could potentially "relate to" a conceivable subject of legislation, for Congress has broad legislative powers that touch a vast number of subjects. The President's financial records could relate to economic reform, medical records to health reform, school transcripts to education reform, and so on. Indeed, at argument, the House was unable to identify *any* type of information that lacks some relation to potential legislation.

Without limits on its subpoena powers, Congress could "exert an imperious controul" over the Executive Branch and aggrandize itself at the President's expense, just as the Framers feared. And a limitless subpoena power would transform the "established practice" of the political branches. Instead of negotiating over information requests, Congress could simply walk away from the bargaining table and compel compliance in court. . . .

The interbranch conflict here does not vanish simply because the subpoenas seek personal papers or because the President sued in his personal capacity. The President is the only person who alone composes a branch of government. As a result, there is not always a clear line between his personal and official affairs. "The interest of the man" is often "connected with the constitutional rights of the place." The Federalist No. 51. Given the close connection between the Office of the President and its occupant, congressional demands for the President's papers can implicate the relationship between the branches regardless whether those papers are personal or official. Either way, a demand may aim to harass the President or render him "complaisan[t] to the humors of the Legislature." In fact, a subpoena for personal papers may pose a heightened risk of such impermissible purposes, precisely because of the documents' personal nature and their less evident connection to a legislative task. . . .

In addition, separation of powers concerns are no less palpable here simply because the subpoenas were issued to third parties. Congressional demands for the President's information present an interbranch conflict no matter where the information is held—it is, after all, the President's information. . . .

E

Congressional subpoenas for the President's personal information implicate weighty concerns regarding the separation of powers. Neither side, however, identifies an approach that accounts for these concerns. For more than two centuries, the political branches have resolved information disputes using the wide variety of means that the Constitution puts at their disposal. The nature of such interactions would be transformed by judicial enforcement of either of the approaches suggested by the parties, eroding a "[d]eeply embedded traditional way[ ] of conducting government." [*Youngstown,* Frankfurter, J., concurring)].

A balanced approach is necessary, one that takes a "considerable impression" from "the practice of the government, and "resist[s]" the "pressure inherent within each of the separate Branches to exceed the outer limits of its power." We therefore conclude that, in assessing whether a subpoena directed at the President's personal information is "related to, and in furtherance of, a legitimate task of the Congress," courts must perform a careful analysis that takes adequate account of the separation of powers principles at stake, including both the significant legislative interests of Congress and the "unique position" of the President.

First, courts should carefully assess whether the asserted legislative purpose warrants the significant step of involving the President and his papers. [Congress] may not rely on the President's information if other sources could reasonably provide

Congress the information it needs in light of its particular legislative objective. The President's unique constitutional position means that Congress may not look to him as a "case study" for general legislation.

Unlike in criminal proceedings, where "[t]he very integrity of the judicial system" would be undermined without "full disclosure of all the facts," efforts to craft legislation involve predictive policy judgments that are "not hamper[ed] . . . in quite the same way" when every scrap of potentially relevant evidence is not available. While we certainly recognize Congress's important interests in obtaining information through appropriate inquiries, those interests are not sufficiently powerful to justify access to the President's personal papers when other sources could provide Congress the information it needs.

Second, to narrow the scope of possible conflict between the branches, courts should insist on a subpoena no broader than reasonably necessary to support Congress's legislative objective. . . .

Third, courts should be attentive to the nature of the evidence offered by Congress to establish that a subpoena advances a valid legislative purpose. The more detailed and substantial the evidence of Congress's legislative purpose, the better. That is particularly true when Congress contemplates legislation that raises sensitive constitutional issues, such as legislation concerning the Presidency. In such cases, it is "impossible" to conclude that a subpoena is designed to advance a valid legislative purpose unless Congress adequately identifies its aims and explains why the President's information will advance its consideration of the possible legislation.

Fourth, courts should be careful to assess the burdens imposed on the President by a subpoena. We have held that burdens on the President's time and attention stemming from judicial process and litigation, without more, generally do not cross constitutional lines. See *Vance; Clinton.* But burdens imposed by a congressional subpoena should be carefully scrutinized, for they stem from a rival political branch that has an ongoing relationship with the President and incentives to use subpoenas for institutional advantage.

Other considerations may be pertinent as well; one case every two centuries does not afford enough experience for an exhaustive list.

When Congress seeks information "needed for intelligent legislative action," it "unquestionably" remains "the duty of *all* citizens to cooperate." Congressional subpoenas for information from the President, however, implicate special concerns regarding the separation of powers. The courts below did not take adequate account of those concerns. The judgments of the Courts of Appeals for the D. C. Circuit and the Second Circuit are vacated, and the cases are remanded for further proceedings consistent with this opinion.

It is so ordered.

JUSTICE THOMAS, dissenting. . . .

I would hold that Congress has no power to issue a legislative subpoena for private, nonofficial documents—whether they belong to the President or not. Congress may be able to obtain these documents as part of an investigation of the President, but to do so, it must proceed under the impeachment power. Accordingly, I would reverse the judgments of the Courts of Appeals. . . .

At the time of the founding, the power to subpoena private, nonofficial documents was not included by necessary implication in any of Congress' legislative powers. . . .

Congress' legislative powers do not authorize it to engage in a nationwide inquisition with whatever resources it chooses to appropriate for itself. The majority's solution—a nonexhaustive four-factor test of uncertain origin—is better than nothing. But the power that Congress seeks to exercise here has even less basis in the Constitution than the majority supposes. I would reverse in full because the power to subpoena private, nonofficial documents is not a necessary implication of Congress' legislative powers. If Congress wishes to obtain these documents, it should

proceed through the impeachment power. Accordingly, I respectfully dissent.

JUSTICE ALITO, dissenting.

JUSTICE THOMAS makes a valuable argument about the constitutionality of congressional subpoenas for a President's personal
documents. In these cases, however, I would assume for the sake
of argument that such subpoenas are not categorically barred.
Nevertheless, legislative subpoenas for a President's personal
documents are inherently suspicious. Such documents are sel-
dom of any special value in considering potential legislation, and
subpoenas for such documents can easily be used for improper
non-legislative purposes. Accordingly, courts must be very sensitive to separation of powers issues when they are asked to approve
the enforcement of such subpoenas. . . .

Whenever such a subpoena comes before a court, Congress
should be required to make more than a perfunctory showing that
it is seeking the documents for a legitimate legislative purpose
and not for the purpose of exposing supposed Presidential wrongdoing. The House can inquire about possible Presidential wrongdoing pursuant to its impeachment power, but the Committees do
not defend these subpoenas as ancillary to that power.

Instead, they claim that the subpoenas were issued to gather
information that is relevant to legislative issues, but there is disturbing evidence of an improper law enforcement purpose. In
addition, the sheer volume of documents sought calls out for
explanation. . . .

[The] House should provide a description of the type of legislation being considered, and while great specificity is not necessary, the description should be sufficient to permit a court to
assess whether the particular records sought are of any special
importance. The House should also spell out its constitutional authority to enact the type of legislation that it is contemplating,
and it should justify the scope of the subpoenas in relation to the
articulated legislative needs. In addition, it should explain why

the subpoenaed information, as opposed to information available from other sources, is needed. Unless the House is required to make a showing along these lines, I would hold that enforcement of the subpoenas cannot be ordered. Because I find the terms of the Court's remand inadequate, I must respectfully dissent.

Page 436. Before section c of the Note, add the following:

Should the constitutionality of vague delegations turn on a practical assessment of how much power to deviate from congressional will an agency actually has? In Sullivan, Powers But How Much Power? Game Theory and the Nondelegation Principle, 104 Va. L. Rev. 1229 (2018), the author uses insights drawn from game theory to demonstrate that even when agencies are operating under vague or meaningless standards, they often have strong incentives to comply with the desires of Congress. He argues that constitutional insistence on precise delegations should be relaxed in circumstances when agencies have little actual power to depart from congressional will. Does this argument take sufficient account of the political accountability objections to delegation discussed in the text?

Page 437. Before section 5 of the Note, add the following:

In the case that follows, the Court gave the strongest indications yet that it may be prepared to reconsider the nondelegation doctrine.

GUNDY v. UNITED STATES, 588 U.S.___(2019). The Sex Offender Registration and Notification Act (SORNA) requires various individuals characterized as "sex offenders" to register in a national registry and punishes failure to do so as a criminal offense. However, the Act provides that "[the] Attorney General shall have the authority to specify the applicability of the [registration requirements] to sex offenders convicted before the enactment of this chapter."

Pursuant to this authority, the Attorney General issued a rule providing that SORNA applied to all pre-Act offenders. Petitioner was a pre-Act offender convicted of failure to register. He argued that Congress had unconstitutionally delegated legislative power when it authorized the Attorney General to "specify the applicability" of the registration requirement.

The Court affirmed petitioner's conviction. Writing for a plurality of the Court (Justices Ginsburg, Breyer, and Sotomayor joined her opinion), Justice Kagan affirmed the Court's "intelligible principle" test for statutory delegations:

"Given that standard, a nondelegation inquiry always begins (and often almost ends) with statutory interpretation. The constitutional question is whether Congress has supplied an intelligible principle to guide the delegee's use of discretion. So the answer requires construing the challenged statute to figure out what task it delegates and what instructions it provides. . . .

"[SORNA] does not give the Attorney General anything like the 'unguided' and 'unchecked' authority that Gundy says. The provision, in Gundy's view, 'grants the Attorney General plenary power to determine SORNA's applicability to pre-Act offenders—to require them to register, or not, as she sees fit, and to change her policy for any reason and at any time.' If that were so, we would face a nondelegation question. But it is not. This Court has already interpreted [SORNA] to say something different—to require the Attorney General to apply SORNA to all pre-Act offenders as soon as feasible. [The Court cites its earlier decision, Reynolds v. United States, 565 U.S. 432 (2012)]. . . .

"Now that we have determined what [SORNA] means, we can consider whether it violates the Constitution. The question becomes: Did Congress make an impermissible delegation when it instructed the Attorney General to apply SORNA's registration requirements to pre-Act offenders as soon as feasible?

"In this context, the delegation in SORNA easily passes muster. The statute conveyed Congress's policy that the Attorney General require pre-Act offenders to register as soon as feasible. Under the law, the feasibility issues he could address were administrative—and, more specifically, transitional in nature. [The] Act informed the Attorney General that he did not have forever to work things out. By stating its demand for a 'comprehensive' registration system and by defining the 'sex offenders' required to register to include pre-Act offenders, Congress conveyed that the Attorney General had only temporary authority. [That] statutory authority, as compared to delegations we have upheld in the past, is distinctly small-bore. It falls well within constitutional bounds.

"Indeed, if SORNA's delegation is unconstitutional, then most of Government is unconstitutional—dependent as Congress is on the need to give discretion to executive officials to implement its programs. [Among] the judgments often left to executive officials are ones involving feasibility. In fact, standards of that kind are ubiquitous in the U.S. Code."

Justice Alito concurred in the judgment: "The Constitution confers on Congress certain 'legislative [p]owers' and does not permit Congress to delegate them to another branch of government. Nevertheless, since 1935, the Court has uniformly rejected nondelegation arguments and has upheld provisions that authorized agencies to adopt important rules pursuant to extraordinarily capacious standards.

"If a majority of this Court were willing to reconsider the approach we have taken for the past 84 years, I would support that effort. But because a majority is not willing to do that, it would be freakish to single out the provision at issue here for special treatment.

"Because I cannot say that the statute lacks a discernable standard that is adequate under the approach this Court has taken for many years, I vote to affirm."

Justice Gorsuch, joined by Chief Justice Roberts and Justice Thomas, dissented: "The Constitution promises that only the people's elected representatives may adopt new federal laws restricting liberty. Yet the statute before us scrambles that design. It purports to endow the nation's chief prosecutor with the power to write his own criminal code governing the lives of a half-million citizens. Yes, those affected are some of the least popular among us. But if a single executive branch official can write laws restricting the liberty of this group of persons, what does that mean for the next?

"Today, a plurality of an eight-member Court endorses this extraconstitutional arrangement but resolves nothing. Working from an understanding of the Constitution at war with its text and history, the plurality reimagines the terms of the statute before us and insists there is nothing wrong with Congress handing off so much power to the Attorney General. But Justice ALITO supplies the fifth vote for today's judgment and he does not join either the plurality's constitutional or statutory analysis, indicating instead that he remains willing, in a future case with a full Court, to revisit these matters. Respectfully, I would not wait. . . .

"If Congress could pass off its legislative power to the executive branch, the '[v]esting [c]lauses, and indeed the entire structure of the Constitution' would 'make no sense.' Without the involvement of representatives from across the country or the demands of bicameralism and presentment, legislation would risk becoming nothing more than the will of the current President. And if laws could be simply declared by a single person, they would not be few in number and the product of widespread social consensus, likely to protect minority interests, or apt to provide stability and fair notice. Accountability would suffer too. Legislators might seek to take credit for addressing a social problem by sending it to the executive for resolution, while at the same time blaming the executive for the problems that attend whatever measures he chooses to pursue. In turn, the executive might point to Congress as the source of the problem. . . .

"Accepting, then, that we have an obligation to decide whether Congress has unconstitutionally divested itself of legislative responsibilities, the question follows: What's the test? . . .

"First, we know that as long as Congress makes the policy decisions when regulating private conduct, it may authorize another branch to 'fill up the details.'. . .

"Second, once Congress prescribes the rule governing private conduct, it may make the application of that rule depend on executive fact-finding. . . .

"Third, Congress may assign the executive and judicial branches certain non-legislative responsibilities. While the Constitution vests all federal legislative power in Congress alone, Congress's legislative authority sometimes overlaps with authority the Constitution separately vests in another branch. So, for example, when a congressional statute confers wide discretion to the executive, no separation-of-powers problem may arise if 'the discretion is to be exercised over matters already within the scope of executive power.' . . .

"Before the 1930s, federal statutes granting authority to the executive were comparatively modest and usually easily upheld. But then the federal government began to grow explosively. And with the proliferation of new executive programs came new questions about the scope of congressional delegation. [Justice Gorsuch discusses the Court's decisions in *Schechter Poultry* and *Panama Refining*.] . . .

"[Congress] responded by writing a second wave of New Deal legislation more '[c]arefully crafted' to avoid the kind of problems that sank [earlier] statutes. And since that time the Court hasn't held another statute to violate the separation of powers in the same way. Of course, no one thinks that the Court's quiescence can be attributed to an unwavering new tradition of more scrupulously drawn statutes. Some lament that the real cause may have to do with a mistaken 'case of death by association' because *Schechter Poultry* and *Panama Refining* happened to be handed down during the same era as certain of the Court's now-discredited substantive due process decisions. But maybe the most likely explanation of all lies in the story of the evolving 'intelligible principle' doctrine. . . .

"For two decades, no one thought to invoke the 'intelligible principle' comment as a basis to uphold a statute that would have failed more traditional separation-of-powers tests. In fact, the phrase sat more or less silently entombed until the late 1940s. Only then did lawyers begin digging it up in earnest and arguing to this Court that it had somehow displaced (*sub silentio* of course) all prior teachings in this area.

"This mutated version of the 'intelligible principle' remark has no basis in the original meaning of the Constitution, in history, or even in the decision from which it was plucked. . . .

"The statute here [sounds] all the alarms the founders left for us. Because Congress could not achieve the consensus necessary to resolve the hard problems associated with SORNA's application to pre-Act offenders, it passed the potato to the Attorney General. And freed from the need to assemble a broad supermajority for his views, the Attorney General did not hesitate to apply the statute retroactively to a politically unpopular minority. . . .

"It would be easy enough to let this case go. After all, sex offenders are one of the most disfavored groups in our society. But the rule that prevents Congress from giving the executive *carte blanche* to write laws for sex offenders is the same rule that protects everyone else. . . .

"Nor would enforcing the Constitution's demands spell the doom for what some call the 'administrative state.' The separation of powers does not prohibit any particular policy outcome, let alone dictate any conclusion about the proper size and scope of government. Instead, it is a procedural guarantee that requires Congress to assemble a social consensus before choosing our nation's course on policy questions like those implicated by SORNA. What is more, Congress is hardly bereft of options to accomplish all it might wish to achieve. It may always authorize executive branch officials to fill in even a large number of details, to find facts that trigger the generally applicable rule of conduct specified in a statute, or to exercise non-legislative powers. Congress can also commission agencies or other experts to study and recommend legislative language. Respecting the separation of powers forecloses no substantive outcomes. It only requires us to respect along the way one of the most vital of the procedural protections of individual liberty found in our Constitution."

Justice Kavanaugh took no part in the consideration or decision of the case.

Consider Bamzai, Delegation and Interpretive Discretion: *Gundy, Kisor,* and the Formulation and Future of Administrative Law, 133 Harv. L. Rev. 164,185 (2019):

> Both [Justice Kagan's and Justice Gorsuch's approaches] call for an assessment of the importance of the issue that Congress is delegating to an agency, as well as the boundaries that Congress has imposed to cabin executive discretion. To be sure, the articulation of a standard—"filling up the details" versus "intelligible principle"—can affect outcomes in the application of that standard. But the two approaches are not analytically different. They both require consideration of the same set of factors. Depending on the standard of review used in applying them, it may be that the daylight between these two articulations is marginal.

Gundy has inspired an academic debate about the legality of delegation "at the Founding." On the one hand, Ilan Wurman finds "innumerable statements from the Founding period that implicitly endorse a nondelegation doctrine." Ilan Wurman, Nondelegation at the Founding, 130 Yale L.J. 1490, 1495 (2021). On the other hand, Nicholas Parillo offers a "major counterexample":

> A fiscal shortfall struck in 1798 that pushed Congress to exercise, for the first time, its constitutional power to levy a "direct" tax (that is, roughly speaking, a tax on property[5]).

Congress decided to raise $2 million nationwide and, per the Constitution's requirement for direct taxes, apportioned that sum among the states according to each state's free population plus three-fifths of its slave population. . . . In each state, slaveholders were to pay fifty cents for each enslaved person they owned. Once the sum levied on a state's slaveholders was calculated, the remainder of the state's quota—which proved to be the large majority of the quota in every one of the twelve states for which records survive, including major slave states—was to be paid by the owners of the state's real estate in proportion to the value of their respective properties. . . . Well over 1,500 frontline federal assessors fanned out across the nation to assign a value to literally every house and farm in every state, and a corps of more than 600 higher-level federal assessors decided appeals from owners who thought they had been assessed out of proportion to properties in their local area. . . . Yet for all the work these officials did, there was one problem they were not positioned to solve: the danger that officials in some parts of a state might generally value real estate in their respective areas in a way that was out of proportion to what officials did in other parts of the state. To address this problem, Congress established in each state a board of federal tax commissioners, appointed by the President and confirmed by the Senate, with power to divide the state into federal assessment districts and to raise or lower all assessments within any district by any percentage amount "as *shall appear to be just and equitable*"— a phrase the statute did not define. Each federal board's district-wide mass revisions were final. There was no review by any other official, nor by any court. Intrastate mass tax valuation revisions practically identical to those authorized under the direct tax of 1798 were held not to be adjudications for due-process purposes. . . . Thus, the 1798 direct tax provides a clear Founding-era example of congressional delegation of rulemaking authority in a context that was both coercive and domestic: the taxation of real estate.

Nicholas R. Parrillo, A Critical Assessment of the Originalist Case Against Administrative Regulatory Power: New Evidence from the Federal Tax on Private Real Estate in the 1790s, 130 Yale L.J. 1288, 1303-06 (2021).

Page 445.   At the end of section 1 of the Note, add the following:

Consider the extent to which these cases, and the cases discussed in the remainder of this chapter, reflect a broader, unresolved controversy over the constitutionality of a modern "administrative state" that vests broad lawmaking power in agencies that have both adjudicative and rulemaking authority. See, e.g., P. Hamburger, The Administrative Threat 22 (2017):

> The Constitution establishes only regular avenues of power, and thereby blocks irregular or extralegal power. To be precise, it blocks extralegal lawmaking by placing legislative power exclusively in Congress, and it prevents extralegal adjudication by placing judicial power exclusively in the courts.
>
> It thus authorizes only two pathways for governments to bind Americans, in the sense of imposing legal obligation on them. [These] are [the government's] lawful options. Other attempts to bind Americans, whether with rules or adjudications, are unconstitutional.

Compare Metzger, 1930s Redux: The Administrative State Under Siege, 131 Harv. L. Rev. 1, 7 (2017):

> [The] administrative state is essential for actualizing constitutional separation of powers today, serving both to constrain executive power and to mitigate the dangers of presidential unilateralism while also enabling effective governance.

[Anti-administrativists] fail to recognize that the key administrative state features that they condemn, such as bureaucracy with its internal oversight mechanisms and expert civil service, are essential for the accountable, constrained, and effective exercise of executive power.

In Nourse, Reclaiming the Constitutional Text from Originalism: The Case of Executive Power, 106 Cal. L. Rev. 1 (2018), the author relies on the necessary and proper clause in support of Congress' power to shield executive branch officials from removal. The clause grants Congress the power to "make all Laws which shall be necessary and proper for carrying into Execution all [Powers] vested by this Constitution [in] any Department or Officer thereof." According to the author, this clause "gives Congress the power to assist the President in his enumerated power to faithfully execute the law." Therefore

Congress has the power to assist in implementation by providing institutions and offices to aid the executive. . . .

The only real textual limit on Congress's power to assist the President in execution is that the law must be "proper." It seems fairly easy, however, to argue that it is proper to restrain Presidents from removing the heads of departments for purely arbitrary or partisan reasons. If Congress, for example, wants to maintain market or legal stability across administrations and to ensure this by preventing dismissal of officers for political or arbitrary reasons, that presumably is a "proper" reason because it aids in the execution of the law.

Does it follow from this argument that Congress could limit the President's authority to remove his Secretary of State? Could the limitation extend "across administrations" by preventing the President from removing a Secretary of State appointed by a prior President? What about a restriction on the removal of a President's Press Secretary?

Page 448.   Before section 5 of the Note, add the following:

Compare Lucia v. Securities and Exchange Comm'n, ___ S. Ct. ___ (2018). The Securities and Exchange Commission delegates many administrative proceedings to administrative law judges (ALJs), who are appointed by SEC staff members, rather than by the Commission itself. The ALJs hear enforcement actions and exercise authority comparable to that of a federal district judge conducting a bench trial. At the conclusion of hearings, the ALJs issue "initial decisions" setting out findings regarding material facts and appropriate relief. The Commission can review ALJ decisions, but if it opts against review, the decisions are final and are deemed the action of the Commission.

In a 6-3 decision, the Court, per Justice Kagan, held that ALJs were "Officers of the United States" and therefore had to be appointed by the President, courts of law, or heads of department. Because staff members of the Commission fit into none of these categories, the appointments were unconstitutional.

Relying on its earlier decision in Freytag v. Commissioner, 501 U.S. 868 (1991), the Court held that ALJs were "Officers" because they held "a continuing office," and exercised "significant discretion" when carrying out "important functions." The Court relied on the fact that ALJs "critically shape the administrative record" and have the authority to issue final decisions.

Justice Thomas, joined by Justice Gorsuch, wrote a concurring opinion. Justice Breyer, joined by Justice Ginsburg and, in part, by Justice Sotomayor, concurred in the judgment in part and dissented in part. Justice Sotomayor, joined by Justice Ginsburg, dissented.

Compare *Lucia* to Financial Oversight and Management Bd. for Puerto Rico v. Aurelius Investment, LLC. In a 9-0 decision written by Justice Breyer, the Court held that officials whose duties are primarily local and who are appointed pursuant to Congress' powers to exercise legislative powers in the District of Columbia and in United States territories were not "officers of the

United States" within the meaning of Article II, section 2. A statute granting the president power to appoint these officers without the advice and consent of the Senate was therefore constitutional. Justices Thomas and Sotomayor each filed separate opinions concurring in the judgment.

4b. Who, though, is a "principal officer" for the purposes of the Appointment Clause? In *Edmond v. United States*, 520 U.S. 651 (1997), the Court answered this question in respect to judges of the Coast Guard Court of Criminal Appeals. These were appointed by the Secretary of Transportation. The Court held that the judges were inferior officers because they were effectively supervised by a combination of Presidentially nominated and Senate confirmed officers in the Executive Branch. *Edmond* explained that an inferior officer is "directed and supervised at some level by others who were appointed by Presidential nomination with the advice and consent of the Senate." The Coast Guard judges in question had "no power to render a final decision on behalf of the United States unless permitted to do so by other Executive officers."

At issue in *United States v. Arthrex*, ___ S Ct. ___ (2021), was the validity of a patent previously issued by the Patent and Trademark Office. The patent was challenged before the Patent Trial and Appeal Board in a process called "inter partes review." This Board is made up of Administrative Patent Judges (APJs), who are appointed by the Secretary of Commerce. Another presidential appointee, the Director of the Patent and Trademark Office, has "administrative oversight" over APJs: fixing their salaries; deciding whether to institute inter partes review; selecting APJs for particular matters; promulgating regulations and prospective guidance; and deciding which past decisions are "precedential." The Director has no power to issue or reconsider decisions on patentability.

A patent holder whose patent had been found invalid challenged the Board's power to act under the Appointments Clause. The Federal Circuit held that the APJs were principal officers whose appointments were unconstitutional because no other presidential appointee could review their decisions or remove them at will. To remedy this constitutional violation, the Federal Circuit invalidated the APJs' tenure protections, making them removable at will by the Secretary.

A 5-4 majority of the Court, with Chief Justice Roberts writing, agreed that the APJs were "principal officers" under the Appointment Clause. A different majority, again with Roberts writing, found that the appropriate remedy was not to invalidate the APJs' tenure protection, but instead to remand the dispute to the Acting Director to decide whether to rehear it. Applying *Edmond*, Chief Justice Roberts distinguished APJs from the Coast Guard's judges because no presidential appointee "direct[s] and supervise[s]" the work of APJs in using patentability decisions. "APJs have the 'power to render a final decision on behalf of the United States' without any such review by their nominal superior or any other principal officer in the Executive Branch. The only possibility of review is a petition for rehearing, but Congress unambiguously specified that "[o]nly the Patent and Trial Appeal Board may grant rehearings." Such review simply repeats the arrangement challenged as unconstitutional in this suit." The resulting "diffusion of accountability" was at odds with the Appointment Clause's ends. In contrast, Chief Justice Roberts observed that the "norm" in the administrative state was for principal officers to have the capacity to review decisions made by inferior adjudicative officers. Such "higher-level agency reconsideration" by the agency head is "the standard way to maintain political accountability and effective oversight for adjudication."

Turning to remedies, Chief Justice Roberts rejected the Federal Circuit's invalidation order. Instead, he held that the PTO Director "may review final PTAB decisions and, upon review, may issue decisions himself on behalf of the Board." Nevertheless, "the Director need not review every decision of the PTAB. What matters is that the Director have the discretion to review decisions rendered by APJs. In this way, the President remains responsible for the exercise of executive power — and through him, the exercise of executive power remains accountable to the people."

Justice Gorsuch joined the majority as to the Appointment Clause violation, but not the remedy. Justice Breyer, in an opinion joined by Justices Sotomayor and Kagan, dissented from the Appointment Clause holding but joined the remedial holding because "the current statutory scheme is defective only because the APJ's decisions are not reviewable by the Director alone. The Court's remedy addresses that specific problem, and for that reason I agree with its remedial holding."

In Mascott, Who Are "Officers of the United States"?, 70 Stan. L. Rev. 443 (2018), the author concludes that

> [The] original public meaning of the Article II term "officer" related to neither discretion nor final decisionmaking authority. [In] the Founding era, the term [was] commonly understood to encompass any individual who had ongoing responsibility for a governmental duty. This included even individuals with more ministerial duties like recordkeeping. The only continuing positions excluded [were] (i) positions more like those of "servants" or "attendants" and (ii) "deputies" acting as agents in place of an officer, where the officer was subject to personal legal liability for the deputy's actions.

According to the author, enforcing this understanding would mean that "numerous officials in the modern administrative state currently considered nonofficers might in fact be subject to Article II appointment requirements" including "many positions covered by the competitive [civil] service system." The author concludes that compliance with the Article II would require "far-reaching" change, which is nonetheless "achievable."

> [The] President and department heads may satisfy Article II's requirements by providing a final signoff on a lower-level officers' selection of officials. Officials selected through civil service procedures [could] likely also continue to undergo competitive selection—if certain changes were made to ensure a chain of accountability from the board members

evaluating and ranking candidates up to the President or department head with the final appointment authority.

In Ortiz v. United States, 138 S. Ct. 2165 (2018), the Court held that the appointments clause posed no obstacle to an individual serving as an inferior officer on one Article I court while simultaneously serving as a principal officer on another Article I court.

Page 457.   Before the Note, add the following:

SEILA LAW v. CONSUMER FINANCIAL PROTECTION COMMISSION

___U.S.___ (2020)

CHIEF JUSTICE ROBERTS delivered the opinion of the Court with respect to Parts I, II, and III.

In the wake of the 2008 financial crisis, Congress established the Consumer Financial Protection Bureau (CFPB), an independent regulatory agency tasked with ensuring that consumer debt products are safe and transparent. In organizing the CFPB, Congress deviated from the structure of nearly every other independent administrative agency in our history. Instead of placing the agency under the leadership of a board with multiple members, Congress provided that the CFPB would be led by a single Director, who serves for a longer term than the President and cannot be removed by the President except for inefficiency, neglect, or malfeasance. The CFPB Director has no boss, peers, or voters to report to. Yet the Director wields vast rulemaking, enforcement, and adjudicatory authority over a significant portion of the U. S. economy. The question before us is whether this arrangement violates the Constitution's separation of powers. . . .

The President's power to remove — and thus supervise — those who wield executive power on his behalf follows from the text of

Article II, was settled by the First Congress, and was confirmed in the landmark decision Myers v. United States. Our precedents have recognized only two exceptions to the President's unrestricted removal power. In *Humphrey's Executor* we held that Congress could create expert agencies led by a group of principal officers removable by the President only for good cause. And in United States v. Perkins, 116 U.S. 483 (1886) and Morrison v. Olson we held that Congress could provide tenure protections to certain inferior officers with narrowly defined duties.

We are now asked to extend these precedents to a new configuration: an independent agency that wields significant executive power and is run by a single individual who cannot be removed by the President unless certain statutory criteria are met. We decline to take that step. While we need not and do not revisit our prior decisions allowing certain limitations on the President's removal power, there are compelling reasons not to extend those precedents to the novel context of an independent agency led by a single Director. Such an agency lacks a foundation in historical practice and clashes with constitutional structure by concentrating power in a unilateral actor insulated from Presidential control.

We therefore hold that the structure of the CFPB violates the separation of powers. We go on to hold that the CFPB Director's removal protection is severable from the other statutory provisions bearing on the CFPB's authority. The agency may therefore continue to operate, but its Director, in light of our decision, must be removable by the President at will.

I ...

[In this section of the opinion, the Court relates the history that led to the CFBC's creation and details its extensive powers].

The agency has the authority to conduct investigations, issue subpoenas and civil investigative demands, initiate administrative adjudications, and prosecute civil actions in federal court. To remedy violations of federal consumer financial law, the CFPB may seek restitution, disgorgement, and injunctive relief, as well as civil penalties of up to $1,000,000 (inflation adjusted) for each day that a violation occurs. Since its inception, the CFPB has obtained over $11 billion in relief for over 25 million consumers, including a $1 billion penalty against a single bank in 2018.

The CFPB's rulemaking and enforcement powers are coupled with extensive adjudicatory authority. . . .

Rather than create a traditional independent agency headed by a multimember board or commission, Congress elected to place the CFPB under the leadership of a single Director. The CFPB Director is appointed by the President with the advice and consent of the Senate. The Director serves for a term of five years, during which the President may remove the Director from office only for "inefficiency, neglect of duty, or malfeasance in office."

Unlike most other agencies, the CFPB does not rely on the annual appropriations process for funding. Instead, the CFPB receives funding directly from the Federal Reserve, which is itself funded outside the appropriations process through bank assessments. . . .

B . . .

[In 2017, the CFPB issued a civil investigation demand directed at Seila Law. Seilia responded by claiming that the agency's leadership by a single director removable only for cause was unconstitutional. The agency declined to address the claim and filed a petition to enforce the demand in District Court. The District Court rejected Seila's argument, and the Court of Appeals affirmed. Before the Supreme Court, the government sided with Seila, so the Court appointed an amicus to argue on behalf of the Court of Appeals decision.] . . .

II . . .

[In this portion of the opinion, the Court rejects the arguments that Seila lacked standing, that a challenge to the tenure provision should be made only in the context of an effort to remove the director, and that there was no case or controversy because the government agreed with Seila's position].

III

We hold that the CFPB's leadership by a single individual removable only for inefficiency, neglect, or malfeasance violates the separation of powers. . . .

A

Article II provides that "[t]he executive Power shall be vested in a President," who must "take Care that the Laws be faithfully executed." Art. II, § 1, cl. 1; id., § 3. The entire "executive Power" belongs to the President alone. But because it would be "impossib[le]" for "one man" to "perform all the great business of the State," the Constitution assumes that lesser executive officers will "assist the supreme Magistrate in discharging the duties of his trust." 30 Writings of George Washington 334 (J. Fitzpatrick ed. 1939).

These lesser officers must remain accountable to the President, whose authority they wield. [That] power, in turn, generally includes the ability to remove executive officials, for it is "only the authority that can remove" such officials that they "must fear and, in the performance of [their] functions, obey." [quoting Bowsher]. . . .

The Court recognized the President's prerogative to remove executive officials in *Myers*. . . .

We recently reiterated the President's general removal power in *Free Enterprise Fund*. Although we had previously sustained congressional limits on that power in certain circumstances, we declined to extend those limits to "a new situation not yet encountered by the Court"—an official insulated by two layers of for-cause removal protection. . . .

Free Enterprise Fund left in place two exceptions to the President's unrestricted removal power. First, in *Humphrey's Executor*, decided less than a decade after *Myers*, the Court upheld a statute that protected the Commissioners of the FTC from removal except for "inefficiency, neglect of duty, or malfeasance in office." In reaching that conclusion, the Court stressed that Congress's ability to impose such removal restrictions "will depend upon the character of the office."

[Rightly] or wrongly, the Court viewed the FTC (as it existed in 1935) as exercising "no part of the executive power." Instead, it was "an administrative body" that performed "specified duties as a legislative or as a judicial aid." It acted "as a legislative agency" in "making investigations and reports" to Congress and "as an agency of the judiciary" in making recommendations to courts as a master in chancery. "To the extent that [the FTC] exercise[d] any executive function[,] as distinguished from executive power in the constitutional sense," it did so only in the discharge of its "quasi-legislative or quasi-judicial powers."

The Court identified several organizational features that helped explain its characterization of the FTC as non-executive. Composed of five members—no more than three from the same political party—the Board was designed to be "non-partisan" and to "act with entire impartiality." The FTC's duties were "neither political nor executive," but instead called for "the trained judgment of a body of experts" "informed by experience. And the Commissioners' staggered, seven-year terms enabled the agency to accumulate technical expertise and avoid a "complete change" in leadership "at any one time."

In short, *Humphrey's Executor* permitted Congress to give for-cause removal protections to a multimember body of experts, balanced along partisan lines, that performed legislative and judicial functions and was said not to exercise any executive power. Consistent with that understanding, the Court later applied "[t]he philosophy of *Humphrey's Executor*" to uphold for-cause removal protections for the members of the War Claims Commission—a three-member "adjudicatory body" tasked with resolving claims for compensation arising from World War II.

While recognizing an exception for multimember bodies with "quasi-judicial" or "quasi-legislative" functions, *Humphrey's*

Executor reaffirmed the core holding of *Myers* that the President has "unrestrictable power . . . to remove purely executive officers." . . .

We have recognized a second exception for inferior officers in two cases, United States v. Perkins and Morrison v. Olson. In *Perkins* we upheld tenure protections for a naval cadet-engineer. And, in *Morrison*, we upheld a provision granting good-cause tenure protection to an independent counsel appointed to investigate and prosecute particular alleged crimes by high-ranking Government officials. Backing away from the reliance in *Humphrey's Executor* on the concepts of "quasi-legislative" and "quasi-judicial" power, we viewed the ultimate question as whether a removal restriction is of "such a nature that [it] impede[s] the President's ability to perform his constitutional duty." Although the independent counsel was a single person and performed "law enforcement functions that typically have been undertaken by officials within the Executive Branch," we concluded that the removal protections did not unduly interfere with the functioning of the Executive Branch because "the independent counsel [was] an inferior officer under the Appointments Clause, with limited jurisdiction and tenure and lacking policymaking or significant administrative authority."

These two exceptions — one for multimember expert agencies that do not wield substantial executive power, and one for inferior officers with limited duties and no policymaking or administrative authority — "represent what up to now have been the outermost constitutional limits of permissible congressional restrictions on the President's removal power."

B . . .

Unlike the New Deal-era FTC upheld [in *Humphrey's Executor*], the CFPB is led by a single Director who cannot be described as a "body of experts" and cannot be considered "non-partisan" in the same sense as a group of officials drawn from both sides of the aisle. Moreover, while the staggered terms of the FTC Commissioners prevented complete turnovers in agency leadership and guaranteed that there would always be some Commissioners who had accrued significant expertise, the CFPB's single-Director structure and five-year term guarantee abrupt shifts in agency leadership and with it the loss of accumulated expertise.

In addition, the CFPB Director is hardly a mere legislative or judicial aid. Instead of making reports and recommendations to Congress, as the 1935 FTC did, the Director possesses the authority to promulgate binding rules fleshing out 19 federal statutes, including a broad prohibition on unfair and deceptive practices in a major segment of the U.S. economy. And instead of submitting recommended dispositions to an Article III court, the Director may unilaterally issue final decisions awarding legal and equitable relief in administrative adjudications. Finally, the Director's enforcement authority includes the power to seek daunting monetary penalties against private parties on behalf of the United States in federal court—a quintessentially executive power not considered in *Humphrey's Executor*.

The logic of *Morrison* also does not apply. Everyone agrees the CFPB Director is not an inferior officer, and her duties are far from limited. Unlike the independent counsel, who lacked policymaking or administrative authority, the Director has the sole responsibility to administer 19 separate consumer-protection statutes that cover everything from credit cards and car payments to mortgages and student loans. It is true that the independent counsel in *Morrison* was empowered to initiate criminal investigations and prosecutions, and in that respect wielded core executive power. But that power, while significant, was trained inward to high-ranking Governmental actors identified by others, and was confined to a specified matter in which the Department of Justice had a potential conflict of interest. By contrast, the CFPB Director has the authority to bring the coercive power of the state to bear on millions of private citizens and businesses, imposing even billion-dollar penalties through administrative adjudications and civil actions.

In light of these differences, the constitutionality of the CFPB Director's insulation from removal cannot be settled by *Humphrey's Executor* or *Morrison* alone.

C

The question instead is whether to extend those precedents to the "new situation" before us, namely an independent agency led by a single Director and vested with significant executive power. We decline to do so. Such an agency has no basis in history and no place in our constitutional structure.

1

"Perhaps the most telling indication of [a] severe constitutional problem" with an executive entity "is [a] lack of historical precedent" to support it. An agency with a structure like that of the CFPB is almost wholly unprecedented. . . .

[The Court finds that there are only a handful of isolated incidents in which Congress provided good-cause tenure to principal officers who wielded power alone rather than as members of boards or commissions. It observes that these instances are "modern and contested" and that "they do not involve regulatory or enforcement authority remotely comparable to that exercised by the CFPB"].

2

In addition to being a historical anomaly, the CFPB's single-Director configuration is incompatible with our constitutional structure. Aside from the sole exception of the Presidency, that structure scrupulously avoids concentrating power in the hands of any single individual. . . .

The Framers deemed an energetic executive essential to "the protection of the community against foreign attacks," "the steady administration of the laws," "the protection of property," and "the security of liberty." Accordingly, they chose not to bog the Executive down with the "habitual feebleness and dilatoriness" that comes with a "diversity of views and opinions." Instead, they gave the Executive the "[d]ecision, activity, secrecy, and dispatch" that "characterise the proceedings of one man."

To justify and check that authority — unique in our constitutional structure — the Framers made the President the most democratic and politically accountable official in Government. . . .

The resulting constitutional strategy is straightforward: divide power everywhere except for the Presidency, and render the President directly accountable to the people through regular elections. In that scheme, individual executive officials will still wield significant authority, but that authority remains subject to the ongoing supervision and control of the elected President. . . .

The CFPB's single-Director structure contravenes this carefully calibrated system by vesting significant governmental power in the hands of a single individual accountable to no one. . . .

The CFPB Director's insulation from removal by an accountable President is enough to render the agency's structure unconstitutional. But several other features of the CFPB combine to make the Director's removal protection even more problematic. In addition to lacking the most direct method of presidential control—removal at will—the agency's unique structure also forecloses certain indirect methods of Presidential control.

Because the CFPB is headed by a single Director with a five-year term, some Presidents may not have any opportunity to shape its leadership and thereby influence its activities. [To] make matters worse, the agency's single-Director structure means the President will not have the opportunity to appoint any other leaders—such as a chair or fellow members of a Commission or Board—who can serve as a check on the Director's authority and help bring the agency in line with the President's preferred policies.

The CFPB's receipt of funds outside the appropriations process further aggravates the agency's threat to Presidential control. The President normally has the opportunity to recommend or veto spending bills that affect the operation of administrative agencies. But no similar opportunity exists for the President to influence the CFPB Director. Instead, the Director receives over $500 million per year to fund the agency's chosen priorities. And the Director receives that money from the Federal Reserve, which is itself funded outside of the annual appropriations process. This financial freedom makes it even more likely that the agency will "slip from the Executive's control, and thus from that of the people."

3 . . .

[Amicus] contends that if we identify a constitutional problem with the CFPB's structure, we should avoid it by broadly construing the statutory grounds for removing the CFPB Director from office. The Dodd-Frank Act provides that the Director may be removed for "inefficiency, neglect of duty, or malfeasance in office." In amicus' view, that language could be interpreted to reserve substantial discretion to the President.

We are not persuaded. For one, *Humphrey's Executor* implicitly rejected an interpretation that would leave the President free to remove an officer based on disagreements about agency policy. In addition, while both amicus and the House of Representatives invite us to adopt whatever construction would cure the constitutional problem, they have not advanced any workable standard derived from the statutory language. Amicus suggests that the proper standard might permit removals based on general policy disagreements, but not specific ones; the House suggests that the permissible bases for removal might vary depending on the context and the Presidential power involved. They do not attempt to root either of those standards in the statutory text. Further, although nearly identical language governs the removal of some two-dozen multimember independent agencies, amicus suggests that the standard should vary from agency to agency, morphing as necessary to avoid constitutional doubt.

Amicus and the House also fail to engage with the Dodd-Frank Act as a whole, which makes plain that the CFPB is an "independent bureau." . . .

IV . . .

[This portion of the opinion is joined only by Justices Alito and Kavanaugh. The plurality concludes that the tenure provisions of the statute are severable from the provisions establishing the CFPB and that it therefore need not invalidate the statute as a whole].

* * *

A decade ago, we declined to extend Congress's authority to limit the President's removal power to a new situation, never before confronted by the Court. We do the same today. In our constitutional system, the executive power belongs to the President, and that power generally includes the ability to supervise and remove the agents who wield executive power in his stead. While we have previously upheld limits on the President's removal authority in certain contexts, we decline to do so when it comes to principal officers who, acting alone, wield significant executive power. The Constitution requires that such officials remain dependent on the President, who in turn is accountable to the people.

JUSTICE THOMAS, with whom JUSTICE GORSUCH joins, concurring in part and dissenting in part. . . .

Because the Court takes a step in the right direction by limiting *Humphrey's Executor* I join Parts I, II, and III of its opinion. I respectfully dissent from the Court's severability analysis, however, because I do not believe that we should address severability in this case. . . .

I

[The] Court concludes that it is not strictly necessary for us to overrule Humphrey's Executor. But with today's decision, the Court has repudiated almost every aspect of [the case]. In a future case, I would repudiate what is left of this erroneous precedent. . . .

II

While I think that the Court correctly resolves the merits of the constitutional question, I do not agree with its decision to sever the removal restriction in To resolve this case, I would simply deny the Consumer Financial Protection Bureau (CFPB) petition to enforce the civil investigative demand. . . .

JUSTICE KAGAN, with whom JUSTICE GINSBURG, JUSTICE BREYER, and JUSTICE SOTOMAYOR join, concurring in the judgment with respect to severability and dissenting in part.

Throughout the Nation's history, this Court has left most decisions about how to structure the Executive Branch to Congress and the President, acting through legislation they both agree to. In particular, the Court has commonly allowed those two branches to create zones of administrative independence by limiting the President's power to remove agency heads. The Federal Reserve Board. The Federal Trade Commission (FTC). The National Labor Relations Board. Statute after statute establishing such entities instructs the President that he may not discharge their directors except for cause—most often phrased as inefficiency, neglect of duty, or malfeasance in office. Those statutes, whose language the Court has repeatedly approved, provide the model for the removal restriction before us today. If precedent were any guide, that provision would have survived its encounter with this Court—and so would the intended independence of the Consumer Financial Protection Bureau (CFPB).

Our Constitution and history demand that result. The text of the Constitution allows these common for-cause removal limits. Nothing in it speaks of removal. And it grants Congress authority to organize all the institutions of American governance, provided only that those arrangements allow the President to perform his own constitutionally assigned duties. Still more, the Framers' choice to give the political branches wide discretion over administrative offices has played out through American history in ways that have settled the constitutional meaning. From the first, Congress debated and enacted measures to create spheres of administration—especially of financial affairs—detached from direct presidential control. As the years passed, and governance became ever more complicated, Congress continued to adopt and adapt such measures—confident it had latitude to do so under a Constitution meant to "endure for ages to come." McCulloch v. Maryland. Not every innovation in governance—not every experiment in administrative independence—has proved successful.

And debates about the prudence of limiting the President's control over regulatory agencies, including through his removal power, have never abated. But the Constitution—both as originally drafted and as practiced—mostly leaves disagreements about administrative structure to Congress and the President, who have the knowledge and experience needed to address them. Within broad bounds, it keeps the courts—who do not—out of the picture.

The Court today fails to respect its proper role. It recognizes that this Court has approved limits on the President's removal power over heads of agencies much like the CFPB. Agencies possessing similar powers, agencies charged with similar missions, agencies created for similar reasons. The majority's explanation is that the heads of those agencies fall within an "exception"—one for multimember bodies and another for inferior officers—to a "general rule" of unrestricted presidential removal power. And the majority says the CFPB Director does not. That account, though, is wrong in every respect. The majority's general rule does not exist. Its exceptions, likewise, are made up for the occasion—gerrymandered so the CFPB falls outside them. And the distinction doing most of the majority's work—between multimember bodies and single directors—does not respond to the constitutional values at stake. If a removal provision violates the separation of powers, it is because the measure so deprives the President of control over an official as to impede his own constitutional functions. But with or without a for-cause removal provision, the President has at least as much control over an individual as over a commission—and possibly more. That means the constitutional concern is, if anything, ameliorated when the agency has a single head. Unwittingly, the majority shows why courts should stay their hand in these matters. "Compared to Congress and the President, the Judiciary possesses an inferior understanding of the realities of administration" and the way "political power[ ] operates." *Free Enterprise Fund* (Breyer, J., dissenting).

In second-guessing the political branches, the majority second-guesses as well the wisdom of the Framers and the judgment of history. It writes in rules to the Constitution that the drafters knew well enough not to put there. It repudiates the lessons of American experience, from the 18th century to the present day. And it commits the Nation to a static version of governance, incapable of responding to new conditions and challenges. Congress and the President established the CFPB to address financial practices that had brought on a devastating recession, and could do so again. Today's decision wipes out a feature of that agency its creators thought fundamental to its mission — a measure of independence from political pressure. I respectfully dissent. . . .

Collins v. Yellen, ___ S. Ct. ___ (2021). In *Collins*, the Court applied the holding of *Seila Law* to the Federal Housing Finance Agency (FHFA). Created in 2008 during the financial crisis, the FHFA is an "independent agency" led by a single Director whom the President can remove only "for cause." The FHFA had placed Fannie Mae and Freddie Mac — government-sponsored entities that provide mortgage financing — into conservatorships, and negotiated a series of agreements with the Treasury Departments for new capital. A group of shareholders in Fannie Mae and Freddie Mac sued the FHFA on both statutory and constitutional grounds. The en banc Fifth Circuit reversed the district court's dismissal of the statutory claims and found the Director's removal restriction to violate the Constitution. It concluded that the appropriate remedy was to sever the invalid removal restriction from the statute, but not to invalidate past actions by the Director under which capital had been acquired from the Treasury.

The Supreme Court, in an opinion by Justice Alito, reversed on the statutory ground but held the removal restriction invalid under a "straightforward application of our reasoning in *Seila Law*." The Court rejected several arguments for distinguishing *Seila Law*. First, the Court found the difference in powers between the FHCA and the CFPB at issue in *Seila Law* irrelevant. Second, it held that the FHFA does not "take[] on the status of a private party" by becoming a conservator. Nor did the status of Fannie Mae and Freddie Mac as government-sponsored entities change the analysis. Finally, the Court concluded that even a "modest restriction" on the president's removal power embodied in a "for cause" rule — which allows dismissal for disobeying an instruction — is unconstitutional.

The Court then turned to remedies. It held that "there is no basis for concluding that any head of the FHFA lacked the authority to carry out the functions of the office" simply because of the unconstitutional removal restriction. The Court remanded for consideration of the possibility that the "unconstitutional removal provision inflicted harm" to the plaintiffs. Justice Thomas joined the Court's opinion in full and filed a concurring opinion underscoring that "the Government does not necessarily act unlawfully even if a removal restriction is unlawful in the abstract." Justice Gorsuch filed an opinion concurring in the application of *Seila Law*, but arguing that Directors' past actions had to be set aside as ultra vires.

While agreeing with the Court's statutory analysis, Justices Kagan and Sotomeyer filed opinions expressing disagreement with the "extension of *Seila Law*'s holding."

Page 460.   Before section 5 of the Note, add the following:

In Lucia v. Securities and Exchange Comm'n, 138 S. Ct. 2044 (2018), the Court held that administrative law judges (ALJs) who adjudicated disputes relating to securities laws were "Officers of the United States." (The case is discussed at the supplement to page 448 of the Main Text). Given this holding, does the "double insulation" doctrine mean that statutory restrictions on the removal of ALJs are unconstitutional? In *Lucia*, the Court declined to address this issue. Compare Justice Breyer's opinion concurring in the judgment in part and dissenting in part:

> *If* the *Free Enterprise Fund* Court's holding applies equally to the administrative law judges — and I stress the "if" — then to hold that the administrative law judges are "Officers of the United States" is *perhaps*, to hold that their removal

protections are unconstitutional. This would risk transforming administrative law judges from independent adjudicators into *dependent* decisionmakers, serving at the pleasure of the Commission. Similarly, to apply *Free Enterprise Fund*'s holding to high-level civil servants threatens to change the nature of our merit-based civil service as it has existed from the time of President Chester Alan Arthur.

Justice Breyer pointed to two possible grounds for distinguishing ALJs from the Board members discussed in *Free Enterprise Fund*. First, ALJs "perform adjudicative rather than enforcement or policymaking functions." Second, the kind of "for cause" protection provided for Board members was "unusually high" and more significant than the protection enjoyed by ALJs. Is either of these differences sufficient to distinguish between the two situations?

V
EQUALITY AND THE CONSTITUTION

C. *Equal Protection Methodology: Heightened Scrutiny and the Problem of Race*

Page 540.   Before the Note, and at the end of section 2 of the prior Note, add the following:

In Trump v. Hawaii, 138 S. Ct. 2392 (2018), the Supreme Court upheld a presidential proclamation that placed entry restrictions on foreign nationals from several countries. (The proclamation was commonly referred to as a "travel ban.") (The case is discussed at greater length in the supplement to page 1487 of the Main Volume.)

Challengers, including the state of Hawaii, sued. They alleged, among other things, that the proclamation violated the Constitution because it targeted Muslims, in contravention of the establishment clause of the First Amendment.

In an opinion by Chief Justice Roberts, the Court rejected the argument that heightened scrutiny should apply to the proclamation because it had been "issued for the unconstitutional purpose of excluding Muslims." Instead, the Court applied rational basis review, although it "assume[d] that we may look behind the face of the Proclamation to the extent of applying rational basis review. That standard of review considers whether the entry policy is plausibly related to the Government's stated objective to protect the country and improve vetting processes. As a result, we may consider plaintiffs' extrinsic evidence, but will uphold the policy so long as it can reasonably be understood to result from a justification independent of unconstitutional grounds."

In the course of upholding the ban, the majority rejected the dissent's assertion that there were "stark parallels" between the internment policy at issue in *Korematsu* and the travel ban:

Finally, the dissent invokes Korematsu v. United States . . . . Whatever rhetorical advantage the dissent may see in doing so, *Korematsu* has nothing to do with this case. The forcible relocation of U.S. citizens to concentration camps, solely and explicitly on the basis of race, is objectively unlawful and outside the scope of Presidential authority. But it is wholly inapt to liken that morally repugnant order to a facially neutral policy denying certain foreign nationals the privilege of admission. The entry suspension is an act that is well within executive authority and could have been taken by any other President—the only question is evaluating the actions of this particular President in promulgating an otherwise valid Proclamation.

The dissent's reference to *Korematsu*, however, affords this Court the opportunity to make express what is already obvious: *Korematsu* was gravely wrong the day it was decided, has been overruled in the court of history, and—to be clear—"has no place in law under the Constitution." 323 U.S., at 248 (Jackson, J., dissenting).

Page 557.   At the end of section 4 of the Note, add the following:

In Abbott v. Perez, 138 S. Ct. 2305 (2018), the Court addressed the legality of several congressional and state legislative districts drawn in Texas after the 2010 census. The districts were originally drawn by the state legislature in 2011, but because that plan was immediately challenged in court, it never officially went into effect. Instead, the districts were put into effect by being included in an interim judicial remedy. They were then reenacted unchanged by the legislature in 2013.

The Court, in an opinion by Justice Alito, rejected the challengers' claim that the districts had been drawn for the purpose of diluting the voting strength of racial minorities. The Court gave little weight to the district court's finding that the plan was tainted by the discriminatory motivations of legislators in 2011:

> The allocation of the burden of proof and the presumption of legislative good faith are not changed by a finding of past discrimination. "[P]ast discrimination cannot, in the manner of original sin, condemn governmental action that is not itself unlawful." The "ultimate question remains whether a discriminatory intent has been proved in a given case." . . . But we have never suggested that past discrimination flips the evidentiary burden on its head.

The Court distinguished *Hunter* as addressing "a very different situation":

> *Hunter* involved an equal protection challenge to an article of the Alabama Constitution adopted in 1901 at a constitutional convention avowedly dedicated to the establishment of white supremacy. The article disenfranchised anyone convicted of any crime on a long list that included many minor offenses. The court below found that the article had

been adopted with discriminatory intent, and this Court accepted that conclusion. The article was never repealed, but over the years, the list of disqualifying offenses had been pruned, and the State argued that what remained was facially constitutional. This Court rejected that argument because the amendments did not alter the intent with which the article, including the parts that remained, had been adopted. But the Court specifically declined to address the question whether the then-existing version would have been valid if "[re]enacted today."

In these cases, we do not confront a situation like the one in *Hunter*. Nor is this a case in which a law originally enacted with discriminatory intent is later reenacted by a different legislature. The 2013 Texas Legislature did not reenact the plan previously passed by its 2011 predecessor. Nor did it use criteria that arguably carried forward the effects of any discriminatory intent on the part of the 2011 Legislature. Instead, it enacted, with only very small changes, plans that had been developed by the Texas court. . . .

Instead of holding the plaintiffs to their burden of overcoming the presumption of good faith and proving discriminatory intent, [the district court] reversed the burden of proof. It imposed on the State the obligation of proving that the 2013 Legislature had experienced a true "change of heart" and had "engage[d] in a deliberative process to ensure that the 2013 plans cured any taint from the 2011 plans." . . .

In holding that the District Court disregarded the presumption of legislative good faith and improperly reversed the burden of proof, we do not suggest either that the intent of the 2011 Legislature is irrelevant or that the plans enacted in 2013 are unassailable because they were previously adopted on an interim basis by the Texas court. Rather, both the intent of the 2011 Legislature and the court's adoption of the interim plans are relevant to the extent that they naturally give rise to—or tend to refute—inferences regarding the intent of the 2013 Legislature. They must be weighed together with any other direct and circumstantial evidence of that Legislature's intent. But when all the relevant evidence in the record is taken into account, it is plainly insufficient to prove that the 2013 Legislature acted in bad faith and engaged in intentional discrimination.

Page 609.   At the end of section 3 of the Note, add the following:

Compare the treatment of standing in the *Shaw* racial-gerrymandering cases to the treatment of standing in political-gerrymandering cases. In Gill v. Whitford, 138 S. Ct. 1916 (2018), the plaintiffs filed a suit claiming that the state legislative redistricting plan drafted by the legislature unconstitutionally diluted Democratic voters' voting strength statewide in violation of the equal protection clause and the First Amendment. (*Gill* is considered at greater length in the supplement to page 114 of the Main Volume.)

The Court, in an opinion by Chief Justice Roberts, held that the plaintiffs had not yet provided sufficient evidence of a concrete and particularized injury to establish Article III standing. It emphasized that the right to vote is "individual and personal in nature," and thus a plaintiff's claim that his voting strength has been diluted is "district specific." Citing *Hays*, the Court emphasized that a voter can assert a concrete claim only with respect to the district in which he lives. Thus, it rejected the assertion that the plaintiffs' claims were statewide in nature:

> Here, the plaintiffs' partisan gerrymandering claims turn on allegations that their votes have been diluted. That harm arises from the particular composition of the voter's own district, which causes his vote—having been packed or cracked—to carry less weight than it would carry in another, hypothetical district. Remedying the individual

voter's harm, therefore, does not necessarily require restructuring all of the State's legislative districts. It requires revising only such districts as are necessary to reshape the voter's district—so that the voter may be unpacked or uncracked, as the case may be.

And the Court rejected the claim that the plaintiffs had suffered impairment of their interest in the overall composition of the legislature: "[O]ur cases to date have not found that this presents an individual and personal injury of the kind required for Article III standing. On the facts of this case, the plaintiffs may not rely on 'the kind of undifferentiated, generalized grievance about the conduct of government that we have refused to countenance in the past.' A citizen's interest in the overall composition of the legislature is embodied in his right to vote for his representative. And the citizen's abstract interest in policies adopted by the legislature on the facts here is a nonjusticiable 'general interest common to all members of the public.' Ex parte Levitt, 302 U.S. 633, 634 (1937) (*per curiam*)."

D. *Equal Protection Methodology: Heightened Scrutiny and the Problem of Gender*

Page 669.   Before the Note, add the following:

In Barr v. American Association of Political Consultants, Inc., ___ U.S. ___ (2020), the Supreme Court held that an exemption to the general federal prohibition on robocalls to cellphones for calls seeking to collect debts owed to the federal government violated the First Amendment. Faced with the question of how to remedy that violation, a majority of the Justices ultimately agreed that the exemption was severable from the statute as a whole, thereby resulting in the prohibition being extended to federal debt collection calls as well. In his separate opinion, Justice Kavanaugh (who announced the judgment of the Court) offered this explanation:

> This is an equal-treatment case, and equal-treatment cases can sometimes pose complicated severability questions.
>
> The "First Amendment is a kind of Equal Protection Clause for ideas." Williams-Yulee v. Florida Bar, 575 U.S. 433, 470 570 (2015) (Scalia, J., dissenting). And Congress violated that First Amendment equal-treatment principle in this case by favoring debt-collection robocalls and discriminating against political and other robocalls.
>
> When the constitutional violation is unequal treatment, as it is here, a court theoretically can cure that unequal treatment either by extending the benefits or burdens to the exempted class, or by nullifying the benefits or burdens for all. See, e.g., Heckler v. Mathews, 465 U.S. 728, 740 (1984). Here, for example, the Government would prefer to cure the unequal treatment by extending the robocall restriction and thereby proscribing nearly all robocalls to cell phones. By contrast, plaintiffs want to cure the unequal treatment by nullifying the robocall restriction and thereby allowing all robocalls to cell phones.

Justice Kavanaugh observed that the Court typically "extends the relevant statutory benefits or burdens to those previously exempted, rather than nullifying the benefits or burdens for all." He then pointed to Morales-Santana as an example of an "equal-treatment case[]" that "raised complex questions about whether it is appropriate to extend benefits or burdens, rather than nullifying the benefits or burdens." And he observed that in addition to "due process, fair notice, or other independent constitutional barriers to extension of benefits or burdens," there can also be "knotty questions about what is the exception and what is the rule."

E.   Equal Protection Methodology: The Problem of Sexual Orientation

Page 690.   At the bottom of the page, add the following:

In Bostock v. Clayton County, ___ U.S. ___ (2020), the Supreme Court held that Title VII of the Civil Rights Act of 1964, which prohibits discrimination in employment "because of" an individual's "sex" reaches discrimination against an individual for being gay or transgender. Writing for the Court, Justice Gorsuch explained that:

[I]t is impossible to discriminate against a person for being homosexual or transgender without discriminating against that individual based on sex. Consider, for example, an employer with two employees, both of whom are attracted to men. The two individuals are, to the employer's mind, materially identical in all respects, except that one is a man and the other a woman. If the employer fires the male employee for no reason other than the fact he is attracted to men, the employer discriminates against him for traits or actions it tolerates in his female colleague. Put differently, the employer intentionally singles out an employee to fire based in part on the employee's sex, and the affected employee's sex is a but-for cause of his discharge. Or take an employer who fires a transgender person who was identified as a male at birth but who now identifies as a female. If the employer retains an otherwise identical employee who was identified as female at birth, the employer intentionally penalizes a person identified as male at birth for traits or actions that it tolerates in an employee identified as female at birth. Again, the individual employee's sex plays an unmistakable and impermissible role in the discharge decision.

In dissent, Justice Alito, joined by Justice Thomas, warned that:

> [D]espite the important differences between the Fourteenth
> Amendment and Title VII, the Court's decision may exert a
> gravitational pull in constitutional cases. Under our prece-
> dents, the Equal Protection Clause prohibits sex-based dis-
> crimination unless a "heightened" standard of review is met.
> Sessions v. Morales-Santana, 582 U.S. ____, ____ (2017);
> United States v. Virginia, 518 U.S. 515, 532–534 (1996).
> By equating discrimination because of sexual orientation
> or gender identity with discrimination because of sex, the
> Court's decision will be cited as a ground for subjecting all
> three forms of discrimination to the same exacting standard
> of review.
>
> Under this logic, today's decision may have effects that
> extend well beyond the domain of federal antidiscrimination
> statutes. This potential is illustrated by pending and recent
> lower court cases in which transgender individuals have
> challenged a variety of federal, state, and local laws and pol-
> icies on constitutional grounds. . . .
>
> Although the Court does not want to think about the con-
> sequences of its decision, we will not be able to avoid those
> issues for long. The entire Federal Judiciary will be mired for
> years in disputes about the reach of the Court's reasoning.

Does the Court's construction of the phrase "discriminate because
of . . . sex" necessarily require that it subject discrimination on
the basis of sexual orientation or gender identity to some form of
heightened scrutiny?

VI
IMPLIED
FUNDAMENTAL
RIGHTS

The Due Process Clause and the
Incorporation Controversy

Page 746.   Before Section D, add the following:

In Timbs v. Indiana, 139 S. Ct. 682 (2019), the Court, in an
opinion by Justice Ginsburg, held that the eighth amendment excessive fines clause was incorporated against the states by the
fourteenth amendment due process clause.

After Timbs pleaded guilty to dealing in a controlled substance
and conspiracy to commit theft, the state sought civil forfeiture
of his $42,000 Land Rover on the ground that it had been used
to facilitate violation of criminal statutes. Timbs claimed that the
forfeiture was grossly disproportionate to the gravity of the offense and therefore constituted an excessive fine, but the Indiana
Supreme Court held that the excessive fine prohibition applied
only to the federal government.

The Supreme Court reversed. Quoting from *McDonald*, the
Court found that the guarantee was "fundamental to our scheme
of ordered liberty" with "dee[p] root[s] in [our] history and tradition." The state argued that even if the general right should be

incorporated, the application of the right to civil forfeiture was neither fundamental nor deeply rooted, but the Court responded that "[in] considering whether the Fourteenth Amendment incorporates a protection contained in the Bill of Rights, we ask whether the right guaranteed—not each and every particular application of that right—is fundamental and deeply rooted."

In an opinion concurring in the judgment, Justice Thomas renewed his argument that Bill of Rights protections should be incorporated through the fourteenth amendment's privileges or immunities clause rather than through the due process clause. In a separate concurrence, Justice Gorsuch acknowledged that "As an original matter [the] appropriate vehicle for incorporation may well be the [Privileges] or Immunities Clause" but stated that "nothing in this case turns on that question, and, regardless of the precise vehicle, there can be no serious doubt that the Fourteenth Amendment requires the States to respect the freedom from excessive [fines]."

In Apodaca v. Oregon, 406 U.S. 404 (1972), a sharply divided Court held that less than unanimous verdicts by criminal juries were constitutionally permissible in state, but not in federal courts. In Ramos v. Louisiana, ___U.S. ___(2020), the Court disavowed Apodaca and held that the sixth amendment requirement of jury unanimity in criminal cases was fully applicable to the states under the fourteenth amendment.

D. Substantive Due Process

Page 780.   Before Section b, add the following:

3. *Voting in the age of Corona.* In Republican National Committee v. Democratic National Committee, ___ U.S. ___ (2020), the Court addressed the constitutional implications of disruptions in voting caused by the Corona Virus. The Wisconsin primary election was scheduled for April 7. Under state law, absentee ballots had to be mailed and postmarked by this date. Because of the health crisis, an unprecedented number of citizens

requested absentee ballots, and it appeared that some voters would not receive their ballots by the April 7 deadline. Plaintiffs filed this action, alleging that the existing deadline unconstitutionally burdened the right to vote. The trial court agreed and issued a preliminary injunction requiring that absentee ballots be counted so long as they were received by April 13.

In a per curiam opinion, joined by five justices, the Court stayed the district court order.

> Extending the date by which ballots may be cast by voters—not just received by the municipal clerks but cast by voters—for an additional six days after the scheduled election day fundamentally alters the nature of the election. [The] plaintiffs themselves did not even ask for that relief in their preliminary injunction motions. [By] changing the election rules so close to the election date and by affording relief that the plaintiffs themselves did not ask for in their preliminary injunction motions, the District Court contravened this Court's precedents and erred by ordering such relief. This Court has repeatedly emphasized that lower federal courts should ordinarily not alter the election rules on the eve of an election.

Justice Ginsburg, joined by Justices Breyer, Sotomayor, and Kagan, dissented:

> A voter cannot deliver for postmarking a ballot she has not received. Yet tens of thousands of voters who timely requested ballots are unlikely to receive them by April 7, the Court's postmark deadline. Rising concern about the COVID-19 pandemic has caused a late surge in absentee-ballot requests. [The] surge [has] overwhelmed election officials, who face a huge backlog in sending ballots. . . .
>
> [Although] initially silent, the plaintiffs specifically requested [an extension of the deadline] at the preliminary-injunction hearing in view of the ever-increasing demand for absentee ballots. . . .

149

If proximity to the election counseled hesitation when the District Court acted several days ago, this Court's intervention today—even closer to the election—is all the more inappropriate.

The Court again stayed a district court order extending a Wisconsin deadline for voting in the November 2020 election. In a concurrence, Justice Gorsuch, joined by Justice Kavanaugh, stated that: "The Constitution provides that state legislatures—not federal judges, not state judges, not state governors, not other state officials—bear primary responsibility for setting election rules." Democratic National Commission v. Wisconsin State Legislature, 141 S. Ct. 28, 29–30 (2020). Are there circumstances in which legislature will shirk this responsibility? Would a state's failure to provide for absentee voting for voters deterred from going to the polls because of the Corona Virus unconstitutionally infringe on the right to vote?

After the November 2020 election, former President Trump and his allies filed 62 law suits challenging election results in states that the Republica ticket lost. 61 of those suits were dismissed; in one case, a Pennsylvania judge found that voters had three days to "cure" ballot errors after election day. William Cummings et al., By the numbers: President Donald Trump's failed efforts to overturn the election, USA TODAY, January 6, 2021, https://www.usatoday.com/in-depth/news/politics/elections/2021/01/06/trumps-failed-efforts-overturn-election-numbers/4130307001/.

E.   *Fundamental Interest and the Equal Protection Clause*

Page 792.   **At the end of the Note, add the following:**

In Rucho v. Common Cause, ___ U.S. ___ (2019), the Court, in an opinion by Chief Justice Roberts, held that partisan gerrymandering posed a nonjusticiable political question. (The case is discussed in greater detail in the supplement to Chapter One of the Main Volume.) The Court conceded that the districting in question, in North Carolina and Maryland, was "highly partisan by any measure" but nonetheless concluded that the claim was not appropriate for judicial resolution.

Although the Court's opinion was couched in terms of justiciability, some passages might be read to express views about the substantive constitutional issue. For example, the Court wrote that "[to] hold that legislators cannot take partisan interest into account when drawing district lines would essentially countermand the Framers' decision to entrust districting to political entities" The Court also observed that "[partisan] gerrymandering claims invariably sound in a desire for proportional representation [but the] Framers certainly did not think proportional representation was required."

Justice Kagan wrote a dissenting opinion that was joined by Justices Ginsburg, Breyer, and Sotomayor.

F. Modern Substantive Due Process: Privacy, Personhood, and Family

Page 887.   At the end of the Note, add the following:

6. *Box.* In Box v. Planned Parenthood of Indiana, 139 S. Ct. 1780 (2019), the Court, in a per curiam opinion and without receiving merits briefs or hearing oral argument, summarily reversed a lower court decision invalidating portions of an Indiana statute that governed the disposition of fetal remains by abortion providers. In the same opinion, the Court denied certiorari with respect to the lower court's decision invalidating a portion of the law that barred the knowing provision of sex-, race-, or disability-selective abortions by abortion providers.

The fetal remains statute had the effect of preventing doctors from incinerating fetal remains along with surgical byproducts. However, it permitted the simultaneous cremation of fetal remains, which Indiana did not generally allow for human remains, and did not affect a woman's right under existing law to determine the final disposition of the aborted fetus.

Planned Parenthood did not argue that the provision created an "undue burden" on the abortion right. Instead, it claimed only that the statute was not rationally related to a legitimate government interest. The Court held that this "deferential" standard was satisfied because the government had a legitimate interest in the proper disposal of fetal remains.

The Court expressed "no view on the merits" with regard to the selective abortion portion of the statute, noting that it was following "our ordinary practice of denying petitions [for certiorari] insofar as they raise legal issues that have not been considered by additional Courts of Appeals."

Justice Sotomayor noted that she would have denied certiorari with regard to both questions.

In a long concurring opinion, Justice Thomas traced the history of the eugenics movement in the United States. He argued that "abortion is an act rife with the potential for eugenic manipulation," that "[w]hatever else might be said about *Casey* it did not decide whether the Constitution requires States to allow eugenic abortions," and that "[enshrining] a constitutional right to an abortion based solely on race, sex, or disability of an unborn child [would] constitutionalize the views of the 20th-century eugenics movement."

In an opinion concurring in part and dissenting in part, Justice Ginsburg argued that the fetal remains provision implicated the right of women to choose an abortion before viability without undue interference from the state, and that the stricter undue burden standard was therefore applicable. Because it was " 'a waste of th[e] Court's resources' to take up a case simply to say that we are bound by the party's 'strategic litigation choice' to invoke rational-basis review alone," she would have denied the petition for certiorari in its entirety.

Suppose a different plaintiff sought an injunction against the fetal remains provision on the ground that it imposed an undue burden on the abortion right. What result? Does the state have a legitimate interest in preventing parents from trying to control the genetic characteristics of their offspring?

Professor Murray argues that "in painting reproductive rights as tools of deracination, Justice Thomas invokes history selectively, overlooking the way in which the denial of reproductive rights—and, specifically, efforts to restrict abortion—were also used to bolster white supremacy and suppress communities of color." Melissa Murray, Race-Ing *Roe*: Reproductive Justice, Racial Justice, and the Battle for *Roe v. Wade*, 134 Harv. L. Rev. 2025, 2089–90 (2021).

7. June Medical Services. In June Medical Services L.L.C. v. Russo, ___ U.S. ___ (2020), the Court in a 4-4-1 decision reaffirmed *Whole Woman's Health*. The case concerned a Louisiana statute that was nearly identical to Texas' admitting privilege law that had been invalidated in *Whole Woman's Health*. After trial, the District Court found that the statute offered no significant health benefits and that the conditions imposed by hospitals on granting admitting privileges would make it impossible for abortion providers to obtain the privileges. Ironically, a large part of the problem was caused by the fact that abortions rarely require hospitalization. Recent hospital experience is often a requirement for obtaining admitting privileges, and many doctors performing abortions lacked this experience because their patients were rarely hospitalized. The District Court further found that the inability to obtain admitting privileges would reduce the number of abortion clinics in the state to one, or at most two, with at most two physicians providing abortions in the entire state. Accordingly, the Court found that the statute imposed a "substantial burden" on the abortion right.

The Court of Appeals reversed. It found that the hospital privileges requirement would help "verify an applicant's surgical

ability, training, education, experience, practice record, and criminal history." It also rejected the District Court's findings that physicians performing abortions would be unable to obtain admitting
privileges.

A four-justice plurality of the Court, in an opinion written by Justice Breyer, held that the case was indistinguishable
from *Whole Woman's Health*, and therefore reversed the Court
of Appeals. The plurality relied heavily on the premise that the
trial court's findings of fact should not be set aside unless clearly
erroneous. Utilizing that standard, the plurality concluded that
"the testimony and other evidence contained in the extensive record developed over a 6-day trial supported the District Court's
ultimate conclusion that '[e]ven if [the statute] could be said to
further women's health to some marginal degree, the burdens it
imposes far outweigh any such benefit,' and thus the Act imposes
an unconstitutional undue burden."

Chief Justice Roberts wrote a separate opinion concurring
in the judgment. He noted that he had joined the dissent in
Whole Woman's Health and "continued to believe that the case
was wrongly decided." However, "[the] legal doctrine of *stare
decisis* requires us, absent special circumstances, to treat like
cases alike. The Louisiana law imposes a burden on access to
abortion just as severe as that imposed by Texas law, for the
same reasons. Therefore Louisiana's law cannot stand under our
precedent."

Chief Justice Roberts nonetheless criticized language in *Whole
Woman's Health* and repeated in the plurality opinion suggesting
that courts should weigh the law's asserted benefits against the
burdens it imposes on abortion access. Instead, he argued that the
Casey test required only that judges determine whether there was
a "substantial obstacle" to the abortion right. "Here the plurality
expressly acknowledges that we are not considering how to analyze an abortion regulation that does not present a substantial obstacle. [In] this case, *Casey's* requirement of finding a substantial
obstacle before invalidating an abortion regulation is therefore
a sufficient basis for the decision, as it was in *Whole Woman's*

Health. In neither case, nor in *Casey* itself, was there call for consideration of a regulation's benefits, and nothing in *Casey* commands such consideration."

Justice Thomas wrote a dissenting opinion. He argued that the physicians challenging the statute lacked standing because they did not claim that their own constitutional rights had been violated. (This portion of the opinion is discussed in the Supplement to Chapter One). He also renewed his argument that Roe v. Wade should be overruled.

Justice Alito, joined by Justice Gorsuch and, in part, by Justices Thomas and Kavanaugh, also dissented. He pointed out that physicians performing abortions stood to benefit if they were denied admitting privileges because the denial would support their claim that the statute was unconstitutional. He therefore criticized the plurality and the District Court for using a "good faith" standard to determine whether physicians had sought admitting privileges. "Because the doctors in question (many of whom are or were plaintiffs in this case) stand to lose, not to gain, by obtaining privileges, the court should require the plaintiffs to show that these doctors sought admitting privileges with the degree of effort that they would expend if their personal interests were at stake." Accordingly, he would have remanded the case to the District Court with directions that the Court should conduct a new trial and apply this standard.

Justices Gorsuch and Kavanaugh each filed separate dissents.

Page 918. At the end of the Note, add the following:

6. *Nonbiological "parents."* Does *Obergefell* entail a recognition of a due process right to parenthood in circumstances where there is no biological relationship between the adult and the child? For an affirmative answer, see NeJaime, The Constitution of Parenthood, 72 Stan. L. Rev. 261, 272 (2020):

In treating same-sex couples and the parent-child relation-ships they form as equally deserving of respect, the Court embraced nonbiological parenthood. . . .

These decisions [grapple] with the due process interest in marriage, not parenthood. Nonetheless, they provide guidance on how to reason about the liberty interest in pa-rental recognition. As *Obergefell* demonstrates, "new in-sights" about the family arrangements worthy of respect and the groups subject to exclusion can reshape understand-ings of the family relationships protected as a matter of due process.

Assuming arguendo that the author is correct, how should the Court determine which nonbiological relationships have constitutional status? Might there be circumstances under which the Constitution required that a child have more than two parents?

G. *Procedural Due Process*

Page 934.   Before the Note, add the following:

Compare *Loudermill* with Department of Homeland Security v. Thuraissigiam, ___ U.S. ___ (2020). A statute provides for the ex-pedited removal of some people seeking admission to the United States if the applicant cannot demonstrate to an asylum officer in a screening interview a "credible fear of persecution" that would justify the grant of asylum. If the asylum officer rejects the claim, the rejection is reviewed by a supervisor and may then be appealed to an immigration judge, but the determination is not reviewable in any Article III federal court. Thuraissigiam entered the United States illegally and was apprehended within twenty-five yards of the border and claimed that he feared returning to Sri Lanka because of persecution based on race, political opinions, or other protected characteristics. The asylum officer determined that Thuraissigiam lacked a credible fear of persecution, and an immigration judge affirmed the determination. Thuraissigiam claimed that these procedures were insufficient to satisfy the due process clause. In a 7-2 decision written by Justice Alito, the Court rejected the claim:

> While aliens who have established connections in this country have due process rights in deportation proceedings the Court long ago held that Congress is entitled to set the conditions for an alien's lawful entry into this country and that, as a result, an alien at the threshold of initial entry cannot claim any greater rights under the Due Process Clause. See *Nishimura Ekiu v. United States*, 142 U.S. 651, 660 (1892). Respondent attempted to enter the country illegally and was apprehended just 25 yards from the border. He therefore has no entitlement to procedural rights other than those afforded by statute.

Justice Thomas filed a concurring opinion. Justice Breyer filed an opinion concurring in the judgment in which Justice Ginsburg joined. Justice Sotomayor filed a dissenting opinion, which was joined by Justice Kagan.

Page 936.   At the end of section 2 of the Note, add the following:

Can the *Din* Court's treatment of the liberty interest in marriage unification be reconciled with its treatment of the liberty to marry in Obergefell v. Hodges (page 900 of the Main Volume)? For a discussion, see Abrams, The Rights of Marriage: *Obergefell, Din,* and the Future of Constitutional Family Law, 103 Cornell L. Rev. 501 (2018).

H.   The Contracts and Takings Clauses

Page 965.   Before section 4 of the Note, add the following:

For yet another rejection of a contract clause claim, see Sveen v. Melin, 138 S. Ct. 1815 (2018). In 1998, Sveen purchased a life insurance policy and named his wife, Melin, as the primary beneficiary. After the policy had been purchased, Minnesota enacted a statute providing that a divorce revokes the designation of a former spouse as a beneficiary. However, the statute operated only as a default rule; a divorce decree could direct that the former spouse remain the beneficiary, or the policyholder could override the revocation.

Sveen and Melin divorced in 2007 and, because the decree made no mention of the insurance policy and Sveen had not revised his beneficiary designation, the statute meant that the proceeds of the policy went to Sveen's contingent beneficiaries. Melin claimed that the statute violated the contract clause, but in an 8-1 decision, the Court, per Justice Kagan disagreed.

According to the Court, there was no need to decide whether the statute was an appropriate means to advance a "significant and legitimate public purpose," because the statute did not substantially impair a contractual obligation. This was true for three reasons. First, the statute was designed to reflect a policyholder's intent and, therefore supported rather than impaired the contractual scheme. Second, the statute was unlikely to disturb any policyholder's expectations because it did no more than what a divorce court might have done if the statute did not exist. Finally, the statute provided only a default rule that the policyholder could undo by renaming his former spouse as the beneficiary.

Justice Gorsuch filed a dissenting opinion.

Page 965.   At the end of the first paragraph of section 2, add the following.

Note that the takings clause prohibits takings for a public use only if just compensation is not paid. What implications does this requirement have for when a violation occurs? In Williamson County Regional Planning Comm'n v. Hamilton Bank of Johnson City, 473 U.S. 172 (1985), the Court held that a property owner whose property had been taken by a local government had not suffered a violation of his rights — and therefore could not bring a federal takings claim in federal court — until a state court had denied his claim for just compensation under state law. The Court reasoned that so long as the possibility of just compensation remained, there was not a constitutional violation. Subsequently, in San Remo Hotel, L.P. v. City and County of San Francisco, 545 U.S. 323 (2005), the Court held that a state court's resolution of a claim for just compensation under state law generally bars a subsequent federal suit. The intersection of the two cases effectively eliminated the possibility of gaining access to a federal court.

In Knick v. Township of Scott, ___ U.S. ___ (2019), the Court overruled *Williamson.* Instead of a necessary ingredient of the constitutional violation, the Court conceptualized compensation as a remedy for a violation that occurred at the moment of the taking. It followed that a property owner was entitled to immediate access to federal court even though there were state procedures available to provide for compensation.

Does it follow from *Knick* that prior to seeking compensation, a property owner is entitled to injunctive relief requiring the return of the property? One might think so given the Court's holding that a violation occurs at the moment the property is seized. But the *Knick* Court held that injunctive relief was not available, not because there had not been a completed violation, but because of traditional equitable principles that prohibit use of injunctions when there is an adequate remedy at law.

Chief Justice Roberts wrote the opinion of the Court. Justice Thomas wrote a concurring opinion, and Justice Kagan, joined by Justices Ginsburg, Breyer, and Sotomayor, dissented.

Page 969.   Before *Mahon*, add the following:

CEDAR POINT NURSERY V. HASSID

___U.S. ___ (2021)

CHIEF JUSTICE ROBERTS delivered the opinion of the Court.

I

The California Agricultural Labor Relations Act of 1975 gives agricultural employees a right to self-organization and makes it an unfair labor practice for employers to interfere with that right. The state Agricultural Labor Relations Board has promulgated a regulation providing, in its current form, that the self-organization rights of employees include "the right of access by union organizers to the premises of an agricultural employer for the purpose of meeting and talking with employees and soliciting their support." Under the regulation, a labor organization may "take access" to an agricultural employer's property for up to four 30-day periods in one calendar year. In order to take access, a labor organization must file a written notice with the Board and serve a copy on the employer. Two organizers per work crew (plus one additional organizer for every 15 workers over 30 workers in a crew) may enter the employer's property for up to one hour before work, one hour during the lunch break, and one hour after work. Organizers may not engage in disruptive conduct, but are otherwise free to meet and talk with employees as they wish. Interference with organizers' right of access may constitute an unfair labor practice, which can result in sanctions against the employer.

Cedar Point Nursery is a strawberry grower in northern California. It employs over 400 seasonal workers and around 100 full-time workers, none of whom live on the property. According to the complaint, in October 2015, at five o'clock one morning, members of the United Farm Workers entered Cedar Point's property without prior notice. The organizers moved to the nursery's trim shed, where hundreds of workers were preparing strawberry plants. Calling through bullhorns, the organizers disturbed operations, causing some workers to join the organizers in a protest and others to leave the worksite altogether. Cedar Point filed a charge against the union for taking access without giving notice. The union responded with a charge of its own, alleging that Cedar Point had committed an unfair labor practice. . . .

Believing that the union would likely attempt to enter their property again in the near future, the growers filed suit in Federal District Court against several Board members in their official capacity. The growers argued that the access regulation effected an unconstitutional *per se* physical taking under the Fifth and Fourteenth Amendments by appropriating without compensation an easement for union organizers to enter their property. They requested declaratory and injunctive relief prohibiting the Board from enforcing the regulation against them. . . .

II.

A

The Takings Clause of the Fifth Amendment, applicable to the States through the Fourteenth Amendment, provides: "[N]or shall private property be taken for public use, without just compensation." The Founders recognized that the protection of private property is indispensable to the promotion of individual freedom. . . . This Court agrees, having noted that protection of property rights is "necessary to preserve freedom" and "empowers persons to shape and to plan their own destiny in a world where governments are always eager to do so for them."

When the government physically acquires private property for a public use, the Takings Clause imposes a clear and categorical obligation to provide the owner with just compensation. The Court's physical takings jurisprudence is "as old as the Republic." The government commits a physical taking when it uses its power of eminent domain to formally condemn property. The same is true when the government physically takes possession of property without acquiring title to it. And the government likewise effects a physical taking when it occupies property—say, by recurring flooding as a result of building a dam. These sorts of physical appropriations constitute the "clearest sort of taking," and we assess them using a simple, *per se* rule: The government must pay for what it takes.

B

The access regulation appropriates a right to invade the growers' property and therefore constitutes a *per se* physical taking. The regulation grants union organizers a right to physically enter and occupy the growers' land for three hours per day, 120 days per year. Rather than restraining the growers' use of their own property, the regulation appropriates for the enjoyment of third parties the owners' right to exclude.

The right to exclude is "one of the most treasured" rights of property ownership. According to Blackstone, the very idea of property entails "that sole and despotic dominion which one man claims and exercises over the external things of the world, in total exclusion of the right of any other individual in the universe." In less exuberant terms, we have stated that the right to exclude is "universally held to be a fundamental element of the property right," and is "one of the most essential sticks in the bundle of rights that are commonly characterized as property."

Given the central importance to property ownership of the right to exclude, it comes as little surprise that the Court has long treated government-authorized physical invasions as takings requiring just compensation. The Court has often described the property interest taken as a servitude or an easement.

For example, in *United States v. Causby* we held that the invasion of private property by overflights effected a taking. The government frequently flew military aircraft low over the Causby farm, grazing the treetops and terrorizing the poultry. The Court observed that ownership of the land extended to airspace that low, and that "invasions of it are in the same category as invasions of the surface." Because the damages suffered by the Causbys "were the product of a direct invasion of [their] domain," we held that "a servitude has been imposed upon the land."

We similarly held that the appropriation of an easement effected a taking in *Kaiser Aetna v. United States*. A real-estate developer dredged a pond, converted it into a marina, and connected it to a nearby bay and the ocean. The government asserted that the developer could not exclude the public from the marina because the pond had become a navigable water. We held that the right to exclude "falls within [the] category of interests that the Government cannot take without compensation." After noting that "the imposition of the navigational servitude" would "result in an actual physical invasion of the privately owned marina" by members of the public, we cited *Causby* and *Portsmouth* for the proposition that "even if the Government physically invades only an easement in property, it must nonetheless pay just compensation."

The upshot of this line of precedent is that government-authorized invasions of property—whether by plane, boat, cable, or beachcomber—are physical takings requiring just compensation. As in those cases, the government here has appropriated a right of access to the growers' property, allowing union organizers to traverse it at will for three hours a day, 120 days a year. The regulation appropriates a right to physically invade the growers' property—to literally "take access," as the regulation provides. It is therefore a *per se* physical taking under our precedents. Accordingly, the growers' complaint states a claim for an uncompensated taking in violation of the Fifth and Fourteenth Amendments.

C

The Ninth Circuit saw matters differently, as do the Board and the dissent. In the decision below, the Ninth Circuit took the view that the access regulation did not qualify as a *per se* taking because, although it grants a right to physically invade the growers' property, it does not allow for permanent and continuous access "24 hours a day, 365 days a year." . . . That position is insupportable as a matter of precedent and common sense. There is no reason the law should analyze an abrogation of the right to exclude in one manner if it extends for 365 days, but in an entirely different manner if it lasts for 364.

To begin with, we have held that a physical appropriation is a taking whether it is permanent or temporary. Our cases establish that "compensation is mandated when a leasehold is taken and the government occupies property for its own purposes, even though that use is temporary."

Next, we have recognized that physical invasions constitute takings even if they are intermittent as opposed to continuous. *Causby* held that overflights of private property effected a taking, even though they occurred on only 4% of takeoffs and 7% of landings at the nearby airport.

The Board also takes issue with the growers' premise that the access regulation appropriates an easement. In the Board's estimation, the regulation does not exact a true easement in gross under California law because the access right may not be transferred, does not burden any particular parcel of property, and may not be recorded. This, the Board says, reinforces its conclusion that the regulation does not take a constitutionally protected property interest from the growers. The dissent agrees, suggesting that the access right cannot effect a *per se* taking because it does not require the growers to grant the union organizers an easement as defined by state property law.

These arguments misconstrue our physical takings doctrine. As a general matter, it is true that the property rights protected by the Takings Clause are creatures of state law. But no one disputes that, without the access regulation, the growers would

have had the right under California law to exclude union organizers from their property. And no one disputes that the access
regulation took that right from them. The Board cannot absolve
itself of takings liability by appropriating the growers' right to
exclude in a form that is a slight mismatch from state easement
law. Under the Constitution, property rights "cannot be so easily
manipulated."

III

The Board, seconded by the dissent, warns that treating the access
regulation as a *per se* physical taking will endanger a host of state
and federal government activities involving entry onto private
property. That fear is unfounded.

First, our holding does nothing to efface the distinction between
trespass and takings. Isolated physical invasions, not undertaken
pursuant to a granted right of access, are properly assessed as individual torts rather than appropriations of a property right.

Second, many government-authorized physical invasions will
not amount to takings because they are consistent with longstanding background restrictions on property rights. . . . [T]he government does not take a property interest when it merely asserts a
"pre-existing limitation upon the land owner's title." For example, the government owes a landowner no compensation for requiring him to abate a nuisance on his property, because he never
had a right to engage in the nuisance in the first place.

These background limitations also encompass traditional common law privileges to access private property. One such privilege
allowed individuals to enter property in the event of public or
private necessity. The common law also recognized a privilege
to enter property to effect an arrest or enforce the criminal law
under certain circumstances. Because a property owner traditionally had no right to exclude an official engaged in a reasonable
search, government searches that are consistent with the Fourth
Amendment and state law cannot be said to take any property
right from landowners.

Third, the government may require property owners to cede a right of access as a condition of receiving certain benefits, without causing a taking. Under this framework, government health and safety inspection regimes will generally not constitute takings. When the government conditions the grant of a benefit such as a permit, license, or registration on allowing access for reasonable health and safety inspections, both the nexus and rough proportionality requirements of the constitutional conditions framework should not be difficult to satisfy.

None of these considerations undermine our determination that the access regulation here gives rise to a *per se* physical taking. Unlike a mere trespass, the regulation grants a formal entitlement to physically invade the growers' land. Unlike a law enforcement search, no traditional background principle of property law requires the growers to admit union organizers onto their premises. And unlike standard health and safety inspections, the access regulation is not germane to any benefit provided to agricultural employers or any risk posed to the public. The access regulation amounts to simple appropriation of private property.

JUSTICE BREYER, with whom JUSTICE SOTOMAYOR and JUSTICE KAGAN join, dissenting.

I

A

Initially it may help to look at the legal problem — a problem of characterization — through the lens of ordinary English. The word "regulation" rather than "appropriation" fits this provision in both label and substance. It is contained in Title 8 of the California Code of Regulations. It was adopted by a state regulatory board, namely, the California Agricultural Labor Relations Board, in 1975. It is embedded in a set of related detailed regulations that describe and limit the access at issue. In addition to the hours of access just mentioned, it provides that union representatives can enter the property only "for the purpose of meeting and talking with employees and soliciting their support"; they have access only to "areas in which employees congregate before and after working" or "at such location or locations as the employees eat their lunch"; and they cannot engage in "conduct disruptive of the employer's property or agricultural operations, including injury to crops or machinery or interference with the process of boarding buses." From the employers' perspective, it restricts when and where they can exclude others from their property.

At the same time, the provision only awkwardly fits the terms "physical taking" and "physical appropriation." The "access" that it grants union organizers does not amount to any traditional property interest in land. It does not, for example, take from the employers, or provide to the organizers, any freehold estate (*e.g.*, a fee simple, fee tail, or life estate); any concurrent estate (*e.g.*, a joint tenancy, tenancy in common, or tenancy by the entirety); or any leasehold estate (*e.g.*, a term of years, periodic tenancy, or tenancy at will). Nor (as all now agree) does it provide the organizers with a formal easement or access resembling an easement, as the employers once argued, since it does not burden any particular parcel of property.

The majority concludes that the regulation nonetheless amounts to a physical taking of property because, the majority says, it "appropriates" a "right to invade" or a "right to exclude" others. It thereby likens this case to cases in which we have held that appropriation of property rights amounts to a physical *per se* taking.

It is important to understand, however, that, technically speaking, the majority is wrong. The regulation does not *appropriate* anything. It does not take from the owners a right to invade (whatever that might mean). It does not give the union organizations the right to exclude anyone. It does not give the government the right to exclude anyone. What does it do? It gives union organizers the right temporarily to invade a portion of the property owners' land. It thereby limits the landowners' right to exclude certain others. The regulation *regulates* (but does not *appropriate*) the owners' right to exclude.

Why is it important to understand this technical point? Because only then can we understand the issue before us. That issue is whether a regulation that *temporarily* limits an owner's right to exclude others from property *automatically* amounts to a Fifth Amendment taking. Under our cases, it does not.

B

Our cases draw a distinction between regulations that provide permanent rights of access and regulations that provide nonpermanent rights of access. They either state or hold that the first type of regulation is a taking *per se,* but the second kind is a taking only if it goes "too far." And they make this distinction for good reason. . . .

[A] taking is not inevitably found just because the interference with property can be characterized as a physical invasion by the government, or, in other words, when it affects the right to exclude.

The majority refers to other cases. But those cases do not help its cause. That is because the Court in those cases . . . did not apply a *"per se* takings" approach. In *United States v. Causby,* for example, the question was whether government flights over a piece of land constituted a taking. The flights amounted to 4% of the takeoffs, and 7% of the landings, at a nearby airport. But the planes flew "in considerable numbers and rather close together." And the flights were "so low and so frequent as to be a direct and immediate interference with the enjoyment and use of the land." Taken together, those flights "destr[oyed] the use of the property as a commercial chicken farm." Based in part on that economic damage, the Court found that the rule allowing these overflights went "too far." . . .

In *Kaiser Aetna v. United States,* the Court considered whether the Government had taken property by converting a formerly "private pond" (with a private access fee) into a "public aquatic park" (with free navigation-related access for the public). The

Court held there was a taking. But in doing so, it applied a *Penn Central,* not a *per se,* analysis. The Court wrote that "[m]ore than one factor contribute[d] to" the conclusion that the Government had gone "far beyond ordinary regulation or improvement." And it found there was a taking.

C

The persistence of the permanent/temporary distinction that I have described is not surprising. That distinction serves an important purpose. We live together in communities. . . . Modern life in these communities requires different kinds of regulation. Some, perhaps many, forms of regulation require access to private property (for government officials or others) for different reasons and for varying periods of time. Most such temporary-entry regulations do not go "too far." And it is impractical to compensate every property owner for any brief use of their land. As we have frequently said, "[g]overnment hardly could go on if to some extent values incident to property could not be diminished without paying for every such change in the general law." Thus, the law has not, and should not, convert all temporary-access-permitting regulations into *per se* takings automatically requiring compensation.

Consider the large numbers of ordinary regulations in a host of different fields that, for a variety of purposes, permit temporary entry onto (or an "invasion of ") a property owner's land. They include activities ranging from examination of food products to inspections for compliance with preschool licensing requirements. [Justice Breyer cites a long list of environmental, health, and safety regulations.]

The majority tries to deal with the adverse impact of treating these, and other, temporary invasions as if they were *per se* physical takings by creating a series of exceptions from its *per se* rule. It says: (1) "Isolated physical invasions, not undertaken pursuant to a granted right of access, are properly assessed as individual

torts rather than appropriations of a property right." *Ante*, at ——.
It also would except from its *per se* rule (2) government access
that is "consistent with longstanding background restrictions on
property rights," including "traditional common law privileges
to access private property." And it adds that (3) "the government
may require property owners to cede a right of access as a condition of receiving certain benefits, without causing a taking." How
well will this new system work? I suspect that the majority has
substituted a new, complex legal scheme for a comparatively simpler old one.

As to the first exception, what will count as "isolated"? How
is an "isolated physical invasion" different from a "temporary"
invasion, sufficient under present law to invoke *Penn Central*?
And where should one draw the line between trespass and takings? Imagine a school bus that stops to allow public school children to picnic on private land. Do three stops a year place the
stops outside the exception? One stop every week? Buses from
one school? From every school? Under current law a court would
know what question to ask. The stops are temporary; no one assumes a permanent right to stop; thus the court will ask whether
the school district has gone "too far." Under the majority's approach, the court must answer a new question (apparently about
what counts as "isolated").

As to the second exception, a court must focus on "traditional
common law privileges to access private property." Just what are
they? . . .

As to the third, what is the scope of the phrase "certain benefits"? Does it include the benefit of being able to sell meat labeled
"inspected" in interstate commerce? What about the benefit of
having electricity? Of sewage collection? Of internet accessibil-
ity? Myriad regulatory schemes based on just these sorts of benefits depend upon intermittent, temporary government entry onto
private property.

Labor peace (brought about through union organizing) is
one such benefit, at least in the view of elected representatives.
They wrote laws that led to rules governing the organizing of

170

agricultural workers. Many of them may well have believed that union organizing brings with it "benefits," including community health and educational benefits, higher standards of living, and (as I just said) labor peace. A landowner, of course, may deny the existence of these benefits, but a landowner might do the same were a regulatory statute to permit brief access to verify proper preservation of wetlands or the habitat enjoyed by an endangered species or, for that matter, the safety of inspected meat. So, if a regulation authorizing temporary access for purposes of organizing agricultural workers falls outside of the Court's exceptions and is a *per se* taking, then to what other forms of regulation does the Court's *per se* conclusion also apply?

VII
FREEDOM OF
EXPRESSION

A. Introduction

Page 1011. After the end of section 2 of the Note, add the following:

See also E. Berkowitz, Dangerous Ideas: A Brief History of Censorship in the West from the Ancients to Fake News 108-118 (2021).

Page 1015. After the quote from John Stuart Mill, add the following:

More than two centuries before Mill's publication of *On Liberty*, John Milton offered somewhat similar observations about the freedom of speech in his *Areopagitica* (1644). Consider Blasi, A Reader's Guide to John Milton's *Areopagitica*, 2017 Sup. Ct. Rev. 273, 293, 298, in which Blasi explains that Milton maintained that freedom of inquiry requires "the liberty to know, to utter, and to argue freely." Indeed, among the most important features of Milton's argument "is the positive value he sees in confronting evil and dangerous ideas." In his view, "the search for understanding would be much worse off were those ideas not to be available as foils and provocations and were authors and readers not seasoned by the experience of engaging them."

Page 1020. At the end of the paragraph at the top of the page, add the following:

Consider Kendrick, Use Your Words: On the "Speech" in "Freedom of Speech," 116 Mich. L. Rev. 667, 668 (2018):

"Freedom of speech" is clearly important in American society. But what is it? Is free speech implicated when a bakery denies service to a same-sex couple shopping for a wedding cake? Is it implicated when a town applies a zoning ordinance to a tattoo parlor? . . .

Most people presented with the question would say that free speech has something to do with activities that we colloquially call speaking, and that these activities are important in some way. But when serving a cake is speech, and tattooing is speech, [we] might wonder whether we have strayed rather far from both the notion of "speech" as a phenomenon and from whatever it is that might make "freedom of speech" important as a legal, political, or moral right. This matters, [because] if freedom of speech is a basic human right, we ought to be able to articulate when it is implicated and when it is not.

Page 1034. At the end of section 2 of the Note, add the following:

For a superb collection of essays reflecting on Justice Holmes's dissenting opinion in Abrams, see Abrams at 100: A Reassessment of Holmes's "Great Dissent," 51 Seton H. L. Rev. 1 (2020).

B.   Content-Based Restrictions: Dangerous Ideas and Information

Page 1060.   At the end of section b of the Note, add the following:

6c. Tsesis, Terrorist Speech on Social Media, 70 Vand. L. Rev. 651, 654-655, 707 (2017):

The Internet is awash with calls for terrorism. [Technically] adept terrorist organizations and their devotees exploit social networking sites to spread ideologies, disseminate instructional videos, consolidate power, and threaten enemies. [Twitter is] an active forum for a variety of terror organizations [and] YouTube is likewise a hub for radical videos available for viewing throughout the world. [In addressing this challenge, some commentators] believe that courts should unfailingly adhere to the *Brandenburg* standard; according to this perspective, only imminently harmful terrorist speech is subject to censure. But this perspective lacks the nuance to distinguish speech made at a private meeting, attended by a few Ku Klux Klan members in that case, and the national — indeed the global — reach of internet terrorist advocacy. [A] federal law against terrorist incitement [is] the most robust way to address the threat of terrorist propaganda on social media while staying true to free speech doctrine.

Page 1062.   At the end of the Note, add the following:

8. So, where are we today? Consider G. Stone & D. Strauss, Democracy and Equality 195-196 (2020):

In the half-century since 1969, the Supreme Court has not upheld a single conviction or other legal action against an individual because his speech in the political arena might cause others to violate the law. Although the Burger, Rehnquist, and Roberts Courts have recognized a few narrowly defined exceptions to Brandenburg based on what the justices perceived to be special circumstances, . . . the bottom line is that the Supreme Court—and lower courts—have continued rigorously to apply Brandenburg to speech in the political realm. In this essential sense, [Brandenburg] profoundly—and correctly—transformed the freedom of speech in our nation.

Page 1066.   At the end of section 8 of the Note, add the following:

Consider Tsesis, Categorizing Student Speech, 102 Minn. L. Rev. 1147, 1203 (2018): "In recent years, courts have increasingly deferred to public school authorities in student speech cases. [This] shift in K-12 had empowered administrators to punish students who express controversial points of view about matters such as pregnancy, abortion, and illegal drugs. [School] is too important a locus for deliberation, petition, and assembly to leave decisions negatively impacting students' free speech rights at the sole discretion of administrators."

Suppose a student engages in speech outside of school. To what extent may the school discipline the student for such speech? Does *Tinker* apply, or should the student have the same freedom of speech when she is outside of school as anyone else? The Court addressed this question in Mahanoy Area School District v. B.L, ___ S.Ct. ___ (2021), in which a high school student who had not been selected for the varsity cheerleading team posted two messages on Snapchat when she was not in school. One of the images showed B.L. and a friend with middle fingers raised, with the caption "Fuck school fuck softball fuck cheer fuck every-thing." Because several students on the cheerleading squad were upset by this post, the school suspended B.L. from participating on the junior varsity cheerleading squad for a year. The Court, in an eight-to-one decision, held that, although the school's au-thority to restrict student speech outside of school is more lim-ited than when it restricts student speech on school grounds, there are still circumstances when the student speech may be so dis-ruptive of the educational process that the school can discipline the student even for speech off of school property. But, without offering a very clear statement of the standard to be applied in this situation, the Court, in an eight-to-one decision, held that this situation did not satisfy that vague standard and that the school's action therefore violated the student's First Amendment rights. The lone dissenter was Justice Thomas, who—taking an origi-nalist approach—argued that the proper standard should be the one in place at the time the Fourteenth Amendment was adopted, and that at that time public schools were assumed to have broad discretion to punish students for their speech, whether on or off school grounds.

Page 1074.   At the end of section 8 of the Note, add the following:

Consider Schauer, Costs and Challenges of the Hostile Audience, 94 Notre Dame L. Rev. 1671, 1685 (2019): "[W]hat is importantly not clear is just how much the authorities must do before taking some sort of action against the speaker or before bringing the entire event to a halt. [Must the municipality] deploy all or most of its police force, even if doing so would create other dangers to safety and security? Must it call on nonlocal law en-forcement authorities, such as county police, state police, or even the National Guard?"

Page 1074. At the end of the first paragraph of section 9 of the Note, add the following, after the citation to Tsesis:

Wright, The Heckler's Veto Today, 68 Case W. Res. L. Rev. 159 (2017); Russomanno, Speech on Campus: How America's Crisis in Confidence is Eroding Free Speech Values, 45 Hastings Const. L.Q. 273 (2018); Wells, Free Speech Hypocrisy: Campus Free Speech Conflicts and the Sub-Legal First Amendment, 89 U. Colo. L. Rev. 533 (2018); Ross, Campus Discourse and Democracy: Free Speech Principles Provide Sound Guidance Even After the Tumult of 2017, 20 U. Pa. J. Const. L. 787 (2018).

Page 1075. At the end of section 9 of the Note, add the following:

For another facet of the "heckler's veto" issue, consider the issue of heckling itself. To what extent does the First Amendment protect the right of audience members to disrupt a speech by making noise? Suppose instead they "heckle" the speaker with uninvited questions and challenges? Is such speech protected by the First Amendment even if it interrupts the speaker? In what circumstances can such heckling constitutionally be prohibited? See Waldron, Heckle: To Disconcert with Questions, Challenges, or Gibes, 2017 Sup. Ct. Rev. 1.

Consider Schauer, Costs and Challenges of the Hostile Audience, 94 Notre Dame L. Rev. 1671, 1695 (2019): "Although it is plain that hecklers do have free speech rights, the argument that they have rights to drown out other speakers seems strained. As long as reasonable and content-neutral time, place, and manner restrictions are permissible, it is at least plausible that some sort of first-come-first-served or other regulations designed to ensure that speakers can at least be heard would be permissible as well."

Page 1081. At the end of the paragraph beginning with the words "On June 22," add the following:

For a fuller account of the Skokie controversy, see P. Strum, When the Nazis Came to Skokie (1999).

Page 1082. At the beginning of the paragraph beginning with the words "On the hate speech issue," add the following:

For a more critical account of the actual effect of hate speech laws in other nations, see N. Strossen, Hate: Why We Should Resist It with Free Speech, Not Censorship (2018).

Page 1095. At the end of section e of the Note, add the following:

Krotoszynski, Whistleblowing Speech and the First Amendment. 93 Ind. L.J. 267 (2018); Stanger, Whistle Blowers (2019).

Page 1096. At the end of section 10 of the Note, add the following:

11. *Keeping secrets in the future.* Consider Strauss, Keeping Secrets, in L. Bollinger & G. Stone, The Free Speech Century 123, 138-138 (2019):

The Pentagon Papers case was a celebrated chapter in the history of the First Amendment, and the principle established by that case has become foundational. The government may keep its secrets, even if they concern matters of great public interest, by prohibiting people within government from leaking them. But once they are leaked, a newspaper may not be enjoined from publishing those secrets, except in extraordinary circumstances. Abstractly, that principle seems hard to justify. Information should be either secret or be disclosed, one might say, and it does not make sense to have everything turn on the fortuity of whether the information has been leaked. But while it is difficult to judge these matters with confidence, the system put in place by the Pentagon Papers decision seems to have worked in the past.

Today there is reason to think it is no longer working as well. There are more people in a position to leak information; it is easier to leak; and it is much easier to leak large amounts of highly sensitive information, as recent events have demonstrated. At the same time, the ability to spread that information throughout the world is not limited, as it was at the time of the Pentagon Papers case, to a handful of newspapers and television networks, run by people who took seriously their obligations to protect national security. We should consider some changes to the Pentagon Papers settlement to adapt to these new circumstances. A First Amendment right of access to government information, coupled with stricter limits on publication, is one possibility; [and] a formal or informal differentiation among media outlets is yet another. . . . [The] stakes are great, on both sides, and the world has changed in ways that make it important to rethink the way we deal with this problem.

12. *The Pentagon Papers Fifty Years On.* As David Strauss notes in the above quote, a great deal has changed since 1971 – the number of government employees and contractors with access to classified information has increased dramatically, the ability of government employees to leak vast amounts of top secret information has changed profoundly from the use of Xerox machines

to the use of thumb drives and other forms of technology, and the number of entities capable of disseminating this information has grown from a relatively few responsible institutions like the *New York Times* and the *Washington Post* to virtually any individual or organization with access to social media. The central question is whether, in light of these changes, it is time to revisit the *Pentagon Papers* resolution. For a diverse set of answers to these questions, see L. Bollinger and G. Stone, National Security, Leaks & Freedom of the Press (2021), which includes a broad range of perspectives on these issues from such contributors as John Brennan, the former head of the CIA; Keith Alexander, the former head of the NSA; Eric Holder, the former Attorney General; David Sanger, the New York Times' leading national security analyst; Ellen Nakashima, the Washington Post's leading national security analyst; and a host of other national security experts, experienced journalists, and First Amendment scholars.

C. Overbreadth, Vagueness, and Prior Restraint

Page 1111. At the end of the paragraph discussing Walker v. City of Birmingham, add the following:

For a critical analysis of the Court's 5-4 decision in *Walker*, see Kennedy, Walker v. City of Birmingham Revisited, 2017 Sup. Ct. Rev. 313, 336:

That people were compelled to resort to political protest to challenge the widespread and blatant racial discrimination in mid-twentieth century America was disgraceful. That they were arrested and jailed by local authorities intent upon suppressing their message is outrageous. That this persecution was

then blessed by the United States Supreme Court was tragic. . . .
Of all the places to proclaim the civilizing hand of the
law, the Supreme Court chose a case that absolved judicial white supremacists and relegated to jail Martin Luther
King, Jr.

D.   Content-Based Restrictions:
Low Value Speech

Page 1119.   At the end of section 1 of the Note, add
the following:

1a. *New York Times v. Sullivan and originalism.* In a concurring opinion in a libel case in which the Supreme Court denied
certiorari in 2019, Justice Clarence Thomas called for the Court
to "reconsider" New York Times v. Sullivan because it was nothing
more than a "policy driven" decision "masquerading as constitutional law." Noting that "from the founding of the Nation until
1964 the law of defamation was 'almost exclusively the business
of state courts and legislatures,'" and that the law of Alabama at
issue in *New York Times* reflected the prevailing view of defamation law at the time that the first amendment was adopted, Thomas
maintained that the decision in *New York Times* represented a
sharp departure from "the original meaning of the Constitution."
Because "the States are perfectly capable of striking an acceptable balance between encouraging robust public discourse and
providing a meaningful remedy for reputational harm," Thomas
called for the Court to "reconsider our jurisprudence in this
area." McKee v. Cosby, 139 S. Ct. 675 (2019). Assuming Justice
Thomas is right that defamation law at the time the first amendment was adopted looked nothing like what the Court required in
New York Times v. Sullivan, is there any way to justify the result in
New York Times?

Page 1121.   At the end of section 5 of the Note, add the following:

5a. Sullivan and investigative reporting. Consider G. Stone & D. Strauss, Democracy and Equality 73 (2020):

One important and probably unanticipated consequence of the Warren Court's decision in Sullivan has been to open the door to a more aggressive and more effective form of investigative journalism. As a result of Sullivan, it became much less risky for both sources and reporters to disclose misconduct by public officials, and in the years since Sullivan, investigative reporting has become an increasingly important check on the abuse of government authority.

Page 1127.   At the end of subsection c of the Note, add the following:

Consider C. Sunstein, Liars: Falsehoods and Free Speech in an Age of Deception 56 (2021):

If public officials are allowed to punish or censor what they characterize as false, they might end up punishing or censoring truth. The reason is that their own judgments may not be reliable. [Worst] of all, their judgments are likely to be self-serving. If [government officials try] to censor speech as "fake news," the real reason might not be that it is fake. The real reason might be that it casts them in a bad light. The truth police are often minions of an authoritarian, trying to keep hold on power. [Officials are likely to] go after those lies and falsehoods that put them in a bad light, and ignore or celebrate those that put them in a good light.

Page 1128.   At the end of section e of the Note, add the following:

f. Suppose government officials or agencies tell lies in order to mislead the American people or to damage the credibility of the press. Should such lies be held to violate the first amendment? See Norton, Government lies and the Press Clause, 89 U. Colo. L. Rev. 453 (2018).

Page 1131.   After the first full paragraph on the page, add the following:

Consider C. Sunstein, Liars: Falsehoods and Free Speech in an Age of Deception at 48 (2021):

In the relatively few years since *Alvarez*, the world has changed dramatically, not least because of the increasing role of social media and the spread of lies and falsehoods on it. [The] plurality in *Alvarez* was myopic in focusing largely on established categories of cases, such as defamation, in which false statements of fact can sometimes be regulated or sanctioned. In the modern era, false statements falling short of libel are causing serious problems for individuals and society; if they cause such problems, there is a legitimate reason that they should be regulable.

Page 1139.   At the end of the paragraph ending in "to escape revenge porn's long shadow," add the following:

For a detailed analysis of this issue, see Citron, Sexual Privacy, 128 Yale L.J. 1870 (2019).

Page 1162.   At the end of section 6 of the Note, add the following:

See Redish and Voils, False Commercial Speech and the First Amendment, 25 Wm. & Mary Bill Rts. J. 765 (2017).

Page 1164.   At the end of the first paragraph on the page, add the following:

For a lively account of the life and times of Anthony Comstock, see A. Werbel, Lust on Trial (2018).

Page 1195.   At the end of Section 6, following the citation to Lakier, add the following:

Is the Court's sharp distinction between high-value and low-value speech too rigid and artificial? Would it be better for the Court to use strict scrutiny only for truly high-value speech, deferential review for low-value speech, and intermediate scrutiny for all types of speech in-between? See Han, Middle-Value Speech, 61 S. Cal. L. Rev. 65 (2017).

Page 1205.   Before Sable Communications v. FCC, add the following:

IANCU v. BRUNETTI, ____U.S. ____ (2019). In *Matal v. Tam*, infra page 1229, the Court unanimously held the Lanham Act's prohibition on the registration of "disparaging" trademarks unconstitutional because the concept of "disparaging" constituted impermissible viewpoint discrimination. In *Iancu*, Brunetti created a clothing line that uses the trademark FUCT. The Patent and

Trademark Office [PTO] denied the application for a registered trademark because the trademark FUCT violated the Lanham Act's prohibition on the registration of "immoral" or "scandalous" trademarks. In an opinion by Justice Kagan, the Court held that the decision of the PTO violated the first amendment because, like the provision forbidding "disparaging" trademarks, the provision forbidding "immoral" or "scandalous" trademarks "similarly discriminates on the basis of viewpoint."

To justify this conclusion, Kagan cited both the dictionary definitions of these terms and the actual application of these terms by the PTO in a range of cases. Kagan observed that, from both perspectives, it was clear that "the statute, on its face, distinguishes between two opposed sets of ideas: those aligned with conventional moral standards and those hostile to them." For example, under these provisions the PTO had disapproved registration for the trademark BONG HITS 4 JESUS "because 'Christians would be morally outraged by a statement that connects Jesus Christ with illegal drug use,'" but approved trademarks such as "PRAISE THE LORD" and "JESUS DIED FOR YOU" because those trademarks "suggested religious faith rather than blasphemy or irreverence."

In light of those decisions, Kagan rejected the argument that the prohibition of "immoral" or "scandalous" trademarks could be understood as viewpoint-neutral. Thus, like the prohibition of "disparaging" trademarks, which the Court had invalidated in *Matal*, the Court concluded that the prohibition of "immoral" or "scandalous" trademarks also violated the First Amendment.

The interesting question in the case is whether the government could constitutionally refuse to register trademarks that use profanity, as was arguably the case in *Iancu*. Although the majority found it unnecessary to address that question, four justices argued that such a law would be constitutional. In a concurring opinion, Justice Alito agreed with Justice Kagan that the Lanham Act could not fairly be interpreted in so narrow a manner, but made clear that, in his view, under a properly drawn statute the government could constitutionally deny trademark registration to the trademark at issue in this case or, indeed, to any other trademark that contains "vulgar terms that play no real part in the expression of ideas." The use of such vulgarity, he argued "is not needed to express any idea and, in fact, as commonly used today, generally signifies nothing except emotion and a severely limited vocabulary." This raises the question whether this situation should be governed by *Cohen* or by *Pacifica*. What do you think?

In separate opinions, Chief Justice Roberts and Justices Sotomayor and Breyer agreed that the law would be unconstitutional if properly interpreted as constituting viewpoint discrimination, but they dissented from the majority's understanding of the statute. In their view, in the words of Chief Justice Roberts, the statutory prohibition of "scandalous" marks could — and should — reasonably be interpreted as forbidding the registration of trademarks only if they "offend because of their mode of expression — marks that are obscene, vulgar, or profane." "Refusing registration to obscene, vulgar, or profane marks," Roberts maintained, does not offend the First Amendment" because such a restriction is not viewpoint-based and because the Lanham Act does not forbid the use of such words in trademarks, but only forbids their registration. Thus, under the statute, "whether such marks can be registered does not affect the extent to which their owners may use them in commerce to identify goods. No speech is being restricted; no one is being punished. The owners of such marks are merely denied certain additional benefits associated with federal trademark registration. The Government, meanwhile, has an interest in not associating itself with trademarks whose content is obscene, vulgar, or profane. The First Amendment," Roberts concluded, "protects the freedom of speech; it does not require the Government to give aid and comfort to those using obscene, vulgar, and profane modes of expression."

Underscoring the reasoning of Chief Justice Roberts, Justice Sotomayor maintained that, properly construed, the Lanham Act's prohibition on the registering of "scandalous" trademarks did not constitute viewpoint discrimination, which would be unconstitutional, but was viewpoint-neutral. Citing *Pacifica*, Sotomayor reasoned that such a restriction is not necessarily unconstitutional. Indeed, she concluded that "prohibiting the registration of obscene, profane, or vulgar marks qualifies as reasonable, viewpoint-neutral, content-based regulation," and that such a restriction is permissible because "the Government has an interest in not promoting certain kinds of speech," as long as the restriction is viewpoint-neutral and serves a reasonable justification.

For an analysis of *Iancu*, see Greenfield, Trademarks, Hate Speech, and Viewpoint Bias, 2018 Sup. Ct. Rev. 183.

Page 1221.　At the end of section e of the Note, add the following:

For the argument that laws forbidding hate speech undermine the political legitimacy of laws prohibiting discrimination, see Weinstein, Hate Speech Bans, Democracy, and Political Legitimacy, 32 Const. Comm. 527 (2017).

Page 1223.　After section j of the Note, add the following:

k. N. Strossen, Hate: Why We Should Resist It with Free Speech, Not Censorship 81, 87, 99 (2018):

[Laws] censoring "hate speech" have predictably been enforced against those who lack political power, including government critics and members of the very minority groups these laws are intended to protect. This concern has been raised repeatedly by international human rights organizations. For example, the [2015 report by the European

Commission Against Racism and Intolerance] observed that although "the duty under international law to criminalize certain forms of hate speech . . . was established to protect members of vulnerable minority groups," members of these groups have "been disproportionately the subject of prosecutions" under European "hate speech" laws.

[For example, although] the 1965 British "hate speech" law was passed to quell growing racism against minority groups, the first person convicted under it was a black man who cursed a white police officer. [Similarly,] Canadian "hate speech" laws also have been enforced to suppress expression of minority speakers and views. [In one instance, for example,] Canadian Customs seized 1,500 copies of a book that various Canadian universities had tried to import from the United States. What was this dangerous racist, sexist book? None other than *Black Looks: Race and Representation*, by the African-American feminist scholar, bell hooks. [And in] 2017, the Austrian Court of Appeal affirmed a lower court ruling that anonymous Facebook posts criticizing Austria's Green Party leader [constituted] illegal "hate speech" [because they called her a] "lousy traitor" and "corrupt bumpkin."

On the international effects of hate speech laws, see also Cleveland, Hate Speech at Home and Abroad, in L. Bollinger & G. Stone, The Free Speech Century 210 (2019).

Page 1229.   At the end of section 2 of the Note, add the following:

Was the Court right in *Matal* to characterize the issue as one of "viewpoint discrimination"? Consider Calvert. Merging Offensive-Speech Cases with Viewpoint-Discrimination Principles, 27 Wm. & Mary Bill Rts. J. 829, 833-837 (2019):

Equating offensiveness with viewpoint discrimination in
Tam [blurs] doctrinal lines. Specifically, the boundary is now
muddled between what traditionally might have been considered offensive-speech cases — *Cohen* and *Pacifica*, most
notably — and viewpoint-discrimination cases in which the
government targets "views taken by speakers" because of
"[the] ideology or the opinion or perspective of the speaker."
[A] word such as "fuck" is censored [because] its usage
"is a cultural taboo" in terms of how one should speak or
talk, and thus it causes offense. Conversely, in the [view-
point] situation, [the restriction] is premised on the underlying substantive position [that] a message conveys. [In]
other words, while viewpoint-discrimination cases are
about what substantive idea is being said and censored, offensive-speech cases are about the emotional impact (rather
than the cognitive meaning) of speech. The latter is an insufficient reason, standing alone, for squelching expression. In
a nutshell, "fuck" is what offended in *Cohen*, not *Cohen*'s
viewpoint about conscription. "Fuck" is not a viewpoint.
[It] is, instead, a word that violates certain norms of civil
discourse in polite society and thus gives offense to some
people by its very utterance. Justice Alito thus was wrong
in *Tam* when he flatly proclaimed, in oversimplistic fashion,
that "[g]iving offense is a viewpoint." Perhaps better put,
giving offense sometimes may be a viewpoint, but giving
offense is not always a viewpoint.

Consider also Greenfield, Trademarks, Hate Speech, and
Solving a Puzzle of Viewpoint Bias, 2018 Sup. Ct. Rev. 183, 228-
29, arguing that another trademark case, Iancu v. Brunetti, supra
page 1205, offers "an important clarification of the Court's doctrine of viewpoint discrimination." Greenfield observes that, after
Iancu, it is clear that *R.A.V.* is best seen as a case about traditional
viewpoint bias, rather than a case that stands for a notion that
limits on the modes or manner of speech discriminate on the basis
of viewpoint. [A] ban on racial epithets applied to both anti-white

and anti-black protesters, for example, is not constitutionally identical to a ban on racial epithets applied to only on side. [We] now know that while the latter is correctly seen as discriminating on the basis of viewpoint, the former is not."

Page 1242. At the end of section 4 of the Note, add the following:

(5) "Liberal constitutional fundamentalism created the free speech orthodoxy that allowed threats, conspiracy theories, defamation, and outright lies to flourish unchecked in the media and on the Internet. In the name of free speech, liberals helped eliminate nearly every potential standard and safeguard against violent rhetoric, false statements, and targeted harassment. [The] Trump era has exposed the hollowness of liberal free speech platitudes: the belief that truth will eventually prevail, that the best answer to bad speech is more speech, and that protecting the free speech rights of the worst people in society is necessary to protect the free speech of all." M.A. Franks, The Cult of the Constitution 16 (2019).

E. Content-Neutral Restrictions: Limitations on the Means of Communication and the Problem of Content Neutrality

Page 1245. At the end of the material on Kovacs v. Cooper, add the following:

Consider the issue of "heckling." Suppose members of the audience at a speech on public or private property decide to "heckle" the speaker. In what circumstances can the government constitutionally order the hecklers to stop? Assuming the government is acting in a content-neutral manner, how should the rule be fashioned? Can the state constitutionally ban all heckling insofar as the speaker objects to it? Should it matter whether the hecklers are (a) attempting to disrupt the event and prevent the speech, or (b) asking hard questions and posing challenges to the speaker, even if she doesn't want to be interrupted? To what extent do members of the audience have a First Amendment right (a) to disrupt the event or (b) to heckle the speaker by asking uninvited questions and making uninvited comments? What is the right First Amendment standard for addressing such situations? For a lively discussion of heckling, see Waldron, Heckle: To Disconcert with Questions, Challenges, or Gibes, 2017 Sup. Ct. Rev. 1.

Page 1264. At the end of section 3 of the Note, add the following:

For the Court's most recent decision on the disclosure issue, see *Americans for Prosperity Foundation v. Bonta*, 594 U.S. ___ (2021), at the insert for page 1366 in this Supplement.

Page 1273. At the end of section 2 of the Note at the top of the page, add the following:

Consider Krotoszynski, Our Shrinking First Amendment: On the Growing Problem of Reduced Access to Public Property for Speech Activity, 78 Ohio St. L.J. 779, 804, 817 (2017): "[T]he Rehnquist and Roberts Court have reset the balance in the government's favor and have done so to a significant degree. Access to government property for expressive purposes is considerably more circumscribed today than it was in the 1960s or 1970s. [A] course correction that places a higher burden of justification on the government for resisting free speech easements on public property would better serve our core commitment to freedom of expression as an essential condition for democratic self-government to flourish."

Page 1284.   At the end of section 2 of the Note, add the following:

3. *The reach of* Lehman*: polling places.* In Minnesota Voters Alliance v. Mansky, 138 S. Ct. 1876 (2018), the Court considered the constitutionality of a state law prohibiting individuals, including voters, from wearing a "political badge, political button, or other political insignia" inside a polling booth on Election Day. Unlike Burson v. Freeman, noted at page 1279 of the Main Text, which prohibited the display or distribution of campaign materials within one hundred feet of a polling place, and thus restricted speech in a public forum, the law in *Minnesota Voters Alliance* was limited only to speech within a polling place. The Court thus concluded that it regulated speech in a nonpublic forum. In such circumstances, the Court explained that the "government may reserve such a forum 'for its intended purposes, [as] long as the regulation on speech is reasonable and not an effort to suppress expression merely because public officials oppose the speaker's view.' "

Applying that test, the Court reasoned that there was "no basis for rejecting Minnesota's determination that some forms of advocacy should be excluded from the polling place." Nonetheless, the Court invalidated the Minnesota law, because even though it served a reasonable purpose and even though it was applied in an even-handed manner, the restriction was too ill-defined to give reasonable guidance to election officials to enable them to apply the law in a reasonably consistent and predictable manner. The Court noted, for example, that it was unclear whether badges, insignias or buttons were forbidden if they supported the ACLU, said "All Lives Matter," endorsed the NRA, or quoted the First Amendment. The Court therefore concluded that "if a State wishes to set its polling place apart as areas free of partisan discord, it must employ a more discernible approach than the one Minnesota has offered here."

4. *State action.* Suppose that, instead of permitting only commercial advertising in its transit vehicles, the city adopted a set of clearly viewpoint-based restrictions. For example, suppose the city permitted only messages that supported the mayor, opposed abortion, opposed same-sex marriage, opposed affirmative action, and so on. Would such a program be constitutional? Assuming that such a program would violate the first amendment, suppose that instead of making such decisions itself the city leased the authority to sell advertising space in its transit vehicles to a private company for a fixed annual fee. Suppose then that the private company, acting wholly independently of the city, adopted the same viewpoint-based restrictions in its own administration of the program. Would the decisions of the private company violate the first amendment? Would the decisions of the private company in such circumstances constitute state action?

Consider Manhattan Community Access Corp. v. Halleck, 139 S. Ct. 1921 (2019): New York law requires cable operators to set aside channels on their cable systems for public access. New York City designated a private nonprofit corporation, Manhattan Neighborhood Network (MNN), to operate the public access channels on Time Warner's cable system in Manhattan. Thereafter, MNN excluded plaintiffs Halleck and Melendez from the public access channels because they had aired a film on MNN's public access channels that was critical of MNN. Halleck and Melendez sued, claiming that MNN had violated their first amendment rights. In a sharply-divided decision, the Court held that MNN's action did not constitute state action and that the first amendment was therefore irrelevant. The Court, in an opinion by Justice Kavanaugh, explained that this could not be deemed state action because the city possessed no property interest in the cable system or in the public access channels. Justice Sotomayor, joined by Justices Ginsburg, Breyer, and Kagan, dissented on the ground that New York City "secured a property interest in public access television channels when it granted a cable franchise to a cable company" and that by accepting "that agency relationship, MNN stepped into the City's shoes and thus qualifies as a state actor."

Page 1298.   Before Section d, add the following:

The Court reaffirmed its analysis in Reed in Barr v. American Association of Political Consultants, ___ U.S. ___ (2020). In 1991, Congress enacted the Telephone Consumer Protection Act, which prohibited robocalls. In 2015, Congress amended the law to create an exception for robocalls made to collect a debt owed to or guaranteed by the United States. The American Association of Political Consultants maintained that this converted the original act into an unconstitutional content-based restriction and that they, too, should therefore be permitted to make robocalls. Although the Court held the exception unconstitutional, the justices divided sharply over the proper standard to be applied. Five justices, invoking *Reed*, embraced the view that, because the government debt exception was content-based, it must be subjected to "strict scrutiny." The other four justices—Breyer, Ginsburg, Kagan and Sotomayor, maintained that, because the challenged law was content-based but not viewpoint-based, it should be subjected only to intermediate scrutiny. Echoing his opinion in *Reed*, Justice Breyer explained his reasoning as follows:

> There are times when using content discrimination to trigger [strict] scrutiny is eminently reasonable. Specifically, when content-based distinctions are used as a method for suppressing particular viewpoints or threatening the neutrality of a traditional public forum, content discrimination triggering strict scrutiny is generally appropriate. [Neither] of those situations is present here. Outside of these circumstances,

content discrimination can at times help determine the strength of a government justification or identify a potential interference with the free marketplace of ideas. But [this] case is not about protecting the marketplace of ideas. It is not about the formation of public opinion or the transmission of the people's will to elected representatives. It is fundamentally about a method of regulating debt collection.

Page 1314.   Before the Note, add the following:

In Agency for International Development v. Alliance for Open Society International, ___ U.S. ___ (2020) (*Agency for International Development II*), the Court, in an opinion by Justice Kavanaugh, held that although the government could not constitutionally require American organizations receiving federal funds to oppose prostitution and sex trafficking, it could constitutionally require foreign organizations receiving funds under the same federal law to oppose prostitution and sex trafficking as a condition of their receipt of funds under the same legislation. The Court explained that although foreign citizens who are in the United States enjoy many constitutional rights, foreign citizens and organizations outside the United States cannot "assert rights under the U.S. Constitution." The Court held that this was so even when the foreign organizations work in partnership with American organizations. Justices Breyer, Ginsburg, and Sotomayor dissented.

Page 1317.   At the end of section 3 of the Note, add the following:

4. *How much should it matter whether the public thinks it is seeing "government speech"?* Consider Hemel and Ouellette, Public Perceptions of Government Speech, 2017 Sup. Ct. Rev. 33, 35-36:

To draw the line between government speech and private expression, the Supreme Court's early government speech cases looked to whether the speaker is a "traditional" government agency or official and to whether the government exercises "control over the message." [In its more recent decisions, however, such as *Summum*, *Walker*, and *Matal*], the Court has placed increasing emphasis on whether members of the public reasonably perceive the relevant expression as government speech. [While] there are strong theoretical reasons to draw the line between government speech and private speech on the basis of public perception, the Court has so far failed to develop a reliable method for determining whether the public perceives expression to be government speech. [It] would seem that the best way to resolve the worry is to ask a representative sample of the population.

The authors conducted a national survey to test the accuracy of some of the Court's assumptions. They found that some "of the speculative claims made by the Justices," such as the assumption in *Summum* that members of the public interpret monuments on government land as conveying a message on the government's behalf, were borne out by their survey, whereas other claims made by the Justices, such as the assumption in *Matal* that members of the public do not treat federal registration of trademarks as government speech, were not confirmed by their survey. The authors also found that individuals are more likely to attribute messages to the government when they agree with the message. Are such surveys a sound way to decide whether the message communicated should be deemed government speech? If not, is there a better way to make such judgments?

Consider also H. Norton, Government Speech and the Constitution 49-51 (2019):

[T]he government's speech is more valuable and less dangerous when its governmental source is apparent to the public.

For this reason, we should require the government to ensure that the governmental source of its message is clear to the public if it wants to claim the government speech defense to parties' Free Speech Clause challenges. Applying this transparency principle to the Court's government speech canon confirms some of its conclusions while revealing that others—especially those early in its learning curve—should come out differently.

[In *Rust v. Sullivan*, for example,] the governmental source of the speech and its restrictions were not apparent to [patients]. Women seeking help from the clinics might well misunderstand the clinics health care professionals to be offering their own independent counsel rather than speaking as the government's agents bound to a governmental script that precluded the discussion of abortion. [If] expression is to be characterized as the government's [the] expression should be delivered in such a way that enables the public to understand it as the government's viewpoint. [The] transparency principles also shows why [*Walker*] was a hard case. . . .

If transparency is critical in this context, what does that tell you about cases like *Walker* and *Summum*? Was the fact that the speech in those case government speech transparent? If not, what could the government have done to make its role in the speech more apparent?

Page 1326. At the end of section 5 of the Note, add the following:

For a recent analysis of the incidental effects doctrine, see Coenen, Free Speech and Generally Applicable Laws: A New Doctrinal Synthesis, 103 Iowa L. Rev. 435 (2018).

**Page 1350.   At the end of section 3 of the Note, add
             the following:**

3a. *Wedding cakes.* Masterpiece Cakeshop v. Colorado Civil
Rights Comm'n, 138 S. Ct. 1719 (2018), posed the question
whether a state law prohibiting discrimination on the basis of sexual orientation could constitutionally require a baker who opposes
same-sex marriage to sell a wedding cake to a same-sex couple.
(The case is also considered in the supplement to page 1519 of the
Main Volume.) The baker argued that for the state to compel him
to make such a cake would violate both his freedom of speech and
freedom of religion. On the speech issue, the baker maintained that
for the state to compel him to make such a cake would require him
to express a message he personally rejects. In assessing his claim,
should it matter whether the couple simply wanted to buy a pre-
made wedding cake from the baker? Whether they wanted the baker
to make a cake with figures of two men on top of the cake? Whether
they wanted the cake to include the words "Congratulations Charlie
and Dave!!"? Would those who see the cake be likely to attribute its
message to the baker? Should that matter?

The Supreme Court avoided deciding the compelled speech
question, although in his opinion for the Court Justice Kennedy
observed: "The free speech aspect of this case is difficult, for few
persons who [see] a beautiful wedding cake [would think] of its
creation as an exercise of protected speech." But, he added: "If a
baker refused to design a special cake with words or images cel-
ebrating the marriage, [that] might be different from a refusal to
sell any cake at all. In deciding whether a baker's creation can be
protected, these details might make a difference."

Although the Court did not decide the compelled speech question, Justice Thomas, in a concurring opinion joined by Justice
Gorsuch, argued that the application of the statute to the baker
in this case compelled him to convey a message he did not want
to convey. Although conceding that the mere act of producing
and selling wedding cakes is not in itself necessarily expressive

behavior, Thomas argued that in this case the baker's act of "creating and designing custom wedding cakes [is] expressive." This was so, he maintained, because the baker "considers himself an artist," he "takes exceptional care with each cake that he creates," and a wedding cake's "primary purpose" is not so much to be eaten, as "to mark the beginning of a new marriage and to celebrate the couple." Thus, by forcing the baker "to create custom wedding cakes for same-sex weddings," the challenged law "requires him to, at the very least, acknowledge that same-sex weddings are 'weddings' and suggest that they should be celebrated—the precise message he believes his faith forbids." Invoking *Hurley*, Thomas concluded that the "First Amendment prohibits [the state] from requiring" the baker "to 'affir[m] . . . a belief with which [he] disagrees.' "

3b. *State-mandated notices in "crisis pregnancy centers."* In National Institute of Family and Life Advocates v. Becerra, 138 S. Ct. 2361 (2018), the Court considered the constitutionality of the California Reproductive Freedom, Accountability, Comprehensive Care, and Transparency Act (FACT Act), which provides that licensed medical facilities that provide women with assistance involving pregnancy or family planning must post a notice informing their patients that "California has public programs that provide immediate free or low-cost access to comprehensive family planning services, prenatal care, and abortion for eligible women." The Act provides further that unlicensed clinics offering similar services must post a notice making clear that California has not licensed the clinics to provide medical services. The stated purpose of the FACT Act was to "ensure that California residents make their personal reproductive health care decisions knowing their rights and the health care services available to them."

The FACT Act was challenged by two "crisis pregnancy centers," one licensed and one unlicensed. "Crisis pregnancy centers" are "pro-life" organizations that offer a limited range of free options to women but, according to the state, "aim to discourage and prevent women from seeking abortions." There are approximately 200 such centers in California. The crisis pregnancy centers that challenged the Act maintained that the requirement that they post the mandated notices abridged their freedom of speech. The District Court denied their motion for a preliminary injunction, and the Ninth Circuit affirmed.

The Supreme Court, in a 5-4 decision, reversed. Justice Thomas delivered the opinion of the Court:

> The licensed notice is a content-based regulation of speech. By compelling individuals to speak a particular message, such notices "alte[r] the content of [their] speech." [Here], for example, licensed clinics must provide a government-drafted script about the availability of state-sponsored services, as well as contact information for how to obtain them. One of those services is abortion — the very practice that petitioners are devoted to opposing. By requiring petitioners to inform women how they can obtain state-subsidized abortions — at the same time petitioners try to dissuade women from choosing that option — the licensed notice plainly "alters the content" of petitioners' speech.

The Court thus held that "strict scrutiny" was the appropriate standard in this case. Because the lower courts, which characterized the law as a regulation of "professional" speech, applied a less demanding standard of review, the Court reversed, noting that the Act could not pass muster under the proper — and more demanding — standard of review.

Justice Breyer, joined by Justices Ginsburg, Sotomayor, and Kagan, dissented. Breyer maintained that the Court's decision was clearly inconsistent with past precedents. In Planned Parenthood v. Casey, 505 U.S. 833 (1992), for example, the Court upheld a state law that required doctors to inform women considering an abortion about the nature of the abortion procedure, the health risks of abortion and of childbirth, and the availability of printed materials describing the fetus, medical assistance for childbirth, potential child support, and the agencies that would provide adoption services (and other alternatives to abortion). Similarly, in

Zauderer v. Office of Disciplinary Counsel, 471 U.S. 626 (1985), the Court upheld a disciplinary rule requiring attorneys to disclose in their advertisements that clients would have to pay "costs" even if their lawsuits were unsuccessful. Breyer maintained that these and other precedents made clear that "professional" speech, of the sort involved in this case, could be regulated consistent with the First Amendment under the more deferential standard of review applied by the lower courts, and that the Court was wrong to apply strict scrutiny in this case.

In light of this decision, what should be the outcome in cases that involve laws requiring organizations that perform legal abortions to advise patients about alternative ways to deal with unwanted pregnancies? See, e.g., Texas Medical Providers Performing Abortion Services v. Lakey, 667 F.3d 570 (5th Cir. 2012) (upholding a Texas law that prohibits a woman from getting an abortion unless her physician first performs an ultrasound, places the ultrasound images in her view, describes the images to her, makes fetal heart sounds audible, if possible, and describes those sounds to her, whether or not she wants to see or hear them).

For a critical analysis of *Becerra*, see Chemerinsky & Goodwin, Constitutional Gerrymandering Against Abortion Rights: NIFLA v. Becerra, 94 N.Y.U. L. Rev. 61, 66-67 (2019), asserting that "this case is primarily about five conservative Justices' hostility to abortion rights. The Court ignored legal precedent, failed to weigh the interests at stake in its decision, and applied a more demanding standard based on content of speech. [Unless] the Court is willing to invalidate disclosure laws across a vast array of consumer protections, the Court seems to be uniquely unprotective of women's reproductive rights."

Page 1350.   Replace section 5 of the Note with the following:

5. *Union dues.* May a state compel government employees to pay union dues? In Abood v. Detroit Board of Education, 431 U.S.

209 (1977), the Court upheld a state statute authorizing unions representing government employees to charge members dues insofar as the dues are used to support collective bargaining and related activities, but invalidating the statute insofar as the union uses the dues "to contribute to political candidates and to express political views unrelated to its duties as exclusive bargaining representative."

In subsequent decisions, the Court refined this holding. See Ellis v. Brotherhood of Railway, Airline & Steamship Clerks, 466 U.S. 85 (1984) (compelled contributions may constitutionally be used to pay for union conventions, social activities, and publications); Keller v. State Bar of California, 496 U.S. 1 (1990) (an integrated state bar association may not use compulsory dues to finance political and ideological activities with which particular members disagree when such expenditures are not "necessarily or reasonably incurred for the purpose of regulating the legal profession or improving the quality of legal services"); Lehnert v. Ferris Faculty Association, 500 U.S. 507 (1991) (a union may constitutionally charge dissenting employees only for those activities that are (1) "germane" to collective bargaining; (2) justified by the government's interests in labor peace and avoiding free riders; and (3) not significantly burdening of speech); Davenport v. Washington Education Association, 551 U.S. 177 (2007) (a state may constitutionally require public-sector unions to receive affirmative authorization from nonmembers before spending their agency fees for election-related purposes); Knox v. Service Employees International Union, 567 U.S. 310 (2012) (when a public-sector union imposes a special assessment or mid-year dues increase, the union cannot constitutionally require nonmembers to pay the increased amount unless they choose to opt in by affirmatively consenting).

In Harris v. Quinn, 134 S. Ct. 2618 (2014), the Court, in a 5-4 decision, seriously called *Abood* into question, but found it unnecessary to resolve the issue. In Janus v. American Federation of State, County, and Municipal Employees, 138 S. Ct. 2448 (2018), however, the Court, in another 5-4 decision, overruled *Abood*, holding that the state cannot constitutionally compel its employees to pay dues to public-sector labor unions that represent them, even if the dues are limited to paying only for collective bargaining and other activities designed to benefit all employees. Writing for the Court, Justice Alito maintained that it violates the First Amendment for the state to compel individuals to pay fees "to endorse ideas they find objectionable" unless the government can satisfy the standard of "exacting scrutiny." Alito reasoned that neither the state's interest in preserving "labor peace" nor its interest in avoiding "free riders" was sufficient to meet this standard. Henceforth, Alito concluded, "neither an agency fee nor any other payment to the union may be deducted from a non-member's wages, nor may any other attempt be made to collect such a payment, unless the employee affirmatively consents to pay."

Justice Kagan, joined by Justices Ginsburg, Breyer and Sotomayor, dissented:

> For over 40 years, [*Abood*] struck a stable balance between public employees' First Amendment rights and government entities' interests in running their workforces as they thought proper. Under that decision, a government entity could require public employees to pay a fair share of the cost that a union incurs when negotiating on their behalf over terms of employment. But no part of that fair-share payment could go to any of the union's political or ideological activities.
>
> [The] Court's decisions have long made plain that government entities have substantial latitude to regulate their employees' speech—especially about terms of employment—in the interest of operating their workplaces effectively. *Abood* allowed governments to do just that. While protecting public employees' expression about non-workplace matters, the decision enabled a government to advance important managerial interests—by ensuring the

presence of an exclusive employee representative to bargain with.

Not any longer. [Today's] decision will have large-scale consequences. Public employee unions will lose a secure source of financial support. State and local governments that thought fair-share provisions furthered their interests will need to find new ways of managing their work-forces. Across the country, the relationships of public employees and employers will alter in both predictable and wholly unexpected ways.

Rarely if ever has the Court overruled a decision—let alone one of this import—with so little regard for the usual principles of *stare decisis*. There are no special justifications for reversing *Abood*. It has proved workable. No recent developments have eroded its underpinnings. And it is deeply entrenched, in both the law and the real world. More than 20 States have statutory schemes built on the decision. Those laws underpin thousands of ongoing contracts involving millions of employees. Reliance interests do not come any stronger than those surrounding *Abood*. And likewise, judicial disruption does not get any greater than what the Court does today.

Consider: Andrias, Janus's Two Faces, 2018 Sup. Ct. Rev. 21, 51:

Janus is unlikely to be the last case in which the Court strikes down regulation on the ground that it requires individuals or corporations to subsidize messages with which they disagree. Conservative judges on the D.C. Circuit have used a similar theory against numerous governmental regulations. For example, drawing on First Amendment principles, a panel of the D.C. Circuit concluded that requiring an employer to inform workers of their legal right to organize a union via an official posting violated the NLRA's statutory "free speech" provisions. [Indeed, in] the aftermath of *Janus*, employers are pressing the argument [even further], arguing, for example, that their own free speech rights are violated when employees are granted rights by the National Labor Relations Act to wear union buttons at work; such buttons, the argument runs, carry a message with which the employer disagrees. *Janus* suggests that at least several Justices on the Supreme Court may sympathize with this claim.

Page 1352.   At the end of section 6 of the Note, add the following:

Consider Baude & Volokh, Compelled Subsidies and the First Amendment, 132 Harv. L. Rev. 171, 180-181 (2018):

[R]equiring people only to pay money, whether to private organizations or to the government, is not a First Amendment problem at all. The employees in *Janus* were not compelled to speak or to associate. They were compelled to pay, just as we are all compelled to pay taxes; our having to pay taxes doesn't violate our First Amendment rights, even when the taxes are used for speech we disapprove of. [Requiring] someone to pay money is not requiring them to believe, to speak, or to associate, even if the money is spent for political purposes. [Indeed, requiring] people to pay money that can be used for speech with which they disagree is utterly commonplace. [After] all, each of us must pay taxes that will in part go to spread opinions many of us disbelieve and abhor – military recruiting campaigns, antidrug campaigns, publicity for or against abortion or contraception, [and] a vast array of other messages. [The] government cannot require us to say things as part of its program. [But] it can certainly require us to pay for speech by others. You can refuse to say the Pledge of Allegiance, but you can't require the government to refund the portion of your taxes that it spends on patriotic observances.

For an engaging analysis of the compelled speech issue, see Greene, "Not in My Name" Claims of Constitutional Right, 98 Boston U. L. Rev. 1475 (2018).

Page 1366.   At the end of section 4 of the Note, add the following:

5. *Disclosure revisited?* In Americans for Prosperity Foundation v. Bonta, 594 U.S. ___ (2021), the Court considered the constitutionality of a California law requiring all tax-exempt charitable organizations that solicit funds in California to disclose to the state Attorney General's Office the identity of all donors contributing $5,000 or more annually to the organization. The State maintained that having this information readily available substantially furthered its ability to police misconduct by charities in the state, including, for example, self-dealing by officers of the charity, diverting charitable contributions for improper purposes, a donor's use of the charity as a pass-through entity, and so on. In the past, the State did a poor job of maintaining the confidentiality of this information, but more recently the State tightened its control of the information to protect the privacy of donors. Two politically conservative organizations, the Thomas More Law Center and the Americans for Prosperity Foundation, challenged the constitutionality of the State's program of collecting the names of all major donors to charities raising funds in the State on the ground that this program violated the First Amendment.

In a six-to-three decision, the Court held the California program unconstitutional. Chief Justice Roberts delivered the opinion of the Court. Invoking *Buckley*, Roberts maintained that the proper standard in reviewing the constitutionality of the challenged program is "exacting scrutiny," which requires both that there is "a substantial relation between the disclosure requirement and a sufficiently important governmental interest" and that the disclosure requirement is "narrowly tailored" to serve the government's interest. Applying that standard, Roberts held that the California disclosure regime was not sufficiently narrowly tailored to achieve the state's important interest in preventing charitable fraud and self-dealing. Put simply, Roberts concluded that the disclosure requirement was overbroad insofar as it applied to thousands of charitable organizations without any reason to believe that they were engaged in unlawful activity. Moreover, he noted that it doesn't matter if there isn't any disclosure of information to the public, because donors might fear that there could be disclosure and that is sufficient to chill their willingness to make contributions.

Justice Sotomayor, joined by Justices Breyer and Kagan, dissented. Sotomayor maintained that in reaching its decision the majority "discards its decades-long requirement that, to establish a cognizable burden on their associational rights, plaintiffs must plead and prove that disclosure will likely expose them to objective harms, such as threats, harassment, or reprisals." In prior decisions, for example, such as Brown v. Socialist Workers '74 Campaign Committee and NAACP v. Alabama, the Court had invalidated disclosure requirements only as applied to particular organizations that were especially vulnerable to the effects of disclosure, not to all organizations across the boards. In short, Sotomayor argued: "Today's analysis marks reporting and disclosure requirements with a bull's-eye. . . . It does not matter if not a single individual risks experiencing a single reprisal from disclosure, or if the vast majority of those affected would happily comply. That is all irrelevant to the Court's determination that [the California] requirement is facially unconstitutional. Neither precedent nor common sense supports such a result."

Page 1385.   At the end of section a of the Note, add the following:

aa. A. Winkler, We the Corporations 372-373 (2018):

[As a result of *Citizens United*, corporate] spending in the next presidential election cycle of 2012 rose dramatically. Corporations were now allowed to spend general treasury funds to finance independent expenditures in favor of, or against, candidates for office. They also gained the right to contribute to "Super PACs"—a special type of political action committee that [was] able to accept unlimited contributions from corporations. [The] Center for Public Integrity [estimated] that in 2012 there was nearly $1 billion in new political spending [from corporations and individuals] traceable to *Citizens United*. . . .

The *Citizens United* decision [triggered] a public backlash. Polls showed that eight in ten Americans were opposed to the Supreme Court's decision. The opposition crossed party lines, with 85 percent of Democrats, 76 percent of Republicans, and 81 percent of Independents saying *Citizens United* was wrongly decided.

aaa. K. Greenfield, Corporations Are People Too (And They Should Act Like It) 135, 169 (2018):

The question of corporate speech turns not only on the purpose of speech, but also on the purpose of corporations. Corporations should receive those speech rights necessary in order to achieve their institutional and social role. That is, corporations as a class of institutional speakers should be able to speak on the questions that arise about that role, and individual corporations should be able to speak on matters that are germane to their own business. The further afield a corporation roams from those areas of focus, the less persuasive its claim to First Amendment protection will become. [Applying this approach to corporate political spending, corporate political activity should] be limited to matters and questions germane to the company's business. [But] corporate speech serving the social and institutional purposes of corporations should be protected. . . .

aaaa. M. Tushnet, Taking Back the Constitution: Activist Judges and the Next Age of American Law 28-33 (2020):

So, what does it mean to have committed originalist justices on the Supreme Court? Consider [*Citizens United*]. The dissenting opinion by Justice John Paul Stevens has a section, "Original Understandings," which argues that the majority "makes the perfunctory attempt to ground its analysis in the principles or understandings of those who drafted and ratified the [First] Amendment." Stevens found "not a scintilla of evidence to support the notion that anyone believed it would preclude regulatory distinctions based on the corporate form." The majority's response? Basically, nothing. [*Citizens United*] is typical of the conservative judicial approach to the First Amendment. [Conservative justices] almost never comment on what the First Amendment means by "the freedom of speech, or of the press" in 1791, but they occasionally wave their hands vaguely in the direction of some high-sounding principles they attribute to the Framers. [Such opportunism] in the service of conservative outcomes is [damaging] to self-styled originalists [because they] purport to hold that originalism is the *only* method of constitutional interpretation that prevents judges from injecting their personal preferences into the Constitution.

Page 1387.   At the end of section d of the Note, add the following:

As a result of the combination of *Citizens United* and *SpeechNow*, Super PACs in the 2016 election received a total of $1.8 billion in contributions. Ten individuals, including such figures as Thomas Steyer ($90 million), Sheldon and Miriam Adelson ($78 million), and Michael Bloomberg ($24,000), contributed a total of $376 million, or roughly 21 percent of all the money contributed to Super PACS in that election. Corporations contributed a total of $85 million. See Abrams, Citizens United: Predictions and Reality, in L. Bollinger & G. Stone, The Free Speech Century 81, 87 (2019).

Page 1399.   At the end of "Final Thoughts," add the following:

Finally, consider Lakier, Imagining an Antisubordinating First Amendment, 118 Colum. L. Rev. 2117 (2018):

Over the past forty years, the political economy of the First Amendment has undergone a significant shift. In the early and mid-twentieth century, litigants that won First Amendment cases tended to be civil rights groups like the NAACP, proponents of minority religions, and other representatives of the marginalized and the disenfranchised. These days, the winners in First Amendment cases are much more likely to be corporations and other economically and politically powerful actors. The result is that today the First Amendment often serves as the "primary guarantor of the privileged" rather than the champion of the powerless it used to be. . . .

What this shift reflects [is] the Court's embrace over the past several decades of a highly formal conception of the First Amendment equality guarantee. Since the New Deal period, the Court has recognized that implicit in the First Amendment guarantee of expressive liberty is a guarantee of expressive equality—that freedom of speech means not only the right to speak but the right to speak on equal terms as other speakers. Over time, however, the Court has significantly changed its understanding of what this means.

For much of the twentieth century, the Court interpreted the guarantee of expressive equality in a manner that was sensitive to the economic, political, and social inequalities that inhibited or enhanced expression. It interpreted the First Amendment, for example, to require that those who lacked other means of expressing themselves be granted access to publicly important spaces (including privately owned public spaces) to do so. It also struck down laws that, although in principle applicable to all, had a disparate impact on the ability of the poor and the powerless to communicate. And it refused to invalidate on First Amendment grounds laws that restricted the speech of the powerful in an effort to enhance the speech of the powerless. It interpreted the First Amendment, in other words, to guarantee—or at least permit—a rough kind of substantive equality in expressive opportunity.

Since the 1970s, however, the Court has moved increasingly far away from this context-sensitive, substantive-equality-promoting view of the First Amendment. It has rejected the idea that courts should take into account inequalities in economic and political power when interpreting the First Amendment command. It has also, for the most part, rejected the idea that the First Amendment permits the government to limit the speech of wealthy or powerful speakers in order to enhance the speech of others. Instead, it has interpreted the guarantee of expressive equality to require—and to require only—formally equal treatment at the government's hands.

It is this change in the Court's conception of what it means to guarantee expressive equality that is largely responsible [for] the "corporate takeover" of the First Amendment. [This] shift is troubling because it undermines [the] robust and inclusive public debate that the First Amendment is supposed to make possible.

See also Kessler and Pozen, The Search for an Egalitarian First Amendment, 118 Colum. L. Rev. 1953 (2018).

F. Freedom of the Press

Page 1401. At the end of Part 1, add the following:

In reflecting of freedom of the press today and in the future, consider T. Zick, The First Amendment in the Trump Era 2-4 (2019):

"[B]oth as a candidate and through the first term of his presidency, Trump has been a relentless critic of both the institutional press and individual reporters. Of course, presidents have always complained about negative press coverage, [but] no former president [has ever] publicly declared "war" on the press or repeatedly referred to the press as the "enemy of the American people." [Among the things Trump has allegedly done] are

* suspending the White House press credentials of reporters who the President believes failed to show him sufficient "respect";
* revoking and threatening to revoke security clearances from former government official who have

engaged in public commentary [that] expressed
criticism of the current Administration;
* issuing an executive order to raise postal rates to
punish online retailer Amazon.com because Jeff
Bezos, its chief shareholder and CEO, owns the
Washington Post, whose coverage of his administration the President finds objectionable; . . .
* threatening to revoke NBC's and other television
stations' broadcast licenses in retaliation for coverage the President dislikes.

Assuming these allegations are true, has President Trump violated the First Amendment? If so, what is the appropriate remedy?

Page 1415.   At the end of section 1 of the Note, add the following:

In *Branzburg*, the Court recognized the awkwardness in holding that the First Amendment gives the press special rights. Part
of the difficulty is the challenge of deciding who gets to assert
the special rights of the press. But suppose the government wants
to give special privileges to "the press." Can it constitutionally
do so?

In *Citizens United*, the five justices in the majority maintained that
the statutory provision in the Campaign Finance Act that exempted
media-corporations (like *The New York Times*) from restrictions
on campaign expenditures that applied to non-media-corporations
(like General Motors) violated the First Amendment, because such
a distinction between different types of corporations was "dangerous, and unacceptable." 558 U.S., at 351. Is this persuasive?

Consider West, Favoring the Press, 106 Cal. L. Rev. 91, 94-95
(2018):

[This] nondiscrimination view of the Press Clause is deeply
flawed for the simple reason that the press is different and

has always been recognized as such. [Indeed,] the legislative practice of determining that the press should be favored in some contexts, so as to further a public good, dates back to the birth of the nation. Since then, federal and state legislatures, courts, and other government actors have adopted a wide range of regulations that are not granted to other speakers. These measures include testimonial privileges; enhanced protections from searches and seizures; [special] access to government-controlled places, information, or meetings; [preferred] postal rates; [and so on]. It is [entirely] in keeping with the text, history, and spirit of the First Amendment's Press Clause for the government to, at times, treat press speakers differently.

Page 1416.   At the very beginning of Part 4, add the following:

To what extent can government constitutionally intervene in the marketplace of ideas in an effort to improve our nation's freedom of speech and of the press? Consider Lakier, The Non-First Amendment Law of Freedom of Speech, 134 Harv. L. Rev. 2298 (2021):

The First Amendment dominates both popular and scholarly discussion of freedom of speech in the United States. [It] is easy [to] understand why discussion of freedom of speech and press has tended to be so First Amendment-centric. [But it is] a mistake to presume that the only legal mechanism that protects freedom of speech in the United States is the First Amendment. [Recall, for example,] PruneYard Shopping Center v. Robins, [in which the Court recognized that state law can] provide "rights of expression" that [are] "more expansive than those conferred by the Federal Constitution." [Moreover], local, state, and federal legislators have over the course of the past two centuries enacted hundreds, even perhaps thousands, of laws that are intended to protect the same values and interests that the First Amendment protects. In some cases, they have also empowered regulatory agencies to do the same. To focus solely on the protection that the First Amendment provides is therefore to misunderstand how freedom of speech is actually understood and legally protected in the United States today. [Indeed, as history demonstrates, there is a long history in the United States of] non-First Amendment law of freedom of speech

[This] body of non-First Amendment free speech law is not only extensive in its scope and significant in its effects. It also has deep roots in our regulatory traditions. In fact, the non-First Amendment free speech tradition is for all practical purposes older than the First Amendment tradition itself. In contrast to the First Amendment tradition, which only began to emerge in its modern form in the early decades of the twentieth century, legislatures acted to protect the interests that we today recognize the First Amendment to protect beginning in the mid-eighteenth century, and continued to do so throughout the nineteenth and twentieth centuries in all sorts of ways, [as illustrated by government regulation of the postal service, telegraph, telephone service, radio and television, campaign finance laws, and laws like the one upheld in PruneYard].

Page 1425.   After section 2 of the Note, add the following:

3. *Cable and state action.* In Manhattan Community Access Corp. v. Halleck, 139 S. Ct. 1921 (2019), a New York law required cable operators to set aside channels on their cable systems for public access. New York City designated a private nonprofit corporation, Manhattan Neighborhood Network (MNN), to

operate the public access channels on Time Warner's cable system in Manhattan. Thereafter, MNN excluded plaintiffs Halleck and Melendez from the public access channels because they had aired a film on MNN's public access channels that was critical of MNN. Halleck and Melendez sued, claiming that MNN had violated their first amendment rights. In a sharply-divided decision, the Court held that MNN's action did not constitute state action and that the first amendment was therefore irrelevant. The Court, in an opinion by Justice Kavanaugh, explained that this could not be deemed state action because the city possessed no property interest in the cable system or in the public access channels. Justice Sotomayor, joined by Justices Ginsburg, Breyer, and Kagan, dissented on the ground that New York City "secured a property interest in public access television channels when it granted a cable franchise to a cable company" and that by accepting "that agency relationship, MNN stepped into the City's shoes and thus qualifies as a state actor."

Page 1427.   At the end of section d of the Note, add the following:

e. *Net neutrality*. Consider Bhagwat, When Speech Is Not "Speech," 78 Ohio. St. L.J. 839, 857 (2017):

The basic concern driving net neutrality is that broadband providers, because they possess substantial market power and control bottlenecks that end users must pass through to access the Internet, can use their power to interfere with an open Internet where end users and edge providers can communicate with each other without interference or preferentialism. To prevent that, [the FCC in 2005 adopted net neutrality rules that prohibited] broadband providers from blocking access to particular websites, slowing down access to particular websites, or engaging in "paid prioritization" whereby broadband providers favor some Internet traffic over other traffic in exchange for compensation.

Is the requirement of net neutrality consistent with the First Amendment? Consider cases like *Red Lion*, *Tornillo*, and *Turner*. See U.S. Telecom Ass'n v. FCC, 825 F.3d 674 (D.C. Cir. 2016) (upholding the constitutionality of the FCC's net neutrality rule). In 2018, the FCC proposed repealing the requirement of net neutrality.

Page 1428.   At the end of section 5 of the Note, add the following:

For an argument in support of such a change in Section 230, see Citron and Wittes, The Internet Will Not Break: Denying Bad Samaritans § 230 Immunity, 86 Fordham L. Rev. 401 (2017).

Page 1429.   At the end of section 6 of the Note, add the following:

Consider also Citron, Extremist Speech, Compelled Conformity, and Censorship Creep, 93 Notre Dame L. Rev. 1035 (2018):

Silicon Valley has long been viewed as a full-throated champion of First Amendment values. [But in] an agreement with the European Commission, the dominant tech companies have [recently altered their] policies [in order] to stave off threatened European regulation. Far more than illegal speech or violent terrorist imagery is in EU lawmakers' sights, as too is online radicalization and "fake news." [The] impact of [such] coercion will be far reaching. Unlike national laws that are limited to geographic borders, terms-of-service agreements apply to platforms' services on a global scale. [These] changes are less the result of market choices [by private entities] than of a bowing to [foreign] government pressure.

How should the United States address such potentially powerful foreign influence on American free expression?

7. *The fragility of the free press.* Consider Jones & West, The Fragility of the Free American Press, 112 Nw. U. L. Rev. 567 (2017):

> The President of the United States has boldly declared an all-out "war" on the press, and his primary weapon has been an attack on tradition. Repeatedly and aggressively, President Donald Trump has flouted press-protecting norms and customs that have been long respected by other presidents. [He] has ignored customary media accommodations, criticized or excluded reporters and news organizations perceived as unfriendly, spoken of the press in disparaging and vilifying terms, and even threatened media organizations with lawsuits and retributive governmental actions.
>
> Journalists and scholars have rightly warned us that President Trump's disrespect for the Fourth Estate is troubling and that it threatens to harm the vitality of this important check on our democracy. As grave as these warnings have been, however, they have fallen short of capturing the true seriousness of the situation. This is because the kind of press we value and need in the United States — one that is free, independent, and democracy-enhancing — does not just occur naturally. Nor is it protected by a single, robust constitutional right. Rather, our free press sits atop an increasingly fragile edifice. This edifice is supported by a number of legal and nonlegal pillars, such as the institutional media's relative financial strength, the goodwill of the public, a mutually dependent relationship with government officials, and the backing of sympathetic judges. Each of these supports, however, has weakened substantially in recent years, leaving one remaining pillar to bear more of

the weight. That final pillar is political tradition — a set of customs that demands the President of the United States recognize and respect the vital role of the press. It is this final pillar that Trump has put in his sights.

Page 1429. After the citation to Shiffrin, What's Wrong With the First Amendment, add the following:

In a similar vein, consider Seidman, Can Free Speech Be Progressive? 118 Colum. L. Rev. 2219, 2230-2232 (2018):

> With the receding of Warren Court liberalism, free speech law took a sharp right turn. Instead of providing a shield for the powerless, the First Amendment became a sword used by people at the apex of the American power hierarchy. Among its victims: proponents of campaign finance reform, opponents of cigarette addiction, the LBGTQ community, labor unions, animal-rights advocates, environmentalists, targets of hate speech, and abortion providers. [Citing *Citizens United, Lorillard Tobacco, Boy Scouts v. Dale, Janus, Stevens, Central Hudson, R.A.V.*, and *McCullen.*]
>
> [Indeed, despite all the talk of free speech and progressivism,] over the course of our history, free speech law has only occasionally been of much help to progressive causes and [during] the moderns period, it has often been an important impediment. [In part, this is so] because speech opportunities reflect current property distributions, [and free speech therefore] tends to favor people at the top of the power hierarchy.

Consider also A. Tsesis, Free Speech in the Balance 173-177 (2020):

The Roberts Court majority [has] turned the First Amendment into a judicial weapon against legislative efforts to protect individual rights and advance general welfare through economic and regulatory policy. The Court aggressively wields the First Amendment to strike legislative priorities, in a manner reminiscent of the *Lochner* era's preference for personal autonomy above social policy. [In its] increasingly absolutist sounding free speech reasoning [in cases like *Citizens United, United States v. Stevens*, and *Reed v. Town of Gilbert*, the Roberts Court has refused] to weigh the proportionate value of speech against countervailing government policies and has thus become the guardian of corporate and commercial interests against ordinary regulations for the benefit of natural people.

Page 1430.   After the quote from Strauss, add the following:

On a less positive note, consider Wu, Is the First Amendment Obsolete?, in L. Bollinger & G. Stone, The Free Speech Century 272-273 (2019):

The First Amendment was a dead letter for much of American history. Unfortunately, there is reason to fear it is entering a new period of political irrelevance. We live in a golden age of efforts by governments and other actors to control speech, discredit and harass the press, and manipulate public discourse. Yet as these efforts mount, and as the expressive environment deteriorates, the First Amendment has been confined to a narrow and frequently irrelevant role. . . .

The most important change in the expressive environment can be boiled down to one idea: it is no longer speech itself that is scarce, but the attention of listeners. [E]merging techniques of speech control depend on (1) a range of new punishments, like unleashing "troll armies" to abuse the press and other critics, and (2) "flooding" tactics [that] distort or drown out disfavored speech through the creation and dissemination of fake news, the payment of fake commentators, and the deployment of propaganda robots. [The] use of speech as a tool to suppress speech is [very] challenging for the First Amendment to deal with. [What] might be done in response is a question without an easy answer. One possibility is simply to concede that the First Amendment, built in another era, is not suited to today's challenges. Instead, any answer must lie in the development of better social norms, adoption of journalistic ethics by private speech platforms, or action by the political branches. Perhaps constitutional law has reached its natural limit

To pursue these concerns further, see D. Pozen, ed., The Perilous Public Square: Structural Threats to Free Expression Today (2020), and S. Brison & K. Gelber, Free Speech in the Digital Age (2019), each of which contains a collection of excellent essays addressing these questions.

VIII
THE CONSTITUTION AND RELIGION

A. Introduction: Historical and Analytical Overview

Page 1437.   After section 2 of the Note, add the following:

2a. *A specific historical example.* In Espinoza v. Montana Dep't of Revenue, ___ U.S. ___ (2020), the Court described "the historical record" of aid to religiously affiliated schools as "complex." Chief Justice Roberts's opinion for the Court observed, "In the founding era and the early 19th century, governments provided financial support to private schools, including denominational ones. [Local] governments provided grants to private schools, even religious ones, for the education of the poor. [Early] federal aid (often land grants) went to religious schools. [After] the Civil War, Congress spent large sums on education for emancipated freedmen, often by supporting denominational schools in the South through the Freedmen's Bureau."

In dissent, Justice Breyer responded that "[This] diversity of opinion [makes] no difference. [It] is enough to say that, among those who gave shape to the young Republic were people, including Madison and Jefferson, who perceived a grave threat to individual liberty and communal harmony in tax support for the teaching of religious truths."

2b. *The Blaine Amendment and its state counterparts.* Justice Alito's concurring opinion in *Espinoza* offered a detailed historical account of the anti-Catholic and nativist motivations that underlay the Blaine Amendment (in the U.S. Congress) and its parallels in numerous states. When the little Blaine amendments were adopted, the term "sectarian" was a "code word" for Catholics, Mormons, and Jews — "heretics." Addressing the argument that Montana's ban on aid to sectarian institutions had been "cleansed of its bigoted past" when the provision was reenacted in a constitutional revision in 1973, Justice Alito found it "not so clear that the animus was scrubbed." The reenactment continued to use the terms "sect" and "sectarian," which, in light of the history he recounted, made them "disquieting remnants" and kept the provision "'[t]ethered' to its original 'bias.'" Further, "it is not clear at all that the State 'actually confront[ed]' the provision's 'tawdry past in reenacting it'" (quoting Justice Sotomayor's concurring opinion in Ramos v. Louisiana, 140 S.Ct. 1390 (2020)). Justice Sotomayor's dissent replied, "the constitutional provision [was] adopted in 1972 at a convention where it was met with overwhelming support by religious leaders (Catholic and non-Catholic), even those who examined the history of prior no-aid provisions."

Page 1438.   After the paragraph of section 4 of the Note beginning "In Zelman v. Simmons-Harris," add the following:

In Espinoza v. Montana Dept. of Revenue, 2020 U.S. LEXIS 3518 (June 20, 2020), Chief Justice Roberts's opinion for the Court observed, "An infringement of First Amendment rights [cannot] be justified by a State's alternative view that the infringement advances religious liberty" by "safeguard[ing] the freedom of religious organizations by keeping the government out of their operations." He added, "A school, concerned about government involvement with its religious activities, might reasonably decide for itself not to participate in a government program. But we doubt that the school's liberty is enhanced by eliminating any option to participate in the first place."

Page 1493.   After the Hamburger citation, add the following:

See also Barclay, *The Historical Origins of Judicial Religious Exemptions*, 96 Notre Dame L. Rev. 55 (2020) (arguing that such exemptions can be understood as located within the tradition of "equitable interpretation" in statutory interpretation). Consider (a) whether statutory silence about exemptions—that is, statutory coverage that is on its face universal—is properly subject to equitable interpretation, and (b) whether a federal constitutional obligation can be inferred from a tradition dealing with the role of courts in interpreting state statutes.

B.   The Establishment Clause

Page 1448.   Replace the introductory paragraph with the following:

In Lemon v. Kurtzman, 403 U.S. 602 (1971), the Court identified three "tests" for determining whether a statute violates the establishment clause: "First, the statute must have a secular legislative purpose; second, its principal or primary effect must be one that neither advances nor inhibits religion; finally, the statute must not foster 'an excessive government entanglement with religion.' " In American Legion v. American Humanist Ass'n, 139 S. Ct. 2067 (2020), Justice Alito wrote an opinion, joined by Chief Justice Roberts and Justices Breyer and Kavanaugh, criticizing Lemon's "ambitious[] attempt to find a grand unified theory of the Establishment Clause," Justice Kagan joined a separate opinion by Justice Breyer asserting that "there is no single formula for resolving Establishment Clause challenges," Justice Thomas wrote that he would overrule Lemon, and Justice Gorsuch described Lemon as "a misadventure." Though Lemon no longer has the support of a majority on the Court, its components may often be relevant in considering the constitutionality of specific practices; as Justice Kagan wrote, the "test's focus on purposes and effects [can be] crucial in evaluating [some] government action."

The plurality opinion in American Legion identified "six rough categories [of Establishment Clause cases]: (1) religious references or imagery in public monuments, symbols, mottos, displays, and ceremonies; (2) religious accommodations and exemptions from generally applicable laws; (3) subsidies and tax exemptions; (4) religious expression in public schools; (5) regulation of private religious speech; and (6) state interference with internal church affairs," to which "[a] final, miscellaneous category, including cases involving such issues as Sunday closing laws and church involvement in governmental decisionmaking, might be added." Consider the extent to which that categorization provides a better account of the Court's decisions than does the identification of the more particularized themes, connected to the components of the Lemon test, that provides the organizing principle of the materials that follow. Sections B1 and B2 deal with two ways—coercion and endorsement—in which government practices might be said to "advance" (or inhibit) religion. Section B3 deals with issues that arise in connection with identifying whether a government practice has a religious or a secular purpose. Section B4 discusses cases and problems in which the effects, principal or otherwise, of a government program might be said to advance (or inhibit) religion.

Page 1458.   Add as the first sentence of Note 3:

In American Legion v. American Humanist Ass'n, 139 S. Ct. 2067 (2020), Justice Thomas's separate opinion defined "coercion" as "attempt[ing] to control religious doctrine or personnel, compel religious observance, single out a particular religious denomination for exclusive state subsidization, or punish dissenting worship." As he earlier suggested, that definition might make the Establishment Clause overlap the Free Exercise Clause completely, at least in the context of challenges to state practices under the fourteenth amendment.

Page 1459.   Replace Section B2 with the following:

2. The Nonendorsement Principle, History's Relevance, and De Facto Establishments

Introductory Note: Formulating the Nonendorsement Principle

1. *The initial formulation.* In Lynch v. Donnelly, 465 U.S. 668 (1984), a concurring opinion by Justice O'Connor stated:

> The Establishment Clause prohibits government from making adherence to a religion relevant in any way to a person's standing in the political community.
>
> Government can run afoul of that prohibition in two principal ways. One is excessive entanglement with religious institutions, which may interfere with the independence of the institutions, give the institutions access to government or governmental powers not fully shared by nonadherents of the religion, and foster the creation of political constituencies defined along religious lines. The second and more direct infringement is government endorsement or disapproval of

religion. Endorsement sends a message to nonadherents that they are outsiders, not full members of the political community, and an accompanying message to adherents that they are insiders, favored members of the political community. Disapproval sends the opposite message. . . .

The meaning of a statement to its audience depends both on the intention of the speaker and on the "objective" meaning of the statement in the community. Some listeners need not rely solely on the words themselves in discerning the speaker's intent: they can judge the intent by, for example, examining the context of the statement or asking questions of the speaker. Other listeners do not have or will not seek access to such evidence of intent. They will rely instead on the words themselves; for them the message actually conveyed may be something not actually intended. If the audience is large, as it always is when government "speaks" by word or deed, some portion of the audience will inevitably receive a message determined by the "objective" content of the statement, and some portion will inevitably receive the intended message. Examination of both the subjective and the objective components of the message communicated by a government action is therefore necessary to determine whether the action carries a forbidden meaning.

Lynch found no constitutional violation in the display by the city of Pawtucket of a crèche in a Christmas-season display in the city's business district. Chief Justice Burger's opinion described the setting: "The Pawtucket display comprises many of the figures and decorations traditionally associated with Christmas, including, among other things, a Santa Claus house, reindeer pulling Santa's sleigh, candy-striped poles, a Christmas tree, carolers, cutout figures representing such characters as a clown, an elephant, and a teddy bear, hundreds of colored lights, a large banner that reads "SEASONS GREETINGS," and the crèche at issue here." Applying the nonendorsement test to the display, Justice O'Connor concluded:

> Pawtucket's display of its crèche, I believe, does not com-
> municate a message that the government intends to endorse
> the Christian beliefs represented by the crèche. Although
> the religious and indeed sectarian significance of crèche [is]
> not neutralized by the setting, the overall holiday setting
> changes what viewers may fairly understand to be the pur-
> pose of the display—as a typical museum setting, though
> not neutralizing the religious content of a religious painting,
> negates any message of endorsement of that content. The
> display celebrates a public holiday. [The] holiday itself has
> very strong secular components and traditions. Government
> celebration of the holiday [generally] is not understood to
> endorse the religious content of the holiday, just as gov-
> ernment celebration of Thanksgiving is not so understood.
> The crèche is a traditional symbol of the holiday that is very
> commonly displayed along with purely secular symbols, as
> it was in Pawtucket.
>
> These features combine to make the government's dis-
> play of the crèche in this particular physical setting no more
> an endorsement of religion than such governmental "ac-
> knowledgments" of religion as [printing] of "In God We
> Trust" on coins, and opening court sessions with "God save
> the United States and this honorable court." Those govern-
> ment acknowledgments of religion serve, in the only ways
> reasonably possible in our culture, the legitimate secular
> purposes of solemnizing public occasions, expressing confi-
> dence in the future, and encouraging the recognition of what
> is worthy of appreciation in society. For that reason, and be-
> cause of their history and ubiquity, those practices are not
> understood as conveying government approval of particular
> religious beliefs. The display of the crèche likewise serves a

secular purpose—celebration of a public holiday with traditional symbols. It cannot fairly be understood to convey a
message of government endorsement of religion. It is significant in this regard that the crèche display apparently caused
no political divisiveness prior to the filing of this lawsuit, although Pawtucket had incorporated the crèche in its annual
Christmas display for some years.

2. *Applying the principle.* In County of Allegheny v. American
Civil Liberties Union, 492 U.S. 573 (1989), a majority of the
Court joined Justice Blackmun's opinion adopting Justice
O'Connor's "no endorsement" analysis as a general guide in
establishment clause cases. Shifting majorities on the Court held
unconstitutional a freestanding display of a nativity scene on the
main staircase of a county courthouse, but upheld the display of
a Jewish menorah placed next to the city's Christmas tree and a
statement declaring the city's "salute to liberty." One majority
concluded that the "setting" of the nativity scene, which was
the "single element" in the display, "celebrate[d] Christmas
in a way that has the effect of endorsing a patently Christian
message.'

3. *Justifying the principle.* Leedes, Rediscovering the Link between the Establishment Clause and the Fourteenth Amendment:
The Citizenship Declaration, 26 Ind. L. Rev. 469 (1993), suggests
that the "citizenship declaration" in the first sentence of the fourteenth amendment "prohibits the federal and state governments
from subverting a citizen's status in the political community
because of his or her creed or lack of religious commitment."
Consider the argument in N. Feldman, From Liberty to Equality:
The Transformation of the Establishment Clause, 90 Cal. L. Rev.
673, 677, 718 (2002), that the nonendorsement principle rests on
a mistaken reduction of the establishment clause to a principle
of equality: "Religious minorities are not uniquely vulnerable
to political inequality, and religious discrimination in the United
States has not been noticeably worse than discrimination on the
basis of political ideology, immigrant status, or language. [The]

political-equality approach [cannot] provide a compelling answer to the question 'what is special about religion?' [The] harms associated with [exclusion] are no worse than the harms associated with other sorts of second-class citizenship and identity exclusion."

4. *The appropriate perspective.* Justice O'Connor would prohibit actions reasonably perceived as endorsement or disapproval. Perceived by whom? If by religious minorities, is she correct in concluding that reasonable Jews would not perceive the crèche as endorsement of Christianity? See also Corbin, Ceremonial Deism and the Reasonable Religious Outsider, 57 UCLA L. Rev. 1545 (2010), which draws on the law under title VII of the 1964 Civil Rights Act for the argument that the perspective to adopt for determining whether a ceremonial practice constitutes an establishment of religion is that of the reasonable religious outsider. Consider the observation of S. Feldman, Principle, History, and Power: The Limits of the First Amendment Religion Clauses, 81 Iowa L. Rev. 833, 863 (1996): "In Lynch, the Court supported its conclusion by noting that [nobody] had complained about the crèche even though it had been publicly displayed for forty years. To the Court, this silence meant that the crèche had not generated dissension. [The] Court overlooked the possibility [that] Christian cultural imperialism had produced the silence of religious outgroup members. Silence often demonstrates domination, not consensus."

Suppose the government does not intend to endorse religion, but an observer might infer endorsement from the government's actions. How much must that person know about the government's real position?

5. *De facto establishments.* Consider M. Howe, The Garden and the Wilderness 11-12 (1965):

[Roger Williams's] principle of separation endorsed a host of favoring tributes to faith [so] substantial that they have produced in the aggregate what may fairly be described as a de facto establishment of religion [in which] the religious institution as a whole is maintained and activated by forces not kindled directly by government. [Some] elements of our religious establishment are, of course, reinforced by law. Whenever that situation prevails, as it does, for instance, when the law secures the sanctity of Sunday, the courts are apt to seek out a secular justification for the favoring enactment and, by this evasive tactic, meet the charge that an establishment de jure exists. [Yet] the Supreme Court, by pretending that the American principle of separation is predominantly Jeffersonian and by purporting to outlaw even those aids in religion which do not affect religious liberties, seems to have endorsed a governmental policy aimed at the elimination of de facto establishments.

For an argument that most aspects of "ceremonial deism" violate the Court's establishment clause doctrine, see Epstein, Rethinking the Constitutionality of Ceremonial Deism, 96 Colum. L. Rev. 2083 (1996). In McGowan v. Maryland, 366 U.S. 420 (1961), the Court rejected an establishment clause challenge to laws requiring that most large-scale commercial enterprises remain closed on Sundays. The Court's review of history demonstrated that Sunday closing laws were originally efforts to promote church attendance. "But, despite the strongly religious origin of these laws, nonreligious arguments for Sunday closing began to be heard more distinctly." The Court said that the Constitution "does not ban federal or state regulation of conduct whose reason or effect merely happens to coincide with the tenets of some or all religions." It concluded that, "as presently written and administered, most [Sunday closing laws] are of a secular rather than of a religious character." They "provide a uniform day of rest for all citizens. [To] say that the States cannot prescribe Sunday as a day of rest for these purposes solely because centuries ago such laws had their genesis in religion would give a constitutional interpretation of hostility to the public welfare rather than one of mere separation of church and State." As of 1961, was Howe's characterization of Sunday closing laws more accurate than the Court's? As of the present?

In Elk Grove Unified School District v. Newdow, 542 U.S. 1 (2004), the Court refused, on standing grounds, to consider the merits of a challenge to the constitutionality of the inclusion of the words "under God" in the Pledge of Allegiance. Chief Justice Rehnquist and Justices O'Connor and Thomas disagreed with that holding and wrote opinions explaining why they believed that the constitutional challenge should be rejected on the merits. Chief Justice Rehnquist relied on history to show that "our national culture allows public recognition of our Nation's religious history and character." He wrote, "I do not believe that the phrase 'under God' in the Pledge converts its recital into a 'religious exercise.' . . . Instead, it is a declaration of belief in allegiance and loyalty to the United States flag and the Republic. . . . The phrase [is] in no sense a prayer, nor an endorsement of any religion. . . . Reciting the Pledge, or listening to others recite it, is a patriotic exercise, not a religious one; participants promise fidelity to our flag and our Nation, not to any particular God, faith, or church." Justice O'Connor relied on the endorsement test, and characterized the phrase in the Pledge as an example of permissible "ceremonial deism," although she called it a "close question." Ceremonial deism, which involved "solemnizing an event and recognizing a shared religious history," included expressions that had "legitimate nonreligious purposes." Those purposes were revealed "when a given practice has been in place for a significant portion of the Nation's history, and when it is observed by enough persons that it can fairly be called ubiquitous." Further, ceremonial deism was characterized by the "absence of worship or prayer" and by a "highly circumscribed reference to God." Brief references tend "to confirm that the reference is being used to acknowledge religion or to solemnize an event rather than to endorse religion in any way," and "it makes it easier for those participants who wish to 'opt out' [to] do so without having to reject the ceremony entirely [and] tends to limit the ability of government to express a preference for one religious sect over another." Also, "no religious acknowledgement could claim to be an instance of ceremonial deism if it explicitly favored one particular religious belief system over another." She also observed that "[a]ny coercion that persuades an onlooker to participate in an act of ceremonial deism is inconsequential, as an Establishment Clause matter, because such acts are simply not religious in character."

AMERICAN LEGION v. AMERICAN HUMANIST ASSOCIATION

139 S. Ct. 2067 (2020)

Justice ALITO announced the judgment of the Court and delivered the opinion of the Court with respect to Parts I, II-B, II-C, III, and IV, and an opinion with respect to Parts II-A and II-D, in which THE CHIEF JUSTICE, Justice BREYER, and Justice KAVANAUGH join.

Since 1925, the Bladensburg Peace Cross (Cross) has stood as a tribute to 49 area soldiers who gave their lives in the First World War. . . .

[Although] the cross has long been a preeminent Christian symbol, its use in the Bladensburg memorial has a special significance. [For] nearly a century, the Bladensburg Cross has expressed the community's grief at the loss of the young men who perished, its thanks for their sacrifice, and its dedication to the ideals for which they fought. It has become a prominent community landmark, and its removal or radical alteration at this date would be seen by many not as a neutral act but as the manifestation of "a hostility toward religion that has no place in our Establishment Clause traditions." [The] Religion Clauses of the Constitution aim to foster a society in which people of all beliefs can live together harmoniously, and the presence of the Bladensburg Cross on the land where it has stood for so many years is fully consistent with that aim.

I

A

The cross came into widespread use as a symbol of Christianity by the fourth century, and it retains that meaning today. But there are many contexts in which the symbol has also taken on a secular meaning. Indeed, there are instances in which its message is now almost entirely secular.

A cross appears as part of many registered trademarks held by businesses and secular organizations, including Blue Cross Blue Shield, the Bayer Group, and some Johnson & Johnson products. Many of these marks relate to health care, and it is likely that the association of the cross with healing had a religious origin. But the current use of these marks is indisputably secular.

The familiar symbol of the Red Cross—a red cross on a white background—shows how the meaning of a symbol that was originally religious can be transformed. The International Committee of the Red Cross (ICRC) selected that symbol in 1863 because it was thought to call to mind the flag of Switzerland, a country widely known for its neutrality. The Swiss flag consists of a white cross on a red background. In an effort to invoke the message associated with that flag, the ICRC copied its design with the colors inverted. Thus, the ICRC selected this symbol for an essentially secular reason, and the current secular message of the symbol is shown by its use today in nations with only tiny Christian populations. But the cross was originally chosen for the Swiss flag for religious reasons. So an image that began as an expression of faith was transformed.

The image used in the Bladensburg memorial—a plain Latin cross—also took on new meaning after World War I. "During and immediately after the war, the army marked soldiers' graves with temporary wooden crosses or Stars of David"—a departure from the prior practice of marking graves in American military cemeteries with uniform rectangular slabs. The vast majority of these grave markers consisted of crosses, and thus when Americans saw photographs of these cemeteries, what struck them were rows and rows of plain white crosses. As a result, the image of a simple white cross "developed into a 'central symbol'" of the conflict. . . .

B

Recognition of the cross's symbolism extended to local communities across the country. In late 1918, residents of Prince George's County, Maryland, formed a committee for the purpose of erecting a memorial for the county's fallen soldiers. The committee decided that the memorial should be a cross and hired sculptor and architect John Joseph Earley to design it. Although we do not know precisely why the committee chose the cross, it is unsurprising that the committee — and many others commemorating World War I — adopted a symbol so widely associated with that wrenching event. . . .

The completed monument is a 32-foot tall Latin cross that sits on a large pedestal. The American Legion's emblem is displayed at its center, and the words "Valor," "Endurance," "Courage," and "Devotion" are inscribed at its base, one on each of the four faces. The pedestal also features a 9- by 2.5-foot bronze plaque explaining that the monument is "Dedicated to the heroes of Prince George's County, Maryland who lost their lives in the Great War for the liberty of the world." The plaque lists the names of 49 local men, both Black and White, who died in the war. It identifies the dates of American involvement, and quotes President Woodrow Wilson's request for a declaration of war: "The right is more precious than peace. We shall fight for the things we have always carried nearest our hearts. To such a task we dedicate our lives." . . .

II

A

The Establishment Clause of the First Amendment provides that "Congress shall make no law respecting an establishment of religion." While the concept of a formally established church is straightforward, pinning down the meaning of a "law respecting an establishment of religion" has proved to be a vexing problem. [After] grappling with such cases for more than 20 years, Lemon ambitiously attempted to distill from the Court's existing case law a test that would bring order and predictability to Establishment Clause decisionmaking. . . .

For at least four reasons, the Lemon test presents particularly daunting problems in cases, including the one now before us, that involve the use, for ceremonial, celebratory, or commemorative purposes, of words or symbols with religious associations. Together, these considerations counsel against efforts to evaluate such cases under Lemon and toward application of a presumption of constitutionality for longstanding monuments, symbols, and practices.

B

First, these cases often concern monuments, symbols, or practices that were first established long ago, and in such cases, identifying their original purpose or purposes may be especially difficult. . . .

Second, as time goes by, the purposes associated with an established monument, symbol, or practice often multiply. Take the example of Ten Commandments monuments. [For] believing Jews and Christians, the Ten Commandments are the word of God handed down to Moses on Mount Sinai, but the image of the Ten Commandments has also been used to convey other meanings. They have historical significance as one of the foundations of our legal system, and for largely that reason, they are depicted in the marble frieze in our courtroom and in other prominent public buildings in our Nation's capital. . . .

The existence of multiple purposes is not exclusive to longstanding monuments, symbols, or practices, but this phenomenon is more likely to occur in such cases. Even if the original purpose of a monument was infused with religion, the passage of time may obscure that sentiment. As our society becomes more and more religiously diverse, a community may preserve such monuments, symbols, and practices for the sake of their historical significance or their place in a common cultural heritage.

Third, just as the purpose for maintaining a monument, symbol, or practice may evolve, "[t]he 'message' conveyed . . . may change over time." Consider, for example, the message of the Statue of Liberty, which began as a monument to the solidarity and friendship between France and the United States and only decades later came to be seen "as a beacon welcoming immigrants to a land of freedom."

With sufficient time, religiously expressive monuments, symbols, and practices can become embedded features of a community's landscape and identity. . . .

Fourth, when time's passage imbues a religiously expressive monument, symbol, or practice with this kind of familiarity and historical significance, removing it may no longer appear neutral, especially to the local community for which it has taken on particular meaning. A government that roams the land, tearing down monuments with religious symbolism and scrubbing away any reference to the divine will strike many as aggressively hostile to religion. Militantly secular regimes have carried out such projects in the past, and for those with a knowledge of history, the image of monuments being taken down will be evocative, disturbing, and divisive.

These four considerations show that retaining established, religiously expressive monuments, symbols, and practices is quite different from erecting or adopting new ones. The passage of time gives rise to a strong presumption of constitutionality.

C

The role of the cross in World War I memorials is illustrative of each of the four preceding considerations. Immediately following the war, "[c]ommunities across America built memorials to commemorate those who had served the nation in the struggle to make the world safe for democracy." [The] solemn image of endless rows of white crosses became inextricably linked with and symbolic of the ultimate price paid by 116,000 soldiers. And this relationship between the cross and the war undoubtedly influenced the design of the many war memorials that sprang up across the Nation.

This is not to say that the cross's association with the war was the sole or dominant motivation for the inclusion of the symbol in every World War I memorial that features it. But today, it is all but impossible to tell whether that was so. [And] no matter what the original purposes for the erection of a monument, a community may wish to preserve it for very different reasons. . . .

In addition, the passage of time may have altered the area surrounding a monument in ways that change its meaning and provide new reasons for its preservation. Such changes are relevant here, since the Bladensburg Cross now sits at a busy traffic intersection, and numerous additional monuments are located nearby. . . .

Finally, as World War I monuments have endured through the years and become a familiar part of the physical and cultural landscape, requiring their removal would not be viewed by many as a neutral act. [Thus], a campaign to obliterate items with religious associations may evidence hostility to religion even if those religious associations are no longer in the forefront. . . .

D

While the Lemon Court ambitiously attempted to find a grand unified theory of the Establishment Clause, in later cases, we have taken a more modest approach that focuses on the particular issue at hand and looks to history for guidance. Our cases involving prayer before a legislative session are an example. . . .

[After summarizing the cases described in Note 2 below, Justice Alito concluded:] The practice begun by the First Congress stands out as an example of respect and tolerance for differing views, an honest endeavor to achieve inclusivity and nondiscrimination, and a recognition of the important role that religion plays in the lives of many Americans. Where categories of monuments, symbols, and practices with a longstanding history follow in that tradition, they are likewise constitutional.

III

Applying these principles, we conclude that the Bladensburg Cross does not violate the Establishment Clause.

As we have explained, the Bladensburg Cross carries special significance in commemorating World War I. Due in large part to the image of the simple wooden crosses that originally marked the graves of American soldiers killed in the war, the cross became a symbol of their sacrifice, and the design of the Bladensburg Cross must be understood in light of that background. That the cross originated as a Christian symbol and retains that meaning in many contexts does not change the fact that the symbol took on an added secular meaning when used in World War I memorials.

Not only did the Bladensburg Cross begin with this meaning, but with the passage of time, it has acquired historical importance. It reminds the people of Bladensburg and surrounding areas of the deeds of their predecessors and of the sacrifices they made in a war fought in the name of democracy. As long as it is retained in its original place and form, it speaks as well of the community that erected the monument nearly a century ago and has maintained it ever since. The memorial represents what the relatives, friends, and neighbors of the fallen soldiers felt at the time and how they chose to express their sentiments. And the monument has acquired additional layers of historical meaning in subsequent years. The Cross now stands among memorials to veterans of later wars. It has become part of the community. . . .

[It] is surely relevant that the monument commemorates the death of particular individuals. It is natural and appropriate for those seeking to honor the deceased to invoke the symbols that signify what death meant for those who are memorialized. In some circumstances, the exclusion of any such recognition would make a memorial incomplete. This well explains why Holocaust memorials invariably include Stars of David or other symbols of Judaism. It explains why a new memorial to Native American veterans in Washington, D. C., will portray a steel circle to

240

represent " 'the hole in the sky where the creator lives.'" And this is why the memorial for soldiers from the Bladensburg community features the cross—the same symbol that marks the graves of so many of their comrades near the battlefields where they fell.

IV

The cross is undoubtedly a Christian symbol, but that fact should not blind us to everything else that the Bladensburg Cross has come to represent. For some, that monument is a symbolic resting place for ancestors who never returned home. For others, it is a place for the community to gather and honor all veterans and their sacrifices for our Nation. For others still, it is a historical landmark. For many of these people, destroying or defacing the Cross that has stood undisturbed for nearly a century would not be neutral and would not further the ideals of respect and tolerance embodied in the First Amendment. For all these reasons, the Cross does not offend the Constitution. . . .

JUSTICE BREYER, with whom JUSTICE KAGAN joins, concurring.

I have long maintained that there is no single formula for resolving Establishment Clause challenges. The Court must instead consider each case in light of the basic purposes that the Religion Clauses were meant to serve: assuring religious liberty and tolerance for all, avoiding religiously based social conflict, and maintaining that separation of church and state that allows each to flourish in its "separate spher[e]." . . .

The case would be different, in my view, if there were evidence that the organizers had "deliberately disrespected" members of minority faiths or if the Cross had been erected only recently, rather than in the aftermath of World War I. But those are not the circumstances presented to us here, and I see no reason to order this cross torn down simply because other crosses would raise constitutional concerns.

Nor do I understand the Court's opinion today to adopt a "history and tradition test" that would permit any newly constructed religious memorial on public land. The Court appropriately "looks to history for guidance," but it upholds the constitutionality of the Peace Cross only after considering its particular historical context and its long-held place in the community. A newer memorial, erected under different circumstances, would not necessarily be permissible under this approach. . . .

JUSTICE KAVANAUGH, concurring. . . .

I

Consistent with the Court's case law, the Court today applies a history and tradition test in examining and upholding the constitutionality of the Bladensburg Cross. . . .

[Each] category of Establishment Clause cases has its own principles based on history, tradition, and precedent. And the cases together lead to an overarching set of principles: If the challenged government practice is not coercive and if it (i) is rooted in history and tradition; or (ii) treats religious people, organizations, speech, or activity equally to comparable secular people, organizations, speech, or activity; or (iii) represents a permissible legislative accommodation or exemption from a generally applicable law, then there ordinarily is no Establishment Clause violation. . . .

II

The Bladensburg Cross commemorates soldiers who gave their lives for America in World War I. I agree with the Court that the Bladensburg Cross is constitutional. At the same time, I have deep respect for the plaintiffs' sincere objections to seeing the cross on public land. I have great respect for the Jewish war veterans who in an amicus brief say that the cross on public land sends a message of exclusion. I recognize their sense of distress and alienation. Moreover, I fully understand the deeply religious nature of the cross. It would demean both believers and nonbelievers to say that the cross is not religious, or not all that religious. A case like this is difficult because it represents a clash of genuine and important interests. Applying our precedents, we uphold the constitutionality of the cross. In doing so, it is appropriate to also restate this bedrock constitutional principle: All citizens are equally American, no matter what religion they are, or if they have no religion at all.

The conclusion that the cross does not violate the Establishment Clause does not necessarily mean that those who object to it have no other recourse. The Court's ruling allows the State to maintain the cross on public land. The Court's ruling does not require the State to maintain the cross on public land. The Maryland Legislature could enact new laws requiring removal of the cross or transfer of the land. The Maryland Governor or other state or local executive officers may have authority to do so under current Maryland law. And if not, the legislature could enact new laws to authorize such executive action. The Maryland Constitution, as interpreted by the Maryland Court of Appeals, may speak to this question. And if not, the people of Maryland can amend the State Constitution.

Those alternative avenues of relief illustrate a fundamental feature of our constitutional structure: This Court is not the only guardian of individual rights in America. This Court fiercely protects the individual rights secured by the U. S. Constitution. But the Constitution sets a floor for the protection of individual rights. The constitutional floor is sturdy and often high, but it is a floor. Other federal, state, and local government entities generally possess authority to safeguard individual rights above and beyond the rights secured by the U.S. Constitution.

JUSTICE KAGAN, concurring in part. . . .

Although I agree that rigid application of the Lemon test does not solve every Establishment Clause problem, I think that test's focus on purposes and effects is crucial in evaluating government action in this sphere—as this very suit shows. I therefore do not join Part II-A.

JUSTICE THOMAS, concurring in the judgment.

[Justice Thomas's opinion restated his long-standing position that the Fourteenth Amendment did not make the Establishment Clause applicable to the states, and that the Establishment Clause prohibited only coercion, which he defined as "attempt[ing] to control religious doctrine or personnel, compel religious observance, single out a particular religious denomination for exclusive state subsidization, or punish dissenting worship."]

III

[I] would [overrule] the Lemon test in all contexts. First, that test has no basis in the original meaning of the Constitution. Second, "since its inception," it has "been manipulated to fit whatever result the Court aimed to achieve." . . .

JUSTICE GORSUCH, with whom JUSTICE THOMAS joins, concurring in the judgment.

[Justice Gorsuch's opinion argued that the American Humanist Association and other plaintiffs below lacked standing under Article III, which in his view did not allow standing based on the fact that they were "offended observers" of the Cross. He continued:]

[Lemon] was a misadventure. It sought a "grand unified theory" of the Establishment Clause but left us only a mess. How much "purpose" to promote religion is too much (are Sunday closing laws that bear multiple purposes, religious and secular, problematic)? How much "effect" of advancing religion is tolerable (are even incidental effects disallowed)? What does the "entanglement" test add to these inquiries? Even beyond all that, how "reasonable" must our "reasonable observer" be, and what exactly qualifies as impermissible "endorsement" of religion in a country where "In God We Trust" appears on the coinage, the eye of God appears in its Great Seal, and we celebrate Thanksgiving as a national holiday ("to Whom are thanks being given")? [Today], not a single Member of the Court even tries to defend Lemon against these criticisms — and they don't because they can't. . . .

In place of Lemon, Part II-D of the plurality opinion relies on a more modest, historically sensitive approach, recognizing that "the Establishment Clause must be interpreted by reference to historical practices and understandings." . . .

I [don't] doubt that the monument before us is constitutional in light of the nation's traditions. But then the plurality continues on to suggest that "longstanding monuments, symbols, and practices" are "presumpt[ively]" constitutional. And about that, it's hard not to wonder: How old must a monument, symbol, or practice be to qualify for this new presumption? It seems 94 years is enough, but what about the Star of David monument erected in South Carolina in 2001 to commemorate victims of the Holocaust, or the cross that marines in California placed in 2004 to honor their comrades who fell during the War on Terror? And where exactly in the Constitution does this presumption come from? [What] matters when it comes to assessing a monument, symbol, or practice isn't its age but its compliance with ageless principles. The Constitution's meaning is fixed, not some good-for-this-day-only coupon, and a practice consistent with our nation's traditions is just as permissible whether undertaken today or 94 years ago. . . .

JUSTICE GINSBURG, with whom JUSTICE SOTOMAYOR joins, dissenting.

An immense Latin cross stands on a traffic island at the center of a busy three-way intersection in Bladensburg, Maryland. "[M]onumental, clear, and bold" by day, the cross looms even larger illuminated against the night-time sky. Known as the Peace Cross, the monument was erected by private citizens in 1925 to honor local soldiers who lost their lives in World War I. "[T]he town's most prominent symbol" was rededicated in 1985 and is now said to honor "the sacrifices made [in] all wars," by "all veterans." . . .

The Latin cross is the foremost symbol of the Christian faith, embodying the "central theological claim of Christianity: that the son of God died on the cross, that he rose from the dead, and that his death and resurrection offer the possibility of eternal life." Precisely because the cross symbolizes these sectarian beliefs, it is a common marker for the graves of Christian soldiers. For the same reason, using the cross as a war memorial does not transform it into a secular symbol. [Just] as a Star of David is not suitable to honor Christians who died serving their country, so a cross is not suitable to honor those of other faiths who died defending their nation. Soldiers of all faiths "are united by their love of country, but they are not united by the cross."

By maintaining the Peace Cross on a public highway, the Commission elevates Christianity over other faiths, and religion over nonreligion. Memorializing the service of American soldiers is an "admirable and unquestionably secular" objective. But the Commission does not serve that objective by displaying a symbol that bears "a starkly sectarian message." . . .

I . . .

B

In cases challenging the government's display of a religious symbol, the Court has tested fidelity to the principle of neutrality by asking whether the display has the "effect of 'endorsing' religion." . . .

As I see it, when a cross is displayed on public property, the government may be presumed to endorse its religious content. The venue is surely associated with the State; the symbol and its meaning are just as surely associated exclusively with Christianity. . . .

A presumption of endorsement, of course, may be overcome. A display does not run afoul of the neutrality principle if its "setting . . . plausibly indicates" that the government has not sought "either to adopt [a] religious message or to urge its acceptance by others." The "typical museum setting," for example, "though not neutralizing the religious content of a religious painting, negates any message of endorsement of that content." Similarly, when a public school history teacher discusses the Protestant Reformation, the setting makes clear that the teacher's purpose is to educate, not to proselytize. The Peace Cross, however, is not of that genre.

II . . .

B

The Commission urges in defense of its monument that the Latin cross "is not merely a reaffirmation of Christian beliefs"; rather, "when used in the context of a war memorial," the cross becomes "a universal symbol of the sacrifices of those who fought and died."

The Commission's "[a]ttempts to secularize what is unquestionably a sacred [symbol] defy credibility and disserve people of faith." The asserted commemorative meaning of the cross rests on — and is inseparable from — its Christian meaning: "the crucifixion of Jesus Christ and the redeeming benefits of his passion and death," specifically, "the salvation of man." . . .

C

The Commission nonetheless urges that the Latin cross is a "well-established" secular symbol commemorating, in particular, "military valor and sacrifice [in] World War I." [The] Commission overlooks this reality: The cross was never perceived as an appropriate headstone or memorial for Jewish soldiers and others who did not adhere to Christianity. . . .

D

Holding the Commission's display of the Peace Cross unconstitutional would not, as the Commission fears, "inevitably require the destruction of other cross-shaped memorials throughout the country." When a religious symbol appears in a public cemetery — on a headstone, or as the headstone itself, or perhaps integrated into a larger memorial — the setting counters the inference that the government seeks "either to adopt the religious message or to urge its acceptance by others." In a cemetery, the "privately selected religious symbols on individual graves are best understood as the private speech of each veteran." Such displays are "linked to, and sho[w] respect for, the individual honoree's faith and beliefs." They do not suggest governmental endorsement of those faith and beliefs.

Recognizing that a Latin cross does not belong on a public highway or building does not mean the monument must be "torn down." [In] some instances, the violation may be cured by relocating the monument to private land or by transferring ownership of the land and monument to a private party. . . .

Note: Abandoning the Lemon Test and Replacing It with What?

1. *Endorsement or not?* Consider how Justice O'Connor would have analyzed the display in American Legion using her version of the nonendorsement principle. Lynch could be taken to hold that the crèche, in its setting, had only a secular meaning to informed observers. American Legion might be read to assert that the cross had come to have one meaning for Christian observers, another for other observers. Is that approach consistent with the nonendorsement principle? Justice Alito's opinion referred to "[t]he recent tragic fire at Notre Dame in Paris [as] a striking example [of how a nation can 'come to value [religiously expressive monuments] without necessarily embracing their religious roots']. Although the French Republic rigorously enforces a secular public square, the cathedral remains a symbol of national importance to the religious and nonreligious alike. Notre Dame is fundamentally a place of worship and retains great religious importance, but its meaning has broadened. For many, it is inextricably linked with the very idea of Paris and France. Speaking to the nation shortly after the fire, President Macron said that Notre Dame 'is our history, our literature, our imagination. The place where we survived epidemics, wars, liberation. It has been the epicenter of our lives.' " (Was this an appropriate use of non-U.S. material in constructing constitutional doctrine?)

2. *History as a guide*. What role does history play in American Legion? Note the disagreement between Justices Breyer and Kavanaugh. Justice Kavanaugh appears to conclude that a "history and tradition" test would lead to finding no constitutional violation in noncoercive displays supported by history and tradition, while Justice Breyer appears to conclude that history and tradition, while always relevant, is only one consideration among many.

Consider these observations, from Koppelman, The New American Civil Religion: Lessons for Italy, Geo. Wash. 41 Int'l L. Rev. 961, 866 (2010):

Douglas Laycock thinks that a lesson [is] that "separationist groups should sue immediately when they encounter any religious practice newly sponsored by the government." That is precisely the right lesson. [New] sponsorship of religious practices is far more likely to represent a contemporaneous effort to intervene in a live religious controversy than the perpetuation of old forms.

In Walz v. Tax Commission, section B1, supra, the Court noted that every state had a property tax exemption for churches, and that the federal income tax has since its inception exempted religious organizations. It found "significant" that Congress exempted churches from real estate taxes in 1802. "[An] unbroken practice of according the exemption to churches, openly and by affirmative state action, not covertly or by state inaction, is not something to be lightly cast aside." Justice Brennan, concurring, agreed that "the existence from the beginning of the Nation's life of a practice [is] a fact of considerable import in the interpretation of abstract constitutional language. [The] more longstanding and widely accepted a practice, the greater its impact upon constitutional interpretation." He found two "secular purposes" for the exemption: Churches, like other exempt groups, "contribute to the well-being of the community in a variety of nonreligious ways," and they "uniquely contribute to the pluralism of American society."

Marsh v. Chambers, 463 U.S. 783 (1983), relied on a "unique history" to uphold the constitutionality of opening legislative sessions with prayers led by a state-employed chaplain. The history ran from colonial times to the present and included the first Congress's hiring a chaplain in 1789, only three days before it reached final agreement on the language of the first amendment:

> [Historical] evidence sheds light not only on what the draftsmen intended the Establishment Clause to mean, but also on how they thought that Clause applied to the practice authorized by the First Congress—their actions reveal their intent. [In] light of the unambiguous and unbroken history of more than 200 years, there can be no doubt that the practice of opening legislative sessions with prayer has become part of the fabric of our society.

Town of Greece v. Galloway, 134 S. Ct. 1811 (2014), involved the prayer practices of the town board of Greece, a suburb of Rochester, New York. Starting in 1999, the board opened its meetings with, among other matters, a prayer given by guest chaplains chosen from a list of congregations in the town directory, nearly all of which are Christian. Some of the ministers "spoke in a distinctly Christian idiom," including invoking "the saving sacrifice of Jesus Christ on the cross."

Justice Kennedy wrote an opinion that was in part for the Court, and in part only for himself and Chief Justice Roberts and Justice Alito. The Court upheld the town's practices. It relied heavily on Marsh, which "[must] not be understood as permitting a practice that would amount to a constitutional violation if not for its historical foundation. The case teaches instead that the Establishment Clause must be interpreted 'by reference to historical practices and understandings.' [The] Court's inquiry [must] be to determine whether the prayer practice in the town of Greece fits within the tradition long followed in Congress and the state legislatures." But "[an] insistence on nonsectarian or ecumenical prayer as a single, fixed, standard is not consistent with the tradition of legislative [prayer]. [To] hold that invocations must be nonsectarian would force the legislatures [and] the courts [to] act as supervisors and censors of religious speech, [which] would involve government in religious matters to a far greater degree [than] is the case under the town's current practice."

Justice Kennedy also wrote, "If the course and practice over time shows that the invocations denigrate nonbelievers or religious minorities, threaten damnation, or preach conversion, many present may consider the prayer to fall short of the desire to elevate the purpose of the occasion and to unite lawmakers in their common effort. That circumstance would present a different [case]." Noting that "two remarks" by guest chaplains "strayed from the rationale set out in Marsh," he wrote that "they do not despoil a practice that on the whole reflects and embraces our tradition. Absent a pattern of prayers that over time denigrate, proselytize, or betray an impermissible government purpose, a challenge based solely on the content of a prayer will not likely establish a constitutional violation." The town's efforts to locate guest chaplains were "reasonable," and did "not reflect an aversion or bias on the part of town leaders against minority faiths. So long as the town maintains a policy of nondiscrimination, the Constitution does not require it to search beyond its borders for non-Christian prayer givers in an effort to achieve religious balancing."

Justice Kagan, joined by Justices Ginsburg, Breyer, and Sotomayor, dissented. For Justice Kagan, "[t]he practice [here] differs from the one sustained in [Marsh] because Greece's town meetings involve participation by ordinary citizens, and the invocations given—directly to those citizens—were predominantly sectarian. [Greece's] Board did nothing to recognize religious diversity. [The] Town never sought (except briefly when this suit was filed) to involve, accommodate, or in any way reach out to adherents of non-Christian religions." She agreed that "Greece's

Board [has] legislative functions," but its "meetings are also occasions for ordinary citizens to engage with and petition their government, often on highly individualized matters. That feature calls for Board members to exercise special care to ensure that the prayers offered [respect] each and every member of the community as an equal citizen." The sessions in Marsh at which prayers were offered were "floor sessions [for] elected lawyers. Members of the public take no part. [Greece's] town meetings [revolve] around ordinary members of the community," who "urge [changes] in the Board's policies [and] then, in which are essentially adjudicatory hearings, they request the Board to grant [applications] for various permits."

> Let's say that a Muslim citizen of Greece goes before the Board to [request] some permit. [Just] before she gets to speak her piece, a minister deputized by the Town asks her to pray "in the name of God's only son Jesus Christ." She must think [that] Christian worship has become entwined with local governance. And now she faces a choice—to pray alongside the majority [or] somehow to register her deeply felt difference. [That] is no easy call—especially given that the room is small and her every action [will] be noticed. She does not wish to be rude to her neighbors, nor does she wish to aggravate the Board members whom she will soon be trying to persuade. And yet she does not want to acknowledge Christ's divinity. [So] assume she declines to participate with the others in the first act of the meeting—or even [stands] up and leaves the room. [She] becomes a different kind of citizen. [And] she thus stands at a remove, based solely on religion, from her fellow citizens and her elected representatives. Everything about that situation [infringes] the First Amendment.

Justice Kagan would allow some prayer activities. "What the circumstances here demand is the recognition that we are a pluralistic people. [If] the Town Board had let its chaplains know that they should speak in nonsectarian terms, [then] no one would have valid grounds for complaint. [Or] it might have invited clergy of many faiths to serve as chaplains. [But] Greece could not do what it did: infuse a participatory government body with one (and only one) faith." For her, "[when] a citizen stands before her government, [her] religious beliefs do not enter into the picture. The government she faces favors no particular religion, either by word or by deed. And that government [imposes] no religious tests on its citizens, sorts none of them by faith, and permits no exclusion based on belief. When a person goes to court, a polling place, or an immigration proceeding, [government] officials do not engage in sectarian worship, nor do they ask her to do likewise. They all participate in the business of government not as Christians, Jews, Muslims (and more), but only as Americans—none of them different from any other for that civic purpose."

Justice Alito, joined by Justice Scalia, responded to Justice Kagan in a concurring opinion, calling "the narrow aspect" of her dissent's objections to the holding "really quite niggling." He argued that "there [is] no historical support for the proposition that only generic prayer is allowed," and observed that "as our country has become more diverse, composing a prayer that is acceptable to all members of the community who hold religious beliefs has become [harder.]" Further, "if a town attempts to go beyond simply recommending that a guest chaplain deliver a prayer that is broadly acceptable, [the] town will [encounter] sensitive problems," including possible prescreening or reviewing prayers. The alternative of compiling a list of clergy from numerous traditions to serve as guest chaplains meant that Justice Kagan's objection was only the "[the] town's clerical employees did a bad job in compiling the list" they used.

Consider the extent to which the disagreements in *Town of Greece* foreshadow the competing discussions of the role of history and tradition in American Legion.

3. *Religious pluralism and the political process.* Consider the following argument: Contemporary society is pluralist in religion and in politics. Some religious groups oppose all governmental support of religion; others would support sectarian aid but oppose nondenominational aid; and others would support nondenominational aid. As some of these groups seek to secure legislation, they will have to adjust their programs to obtain majority support. The likely outcome of pluralist political bargaining in contemporary society on matters relating to religion is legislation having relatively modest religious content. The political process is therefore sufficient to guard against the evils at which the establishment clause is directed. Does this argument underestimate the degree to which a "least common denominator" religion may raise serious concern about establishment?

4. *Federalism and alternative responses to the presence of religious symbols.* Justice Kavanaugh writes that the state legislature or other state officials could require removing the cross from public land. Justice Alito writes that the cross's removal "would be seen by many [as] the manifestation of" hostility toward religion. Consider this disagreement in light of Justice Alito's discussion of the possibility of dual meanings: Is it fair to say that Justice Kavanaugh would allow public officials to give removal a secular meaning, while Justice Alito would require them to give it an anti-religious (and therefore prohibited) meaning?

Page 1487.   Before the Note, add the following:

TRUMP v. HAWAII

138 S. Ct. 2392 (2018)

CHIEF JUSTICE ROBERTS delivered the opinion of the Court. . . .

[One week after taking office, President Trump signed an executive order directing the Secretary of Homeland Security to conduct a review of the adequacy of information provided by foreign governments about their nationals seeking entry into the United States. Pending the review, the order suspended the entry of foreign nationals for ninety days from seven predominantly Muslim countries.

[The order produced widespread confusion and protest, and a district court temporarily enjoined it, a decision affirmed by the Court of Appeals. Rather than proceeding further with litigation, the President revoked the order and replaced it with a new order again requiring a worldwide review and temporarily restricting entry (with case-by-case waivers) of foreign nationals from six predominantly Muslim countries. Courts again temporarily enjoined enforcement of the order, but the Supreme Court stayed these injunctions with respect to foreign nationals who lacked "a credible claim of a bona fide relationship with a person or entity in the United States. Trump v. International Refugee Assistance Project, 137 S. Ct. 2080 (2017).

[Upon completion of the world-wide review, the President entered a third order, placing entry restrictions on the nationals of eight foreign states—Chad, Iran, Iraq, Libya, North Korea, Syria, Venezuela, and Yemen. Six of the states are predominantly Muslim. According to the order, the states were selected based upon a review of the methods they utilized to determine whether individuals seeking entry into the United States posed a security threat. The order exempted foreign nationals who had been granted asylum and provided for case-by-case waivers. The state of Hawaii and three individuals brought suit challenging the legality of the order.]

III

[In this section of the opinion, the Court held that the order was justified under power delegated to the President in the Immigration and Naturalization Act]

IV

A

[The Court held that the plaintiffs have standing to raise the claim. This issue is discussed in the supplement to page 118 of the Main Volume]

B

[Plaintiffs argued that the order violated the establishment clause because it operated as a "religious gerrymander" that singled out Muslims because of religious animus. They claimed that the stated reasons for the order were pretextual.

[In support of their argument they relied upon the following facts, many of which are detailed in Justice Sotomayor's dissenting opinion:

- Before he was elected, Candidate Trump stated that he was "calling for a total and complete shutdown of Muslims entering the United States until our country's representatives can figure out what is going on. According to Pew Research, among others, there is great hatred towards Americans by large segments of the Muslim population. [Until] we are able to determine and understand this problem and the dangerous threat it poses, our country cannot be the victims of the horrendous attacks by people that believe only in Jihad, and have no sense of reason or respect for human life."

- Also during the campaign, Trump justified his proposal by saying that Franklin Roosevelt "did the same thing" with respect to internment of Japanese Americans during World War II; told an apocryphal story about General John J. Pershing killing a large group of Muslim insurgents in the Philippines with bullets dipped in pigs' blood; stated that "Islam hates us"; called for surveillance of mosques in the United States; and stated that Muslims "do not respect us at all."

- After signing the first version of the executive order, President Trump explained that Christians would be given

priority for entry as refugees. He stated that the order was
designed "to help" Christians in Syria.
- An advisor to President Trump told the media that "when
  [Donald Trump] first announced it, he said 'Muslim ban.'
  He called me up. He said, 'put a commission together. Show
  me the right way to do it legally.'"
- While litigation about the second order was pending,
  President Trump characterized it as a "watered down version of the first one" that had been tailored at the behest of
  "the lawyers." He stated that he would prefer to "go back
  to the first [order] and go all the way" and that it was "very
  hard" for Muslims to assimilate into Western culture. In a
  tweet, he stated that "People, the lawyers and the courts can
  call it whatever they want, but I am calling it what we need
  and what it is, a TRAVEL BAN! That's right, we need a
  TRAVEL BAN for certain DANGEROUS countries, not
  some politically correct term that won't help protect our
  people."
- After the third order was promulgated, President Trump
  retweeted three anti-Muslim videos entitled "Muslims de-
  stroy a Statue of Virgin Mary!", "Islamist mob pushes teen-
  age boy off roof and beats him to death!" and "Muslim
  migrants beats up Dutch boy on crutches!" When asked
  about the videos, the White House Deputy Press Secretary
  connected them to the order and stated that the "President
  has been talking about these security issues for years now,
  from the campaign trail to the White House" and "has
  addressed these issues with the travel order that he issued
  earlier this year."]

Our Presidents have frequently used their power to espouse
the principles of religious freedom and tolerance on which this
Nation was founded. In 1790 George Washington reassured the
Hebrew Congregation of Newport, Rhode Island that "happily the
Government of the United States . . . gives to bigotry no sanc-
tion, to persecution no assistance [and] requires only that they

who live under its protection should demean themselves as good citizens." President Eisenhower, at the opening of the Islamic Center of Washington, similarly pledged to a Muslim audience that "America would fight with her whole strength for your right to have here your own church," declaring that "[t]his concept is indeed a part of America." And just days after the attacks of September 11, 2001, President George W. Bush returned to the same Islamic Center to implore his fellow Americans—Muslims and non-Muslims alike—to remember during their time of grief that "[t]he face of terror is not the true faith of Islam," and that America is "a great country because we share the same values of respect and dignity and human worth." Yet it cannot be denied that the Federal Government and the Presidents who have carried its laws into effect have—from the Nation's earliest days—performed unevenly in living up to those inspiring words.

Plaintiffs argue that this President's words strike at fundamental standards of respect and tolerance, in violation of our constitutional tradition. But the issue before us is not whether to denounce the statements. It is instead the significance of those statements in reviewing a Presidential directive, neutral on its face, addressing a matter within the core of executive responsibility. In doing so, we must consider not only the statements of a particular President, but also the authority of the Presidency itself.

The case before us differs in numerous respects from the conventional Establishment Clause claim. Unlike the typical suit involving religious displays or school prayer, plaintiffs seek to invalidate a national security directive regulating the entry of aliens abroad. Their claim accordingly raises a number of delicate issues regarding the scope of the constitutional right and the manner of proof. The Proclamation, moreover, is facially neutral toward religion. Plaintiffs therefore ask the Court to probe the sincerity of the stated justifications for the policy by reference to extrinsic statements—many of which were made before the President took the oath of office. These various aspects of plaintiffs' challenge inform our standard of review.

C

[In this section, the Court discusses previous decisions relating to entry into the country and national security considerations. It characterized those decisions as providing for a "circumscribed judicial inquiry" when denial of entry allegedly burdens the constitutional rights of U.S. citizens. The Court's role was limited to determining whether the Executive gave a "facially legitimate and bona fide reason for its action."]

A conventional application of [this principle] would put an end to our review. But the Government has suggested that it may be appropriate here for the inquiry to extend beyond the facial neutrality of the order. For our purposes today, we assume that we may look behind the face of the Proclamation to the extent of applying rational basis review. That standard of review considers whether the entry policy is plausibly related to the Government's stated objective to protect the country and improve vetting processes. As a result, we may consider plaintiffs' extrinsic evidence, but will uphold the policy so long as it can reasonably be understood to result from a justification independent of unconstitutional grounds.

D . . .

The Proclamation is expressly premised on legitimate purposes: preventing entry of nationals who cannot be adequately vetted and inducing other nations to improve their practices. The text says nothing about religion. Plaintiffs and the dissent nonetheless emphasize that five of the seven nations currently included in the Proclamation have Muslim-majority populations. Yet that fact alone does not support an inference of religious hostility, given that the policy covers just 8% of the world's Muslim population and is limited to countries that were previously designated by Congress or prior administrations as posing national security risks.

The Proclamation, moreover, reflects the results of a worldwide review process undertaken by multiple Cabinet officials and their agencies. Plaintiffs seek to discredit the findings of the review, pointing to deviations from the review's baseline criteria resulting in the inclusion of Somalia and omission of Iraq. But as the Proclamation explains, in each case the determinations were justified by the distinct conditions in each country. . . .

Three additional features of the entry policy support the Government's claim of a legitimate national security interest. First, since the President introduced entry restrictions in January 2017, three Muslim-majority countries—Iraq, Sudan, and Chad—have been removed from the list of covered countries. . . .

Second, for those countries that remain subject to entry restrictions, the Proclamation includes significant exceptions for various categories of foreign nationals. . . .

Third, the Proclamation creates a waiver program open to all covered foreign nationals seeking entry as immigrants or nonimmigrants. . . .

Finally, the dissent invokes Korematsu v. United States, 323 U.S. 214 (1944). [*Korematsu* is discussed at page 532 of the Main Volume.] Whatever rhetorical advantage the dissent may see in doing so, *Korematsu* has nothing to do with this case. The forcible relocation of U.S. citizens to concentration camps, solely and explicitly on the basis of race, is objectively unlawful and outside the scope of Presidential authority. But it is wholly inapt to liken that morally repugnant order to a facially neutral policy denying certain foreign nationals the privilege of admission. The entry suspension is an act that is well within executive authority and could have been taken by any other President—the only question is evaluating the actions of this particular President in promulgating an otherwise valid Proclamation. The dissent's reference to *Korematsu*, however, affords this Court the opportunity to make express what is already obvious: *Korematsu* was gravely wrong the day it was decided, has been overruled in the court of history, and—to be clear—"has no place in law under the Constitution." 323 U.S., at 248 (Jackson, J., dissenting).

* * *

Under these circumstances, the Government has set forth a sufficient national security justification to survive rational basis review. We express no view on the soundness of the policy. We simply hold today that plaintiffs have not demonstrated a likelihood of success on the merits of their constitutional claim. The case now returns to the lower courts for such further proceedings as may be appropriate.

JUSTICE KENNEDY, concurring.

I join the Court's opinion in full. There may be some common ground between the opinions in this case, in that the Court does acknowledge that in some instances, governmental action may be subject to judicial review to determine whether or not it is "inexplicable by anything but animus," which in this case would be animosity to a religion. Whether judicial proceedings may properly continue in this case, in light of the substantial deference that is and must be accorded to the Executive in the conduct of foreign affairs, and in light of today's decision, is a matter to be addressed in the first instance on remand.

[In] all events, it is appropriate to make this further observation. There are numerous instances in which the statements and actions of Government officials are not subject to judicial scrutiny or intervention. That does not mean those officials are free to disregard the Constitution and the rights it proclaims and protects. The oath that all officials take to adhere to the Constitution is not confined to those spheres in which the Judiciary can correct or even comment upon what those officials say or do. Indeed, the very fact that an official may have broad discretion, discretion free from judicial scrutiny, makes it all the more imperative for him or her to adhere to the Constitution and to its meaning and its promise.

The First Amendment prohibits the establishment of religion and promises the free exercise of religion. From these safeguards, and from the guarantee of freedom of speech, it follows there is freedom of belief and expression. It is an urgent necessity that officials adhere to these constitutional guarantees and mandates in all their actions, even in the sphere of foreign affairs. An anxious world must know that our Government remains committed always to the liberties the Constitution seeks to preserve and protect, so that freedom extends outward, and lasts.

[A concurring opinion by Justice Thomas and a dissenting opinion by Justice Breyer, in which Justice Kagan joined, have been omitted].

JUSTICE SOTOMAYOR, with whom JUSTICE GINSBURG joins, dissenting.

The United States of America is a Nation built upon the promise of religious liberty. Our Founders honored that core promise by embedding the principle of religious neutrality in the First Amendment. The Court's decision today fails to safeguard that fundamental principle. It leaves undisturbed a policy first advertised openly and unequivocally as a "total and complete shutdown of Muslims entering the United States" because the policy now masquerades behind a façade of national-security concerns. But this repackaging does little to cleanse Presidential Proclamation No. 9645 of the appearance of discrimination that the President's words have created. Based on the evidence in the record, a reasonable observer would conclude that the Proclamation was motivated by anti-Muslim animus. That alone suffices to show that plaintiffs are likely to succeed on the merits of their Establishment Clause claim. The majority holds otherwise by ignoring the facts, misconstruing our legal precedent, and turning a blind eye to the pain and suffering the Proclamation inflicts upon countless families and individuals, many of whom are United States citizens. Because that troubling result runs contrary to the Constitution and our precedent, I dissent. . . .

I . . .

A . . .

The "clearest command" of the Establishment Clause is that the Government cannot favor or disfavor one religion over another. That is so, this Court has held, because such acts send messages to members of minority faiths "'that they are outsiders, not full members of the political community.'" To determine whether plaintiffs have proved an Establishment Clause violation, the Court asks whether a reasonable observer would view the government action as enacted for the purpose of disfavoring a religion. In answering that question, this Court has generally considered the text of the government policy, its operation, and any available evidence regarding "the historical background of the decision under challenge, the specific series of events leading to the enactment or official policy in question, and the legislative or administrative history, including contemporaneous statements made by" the decisionmaker.

B

1

[Justice Sotomayor summarizes the statements made by President Trump that are quoted above.]

2

As the majority correctly notes, "the issue before us is not whether to denounce" these offensive statements. Rather, the dispositive and narrow question here is whether a reasonable observer, presented with all "openly available data," the text and "historical context" of the Proclamation, and the "specific sequence of events" leading to it, would conclude that the primary purpose of the Proclamation is to disfavor Islam and its adherents by excluding them from the country. The answer is unquestionably yes. Taking all the relevant evidence together, a reasonable observer would conclude that the Proclamation was driven primarily by anti-Muslim animus, rather than by the Government's asserted national-security justifications. . . .

Notably, the Court recently found less pervasive official expressions of hostility and the failure to disavow them to be constitutionally significant. [citing Masterpiece Cakeshop v. Colorado

Civil Rights Comm'n, excerpted in the supplement to page 1519 of the Main Volume]

Ultimately, what began as a policy explicitly "calling for a total and complete shutdown of Muslims entering the United States" has since morphed into a "Proclamation" putatively based on national-security concerns. But this new window dressing cannot conceal an unassailable fact: the words of the President and his advisers create the strong perception that the Proclamation is contaminated by impermissible discriminatory animus against Islam and its followers. . . .

[In Parts II and III of her opinion, Justice Sotomayor argues that the Court erred in applying rational basis review to the order, that even utilizing rational basis review, the order is unconstitutional, and that the requirements for a preliminary injunction had been satisfied.]

IV . . .

In holding that the First Amendment gives way to an executive policy that a reasonable observer would view as motivated by animus against Muslims, the majority opinion upends this Court's precedent, repeats tragic mistakes of the past, and denies countless individuals the fundamental right of religious liberty. Just weeks ago, the Court rendered its decision in Masterpiece Cakeshop, which applied the bedrock principles of religious neutrality and tolerance in considering a First Amendment challenge to government action. Those principles should apply equally here. In both instances, the question is whether a government actor exhibited tolerance and neutrality in reaching a decision that affects individuals' fundamental religious freedom. But unlike in Masterpiece, where a state civil rights commission was found to have acted without "the neutrality that the Free Exercise Clause requires," the government actors in this case will not be held accountable for breaching the First Amendment's guarantee of religious neutrality and tolerance. Unlike in Masterpiece, where the majority considered the state commissioners' statements about religion to be persuasive evidence of unconstitutional government action the majority here completely sets aside the President's charged statements about Muslims as irrelevant. That holding erodes the foundational principles of religious tolerance that the Court elsewhere has so emphatically protected, and it tells members of minority religions in our country "'that they are outsiders, not full members of the political community.'"

Today's holding is all the more troubling given the stark parallels between the reasoning of this case and that of Korematsu v. United States, 323 U.S. 214 (1944). In *Korematsu*, the Court gave "a pass [to] an odious, gravely injurious racial classification" authorized by an executive order. Adarand Constructors, Inc. v. Peña, 515 U.S. 200, 275 (1995) (Ginsburg, J., dissenting). As here, the Government invoked an ill-defined national security threat to justify an exclusionary policy of sweeping proportion. As here, the exclusion order was rooted in dangerous stereotypes about, inter alia, a particular group's supposed inability to assimilate and desire to harm the United States. As here, the Government was unwilling to reveal its own intelligence agencies' views of the alleged security concerns to the very citizens it purported to protect. And as here, there was strong evidence that impermissible hostility and animus motivated the Government's policy. Although a majority of the Court in *Korematsu* was willing to uphold the Government's actions based on a barren invocation of national security, dissenting Justices warned of that decision's harm to our constitutional fabric. . . .

Today, the Court takes the important step of finally overruling *Korematsu*, denouncing it as "gravely wrong the day it was decided." This formal repudiation of a shameful precedent is laudable and long overdue. But it does not make the majority's decision here acceptable or right. By blindly accepting the Government's misguided invitation to sanction a discriminatory policy motivated by animosity toward a disfavored group, all in the name of a superficial claim of national security, the Court redeploys the same dangerous logic underlying *Korematsu* and merely replaces one "gravely wrong" decision with another. Our

265

Constitution demands, and our country deserves, a Judiciary willing to hold the coordinate branches to account when they defy our most sacred legal commitments. Because the Court's decision today has failed in that respect, with profound regret, I dissent.

Note: The Meaning of Trump v. Hawaii

1. *The holding.* What does the Court hold with respect to the establishment clause?

2. *The standard of review.* The President's comments are among the matters the Court says "inform" the standard of review. Is that standard "mere" rationality, rationality with bite, or something else? The Court identifies the Proclamation's facial neutrality, its inclusion of only 8 percent of the world's Muslim population, and the interagency process that produced the Proclamation as reasons supporting the Proclamation's rationality. Would those items be sufficient under "rationality with bite"?

3. *"Independent" justification.* The opinion says that the Court "will uphold the policy so long as it can reasonably be understood to result from a justification independent of unconstitutional grounds." Consider these possibilities: (1) The Court will uphold the policy if it would have been adopted even without the unconstitutional grounds (in this context, even if the President had never made his comments nor harbored impermissible motivations). (2) The Court will uphold the policy if there exists a justification independent of the unconstitutional grounds. The possibilities differ in that the first asks about the actual decision-maker while the second asks about a hypothetical decision-maker. Which possibility seems more consistent with the facts of the case? Which is more consistent with the rationales for deference to the executive in the context of national-security related decisions?

4. *The nonendorsement principle.* Why does the Court not apply the nonendorsement principle? What principled basis, if any, is there for distinguishing between the "typical" establishment clause suit and this case? Are the "issues regarding the scope of

the constitutional right and the manner of proof" more "delicate" in this context than in the context of legislative prayers said to have been adopted for constitutionally impermissible reasons?

Page 1488.   At the end of section 2 of the Note, add the following:

2a. Espinoza v. Montana Dep't of Revenue, ___ U.S. ___ (2020): In 2015, the Montana legislature enacted a program giving a tax credit of up to $150 to taxpayers who donated money to a "student scholarship organization." Such organizations use the donations to support scholarship for children at private schools. The Montana Constitution contains a provision, "Aid prohibited to sectarian schools," which bars public agencies from making "direct or indirect appropriation[s] . . . for any sectarian purpose or to aid any church, school, academy or [other] institution controlled in whole or in part by any church, sect, or denomination." The Montana Supreme Court held that this provision barred donors from receiving the tax credit if they made their contributions to an organization that distributed the funds through scholarships given to students who attended religiously affiliated schools. Relying heavily on *Trinity Lutheran*, the Supreme Court reversed, holding that the state's application of its constitutional provision violated the Free Exercise Clause: Under the program donors who contributed to organizations that gave scholarships to students attending private schools not affiliated with religious organizations received the tax credit but those who contributed to organizations that gave scholarships to students attending religiously affiliated schools did not.

Chief Justice Roberts's opinion for the Court rejected the argument, based on Locke v. Davey, that the exclusion of religiously-affiliated schools from the program was permissible as a way of preventing state subsidies of "religious education." Locke v. Davey allowed the state to deny an otherwise available subsidy where the subsidy would have been used to support education specifically for use by those studying to become members of the clergy, which the Chief Justice characterized as a "religious use." He noted as well that "the propriety of state-supported clergy was a central subject of founding-era debates." The Montana program, in contrast, excluded religiously affiliated schools where religion might "permeate" the general curriculum but that did not use the money for religion as such. This was discrimination based on status, not use. And an examination of history showed no "'historic and substantial' tradition" supporting the state's practice.

Justice Thomas (joined by Justice Gorsuch), Justices Alito, and Justice Gorsuch wrote concurring opinions. Justice Gorsuch's opinion, like his separate opinion in *Trinity Lutheran*, expressed skepticism about the coherence and constitutional underpinnings of the Court's distinction between religious uses of funds ("acts") and religious status.

Justice Ginsburg, joined by Justice Kagan, dissented, as did Justice Breyer (joined in part by Justice Kagan) and Justice Sotomayor. Justice Breyer's dissent emphasized the "play in the joints" principle. That principle, he argued, allowed state legislatures and courts to deal with the many forms that government benefits take. "Does one detail affect one religion negatively and another positively? What about a religion that objects to the particular way in which the government seeks to enforce mandatory (say, qualification-related) provisions of a particular benefit program? Or the religious group that for religious reasons cannot accept government support? And what happens when qualification requirements mean that government money flows to one religion rather than another? Courts are ill-equipped to deal with such conflicts. Yet, in a Nation with scores of different religions, many such disagreements are possible." Pointing out that "many faith leaders emphasize the central role of schools to their religious missions," Justice Breyer argued that the state's refusal to fund religious education was more like the program upheld in Locke v. Davey than like the playground repaving program in *Trinity Lutheran*.

Espinosa appears to resolve affirmatively the question posed in the text of this Note asking whether voucher programs must allow their use in religiously affiliated schools.

Is funding public schools but not religiously affiliated private schools an impermissible form of discrimination? The Court's opinion says, "A State need not subsidize private education. But once a State decides to do so, it cannot disqualify some private schools solely because they are religious." Consider the following: *Espinosa* quoted a passage in *Trinity Lutheran* stating that the Free Exercise Clause "protects against even 'indirect coercion,'" and appeared to describe "disqualifying the religious from government aid" as "punish[ing] the free exercise of religion." Referring to parents' decisions to send their children to religious schools, the opinion also said, "the no-aid provision penalizes that decision by cutting families off from otherwise available benefits if they choose a religious private school rather than a secular one, and for no other reason." Do these observations imply that the use of public funds to support public schools but not religiously affiliated private schools violates the Free Exercise Clause? (In context, the reference to "a secular one" in the quoted passage clearly refers to secular private schools, but is there a principled basis for treating the choice between a religiously affiliated private school and a secular public one differently?)

C. *The Free Exercise Clause: Required Accommodations*

Page 1508. After the first paragraph of section 2 of the Note, add the following:

(aa) *What makes a law "general"?* Consider a regulation applicable to a range of activities, including religious ones such as church services, from which other activities are expressly exempted. This issue surfaced prominently as states and cities began to relax comprehensive "stay at home" policies in 2020 during the COVID-19 pandemic. Early stages of "reopening" allowed certain businesses, including golf courses, to operate subject to limits on the number of patrons who could be present at any time and to requirements of "social distancing," that is, requirements that patrons stay several feet away from each other. In some localities, though, churches were not part of the first stages of reopening and so could not lawfully conduct religious services even if they complied with limits on attendance and social distancing requirements.

(1) Should the court examine the reasons for exempting the non-religious activities from the regulation and determine whether those reasons are inapplicable to the religious activities? Suppose a "stay at home" regulation exempts a list of activities designated as "essential," including provision of medical services and selling food but not including religious services. Does doing so amount to express discrimination against religion in a way that the First Amendment prohibits?

Alternatively, consider a defense of the regulation and its exemptions on the basis of risk. In the pandemic case, risk-related characteristics include: whether the activity is conducted indoors or outdoors, how long participants are at the venue, the extent to which singing, shouting, and other actions leading to distribution of droplets from the mouth occur, the size of indoor venues, and the ability of organizers/businesses to control social distancing by participants/customers. Should the government have the burden of establishing that the overall risk from religious activities is greater than the overall risk for (each and every) activity that it exempts from its regulations? If so, by what standard should the government's regulations be assessed? Would it be sufficient if the government's assessment of the comparative risks was reasonable? Or should the exemption be extended to religious activities unless the government can show that the risks associated with those activities are "substantially" higher than those associated with the exempted activities?

Suppose the religious activities could be conducted in a way that satisfied the reasons for exempting the non-religious activities were they to comply with a different set of regulations. Would that make the regulation lack generality?

(2) Should the existence of *any* exemptions lead to a finding of lack of generality? The effect would be to require that religious activities be given "most favored nation" treatment — that is, allowed to occur on conditions no more stringent than those imposed on any non-religious activity.

For brief treatments of these questions see the opinions dealing with a stay application in South Bay Pentecostal Church v. Newsom, 140 S. Ct. 1613 (2020). Chief Justice Roberts, in voting to deny a stay against enforcing California's regulations, which did not exempt religious activities, appeared to adopt a risk-based analysis, writing, "Although California's guidelines place restrictions on places of worship, those restrictions appear consistent with the Free Exercise Clause of the First Amendment. Similar or more severe restrictions apply to comparable secular gatherings, including lectures, concerts, movie showings, spectator sports, and theatrical performances, where large groups of people gather in close proximity for extended periods of time. And the Order exempts or treats more leniently only dissimilar activities, such as operating grocery stores, banks, and laundromats, in which people neither congregate in large groups nor remain in close proximity for extended periods."

Justice Kavanaugh, who would have stayed the regulations, described the failure to provide an exemption as discrimination based on religion. He then asked whether the state had "a compelling justification for distinguishing between (i) religious worship services and (ii) the litany of other secular businesses that are not subject to an occupancy cap," and concluded that it had not provided such a justification because the "Church has agreed to abide by the State's rules that apply to comparable secular businesses," and, quoting from an opinion by the Court of Appeals for the Sixth Circuit, "Assuming all of the same precautions are taken, why can someone safely walk down a grocery store aisle but not a pew?"

Does this adopt the "most-favored-nation" approach? Do the two opinions use the word "comparable" to mean the same thing?

On these and related questions see Zalman Rothschild, "Free Exercise in a Pandemic," University of Chicago Law Review Online, https://lawreviewblog.uchicago.edu/2020/06/10/free-exercise-pandemic/.

(3) *Smith* appears to hold that finding a regulation not to be general subjects the regulation to a *Sherbert*-like test to determine whether the application of the regulation to religious activities serves a compelling interest in a narrowly tailored way. In light of the foregoing analysis of the reasons for finding a regulation not general, could such a test ever be satisfied? Consider exemptions from "stay at home" orders for "essential" services. Even if the First Amendment bars the government from treating religious activities as "non-essential," could the government nonetheless apply the "stay at home" orders to such activities because doing so satisfies a *Sherbert*-like test by applying a risk-based analysis?

(4) Would the analysis differ if, rather than exempting specified activities, the regulation enumerated those activities, including religious ones, to which it applied?

Page 1509.   After note 3, add the following:

4. Tandon v. Newsom, 141 S.Ct. 1294 (2021): California limited in-house gatherings to three households, no matter what the purpose (including religious worship). "California treats some comparable secular activities more favorably than at-home religious exercise, permitting hair salons, retail stores, personal care services, movie theaters, private suites at sporting events and concerts, and indoor restaurants to bring together more than three households at a time." The Court in a per curiam opinion holding that the lower court should have granted an injunction against the limitation on religious gatherings, enumerated three principles.

First, government regulations are not neutral and generally applicable, and therefore trigger strict scrutiny under the Free Exercise Clause, whenever they treat *any* comparable secular activity more favorably than religious exercise. It is no answer that a State treats some comparable secular businesses or other activities as poorly as or even less favorably than the religious exercise at issue.

Second, whether two activities are comparable for purposes of the Free Exercise Clause must be judged against the asserted government interest that justifies the regulation at issue. Comparability is concerned with the risks various activities pose, not the reasons why people gather.

Third, the government has the burden to establish that the challenged law satisfies strict scrutiny. To do so in this context, it must do more than assert that certain risk factors "are always present in worship, or always absent from the other secular activities" the government may allow. Instead, narrow tailoring requires the government to show that measures less restrictive of the First Amendment activity could not address its interest in reducing the spread of COVID. Where the government permits other activities to proceed with precautions, it must show that the religious exercise at issue is more dangerous than those activities even when the same precautions are applied. Otherwise, precautions that suffice for other activities suffice for religious exercise too.

Consider the application of these principles to other contexts. Suppose that, in an effort to discourage automobile congestion and to encourage use of public transportation in its downtown, a city restricts the number of parking spaces all businesses and religious institutions can provide in that neighborhood, while allowing more parking spaces to be provided by business and religious institutions in less dense neighborhoods. Does the more generous treatment in outer neighborhoods trigger the requirement of strict scrutiny?

If so, what considerations are relevant to determining whether the restriction satisfies strict scrutiny? In *Tandon*, Justice Kagan's dissent observed that the court of appeals noted that "when people gather in social settings, their interactions are likely to be longer than they would be in a commercial setting," with participants "more likely to be involved in prolonged conversations," that "private houses are typically smaller and less ventilated than commercial establishments," and that "social distancing and mask-wearing are less likely in private settings and enforcement is more difficult." These reasons were insufficient, in the majority's implicit view, to satisfy the requirements of strict scrutiny.

5. Fulton v. City of Philadelphia, ___ S.Ct. ___ (2021), dealt with the constitutionality of a provision in the city's contracts with foster care providers: "Rejection of referral. Provider shall not reject a child or family including, but not limited to, . . . prospective foster parents or adoptive parents, for Services based . . . upon . . . their sexual orientation . . . unless an exception is granted by the Commissioner or the Commissioner's designee, in his/her sole discretion." The city declined to enter into a contract with Catholic Social Services because CSS would not agree to refer children to same-sex couples. Chief Justice Roberts, writing for the Court, held that the power to grant an exception authorized "individualized determinations" under *Smith*. For that reason the provision was "subject to 'the most rigorous of scrutiny.'" The Court found the interests the city asserted "insufficient." "Maximizing the number of foster families and minimizing liability are important goals, but the City fails to show that granting CSS an exception will put those goals at risk. If anything, including CSS in the program seems likely to increase, not reduce, the number of available foster parents." The city's concern for liability was speculative. The city's interest "in the equal treatment of prospective foster parents and foster children [is] a weighty one," but "[the] creation of a system of exceptions [undermines] the City's contention that its non-discrimination policies can brook not departures. The City offers no compelling reason why it has a

particular interest in denying an exception to CSS while making them available to others." (Note that the record apparently did not show that the City had granted any exceptions from the general non-discrimination policy expressed in the contract provision.)

Justice Alito, joined by Justices Thomas and Gorsuch, argued that the city could redraft the contract provision to drop the provision allowing discretionary exceptions, leaving CSS ineligible for a contract and in a position to challenge the exclusion once again. Consider whether the city might include the provision because it has concerns that some unexpected events might lead it to want to exercise a power to make exceptions even though no such circumstances have yet arisen. Justice Gorsuch, dissenting, joined by Justices Thomas and Alito, disagreed with the Court's interpretation of state and local law, and would have found the ordinance unconstitutional as applied to Catholic Social Services.

Justice Alito, noting that "five sitting Justices" had "called for Smith to be reexamined," also argued that the decision should be overruled. Justice Barrett, while agreeing that "the textual and structural arguments against Smith are "compelling," asked, "What should replace Smith? The prevailing assumption seems to be that strict scrutiny would apply whenever a neutral and generally applicable law burdens religious exercise. Yet I am skeptical about swapping Smith's categorical antidiscrimination approach for an equally categorical struct scrutiny regime, particularly when this Court's resolution of conflicts between generally applicable laws and other First Amendment rights—like speech and assembly—has been much more nuanced." Among the "issues to work through" were these: "Should entities like Catholic Social Services [be] treated differently than individuals? Should there be a distinction between indirect and direct burdens on religious exercises? And if the answer is strict scrutiny, would pre-Smith cases rejecting free exercise challenges to garden-variety laws come out the same way?" Justice Kavanaugh joined Justice Barrett in full; Justice Breyer joined her opinion except for the paragraph criticizing Smith.

D. Permissible Accommodation

Page 1519. After section 3 of the Note, add the following:

MASTERPIECE CAKESHOP LTD. v. COLORADO CIVIL RIGHTS COMM'N, 138 S. Ct. 1719 (2018). After Masterpiece Cakeshop refused to provide a cake to celebrate the out-of-state wedding of a gay couple because of the owner Jack Phillips's religious opposition to same-sex marriage, the Colorado Civil Rights Commission found that the owner had violated the state's anti-discrimination act, which prohibits discrimination based on sexual orientation in a "place of business engaged in any sales to the public. . . ." The Supreme Court reversed the state appeals court's decision upholding the finding of a violation, relying on *Lukumi*.

Writing for the Court, Justice Kennedy said, "The Court's precedents make clear that the baker, in his capacity as the owner of a business serving the public, might have his right to the free exercise of religion limited by generally applicable laws. Still, the delicate question of when the free exercise of his religion must yield to an otherwise valid exercise of state power needed to be determined in an adjudication in which religious hostility on the part of the State itself would not be a factor in the balance the State sought to reach. When the Colorado Civil Rights Commission considered this case, it did not do so with the religious neutrality that the Constitution requires."

That neutrality "was compromised" in several ways. "One commissioner suggested that Phillips can believe 'what he wants to believe,' but cannot act on his religious beliefs 'if he decided to do business in the state.' . . . Standing alone, [this statement] might mean simply that a business cannot refuse to provide services based on sexual orientation, regardless of the proprietor's personal views. On the other hand, [it] might be seen as inappropriate as dismissive [showing] lack of due consideration for

Phillips' free exercise rights and the dilemma he faced. In view of the comments that followed, the latter seems the more likely." Two months later, another commissioner stated, "Freedom of religion and religion has been used to justify all kinds of discrimination throughout history, whether it be slavery, whether it be the holocaust. [And] to me it is one of the most despicable pieces of rhetoric that people can use to [use] their religion to hurt others." Justice Kennedy observed, "To describe a man's faith as 'one of the most despicable pieces of rhetoric that people can use' is to disparage his religion in at least two distinct ways: by describing it as despicable, and also by characterizing it as merely rhetorical. [The] commissioner even went so far as to compare Phillips' invocation and sincerely held religious believes to defenses of slavery and the Holocaust. This sentiment is inappropriate for a Commission charged with the solemn responsibility of fair and neutral enforcement of Colorado's anti-discrimination law." . . .

"Another indication of hostility is the difference in treatment between Phillips' case and the cases of other bakers who objected to a requested case on the basis of conscience and prevailed before the Commission." Those cases involved bakers who refused "to create cakes with images that conveyed disapproval of same-sex marriage, along with religious text. Each time, the [Commission] found that the baker acted lawfully [because] the requested cake including 'wording and images [the baker] deemed derogatory. . . .'"

According to the Court, "the Commission was obliged [to] proceed in a manner neutral toward and tolerant of Phillips' religious beliefs. [Phillips] was entitled to a neutral decisionmaker who would give full and fair consideration to his religious objection as he sought to assert it in all of the circumstances in which this case was presented, considered, and decided."

Justice Kagan, joined by Justice Breyer, concurred. Referring to the treatment of the bakers who refused to provide cakes disapproving same-sex marriage, she wrote, "the bakers did not single out [the customer] because of his religion, but instead treated him in the same way they would have treated anyone else." Justice

Gorsuch, joined by Justice Alito, concurred as well, but disagreed with Justice Kagan's characterization of the other bakers' actions: "In both cases, the effect on the customer was the same: bakers refused service to persons who bore a statutorily protected trait (religious faith and sexual orientation.) But in both cases the bakers refused service intending only to honor a personal conviction." Justice Thomas, joined by Justice Gorsuch, wrote a concurring opinion addressing the free speech claims Phillips advanced.

Justice Ginsburg, joined by Justice Sotomayor, dissented, finding that the matters the Court referred to "do not evidence hostility to religion of the kind we have previously held to signal a free-exercise violation." With respect to the others bakers' actions, "Change [Phillips's customers'] sexual orientation (or sex), and Phillips would have provided the cake. Change [the religion of the customer requesting cakes with derogatory messages] and the bakers would have been no more willing to comply with his request."

Note: The Implications of Masterpiece Cakeshop

1. *Evidence of hostility.* What standard does the Court use to determine that the Commission's actions were hostile to religion? Are the comments of the two Commissioners, which the Court observed were not repudiated by other Commissioners or the state court, susceptible of a non-hostile interpretation? What about the Commission's actions with respect to the bakers who refused to provide cakes with messages they deemed derogatory? In Trump v. Hawaii, 138 S. Ct. 2392 (2018), the Court held that comments by President Trump indicating hostility to Muslims affected the standard of review it applied to determine whether an executive order restricting entry into the United States by citizens of certain specified nations was constitutionally permissible. (The case is discussed at the supplement to page 1487 of the Main Volume.)

2. *The requirement of neutral and respectful consideration of Phillips's claim.* Suppose the Commission rejected Phillips's

claim with an opinion saying, "We have deep respect for your convictions, but the state's anti-discrimination law is completely general and does not authorize us to make any exceptions to accommodate sincerely held religious beliefs." What result under *Smith*? Suppose the two Commissioners (out of five) made the comments cited by the Court, to support their assertion that it was a good policy for the anti-discrimination law to deny the Commission the authority to make exceptions. What result under *Smith*?

3. *The relevance of the finding that bakers who refused to provide cakes with derogatory messages were not held to violate the anti-discrimination law.* Does the Commission's refusal find that the bakers who refused to provide cakes with what they regarded as derogatory messages show that the Colorado statute did authorize the Commission to make exceptions to the statute? If so, shouldn't that trigger the *Smith* exception for the unemployment cases, and bring into play not a requirement of respectful consideration but the Sherbert v. Verner requirement that the state's interest be "compelling"? Alternatively, does the Commission's refusal show that the statute does not authorize exemptions but merely does not extend to refusals to provide service based on the business owner's judgments about derogatoriness, that is, refusals based on some ground not protected under the statute?

4. *Third-party harms.* The Court has not yet decided under what circumstances anti-discrimination laws must accommodate claims that discrimination — usually against LGBTQ people, but sometimes against racial and other minorities — is mandated by religious belief. (Burwell v. Hobby Lobby, 573 U.S. 682 (2014), held that such an accommodation, with respect to a requirement that employers provide access to contraceptive services, was required by the federal Religious Freedom Restoration Act.)

A central issue in the analysis of such claims is to what extent avoiding harms to third parties, whether material or dignitary, is an interest of sufficient magnitude to justify the impairment of religious belief antidiscrimination requirements cause. (Would any accommodations survive a test according to which the presence of any harm to third parties is sufficient to make an accommodation unconstitutional?) Hobby Lobby described the interest in avoiding racial discrimination as compelling, but expressed no view on the interest in avoiding other forms of discrimination. For a range of scholarly views on this question, see Barclay, First Amendment Categories of Harm, 95 Indiana L.J. (forthcoming 2020); Storslee, Religious Accommodation, the Establishment Clause, and Third-Party Harm, 86 U. Chi. L. Rev. 871 (2019); Simson, Permissible Accommodation or Impermissible Endorsement? A Proposed Approach to Religious Exemptions and the Establishment Clause, 106 Kentucky L.J. 535 (2017-2018); Lund, Religious Exemptions, Third Party Harms, and the Establishment Clause, 91 Notre Dame L. Rev. 1375 (2016).

E.   *Free Exercise, Free Speech, and the Right of Expressive Association*

Page 1522.   At the end of the description of *Hosanna-Tabor*, add the following:

The Supreme Court elaborated on the test for determining what positions qualify for the ministerial exemption in Our Lady of Guadalupe School v. Morrisey-Beru, ___U.S. ___ (2020) (holding that teachers at religiously affiliated schools whose employers regard them as having "a vital role in carrying out the church's mission" qualify for the ministerial exemption).

Bostock v. Clayton County, ___ U.S. ___ (2020), held that the federal statutory prohibition on employment discrimination based on sex encompassed discrimination based upon sexual orientation and sexual identity. Justice Gorsuch's opinion mentioned the ministerial exemption cases and the federal Religious Freedom Restoration Act, which he described as "a kind of super statute," and observed, "[How] these doctrines protecting religious liberty interact with Title VII are questions for future cases."

IX
STATE ACTION, BASELINES, AND THE PROBLEM OF PRIVATE POWER

D. Constitutionally Required Departures from Neutrality

Page 1579.   Before Jackson, add the following:

MANHATTAN COMMUNITY ACCESS CORPORATION v. HALLECK

---

139 S. Ct. 1921 (2019)

JUSTICE KAVANAUGH delivered the opinion of the Court.

The Free Speech Clause of the First Amendment constrains governmental actors and protects private actors. To draw the line between governmental and private, this Court applies what is known as the state-action doctrine. Under that doctrine, as relevant here, a private entity may be considered a state actor when it exercises a function "traditionally exclusively reserved to the

State." Jackson v. Metropolitan Edison Co., 419 U.S. 345, 352, 95 S. Ct. 449, 42 L. Ed. 2d 477 (1974).

This state-action case concerns the public access channels on Time Warner's cable system in Manhattan. Public access channels are available for private citizens to use. The public access channels on Time Warner's cable system in Manhattan are operated by a private nonprofit corporation known as MNN. The question here is whether MNN — even though it is a private entity — nonetheless is a state actor when it operates the public access channels. In other words, is operation of public access channels on a cable system a traditional, exclusive public function? If so, then the First Amendment would restrict MNN's exercise of editorial discretion over the speech and speakers on the public access channels.

Under the state-action doctrine as it has been articulated and applied by our precedents, we conclude that operation of public access channels on a cable system is not a traditional, exclusive public function. Moreover, a private entity such as MNN who opens its property for speech by others is not transformed by that fact alone into a state actor. In operating the public access channels, MNN is a private actor, not a state actor, and MNN therefore is not subject to First Amendment constraints on its editorial discretion. We reverse in relevant part the judgment of the Second Circuit, and we remand the case for further proceedings consistent with this opinion.

I

A

Since the 1970s, public access channels have been a regular feature on cable television systems throughout the United States. In the 1970s, Federal Communications Commission regulations required certain cable operators to set aside channels on their cable systems for public access. In 1979, however, this Court ruled that the FCC lacked statutory authority to impose that mandate. See FCC v. Midwest Video Corp., 440 U.S. 689, 99 S. Ct. 1435, 59 L. Ed. 2d 692 (1979). A few years later, Congress passed and

President Reagan signed the Cable Communications Policy Act of 1984. 98 Stat. 2779. The Act authorized state and local governments to require cable operators to set aside channels on their cable systems for public access.

The New York State Public Service Commission regulates cable franchising in New York State and requires cable operators in the State to set aside channels on their cable systems for public access. 16 N.Y. Codes, Rules & Regs. §§ 895.1(f), 895.4(b) (2018). State law requires that use of the public access channels be free of charge and first-come, first-served. §§ 895.4(c)(4) and (6). Under state law, the cable operator operates the public access *1927 channels unless the local government in the area chooses to itself operate the channels or designates a private entity to operate the channels. § 895.4(c)(1).

Time Warner (now known as Charter) operates a cable system in Manhattan. Under state law, Time Warner must set aside some channels on its cable system for public access. New York City (the City) has designated a private nonprofit corporation named Manhattan Neighborhood Network, commonly referred to as MNN, to operate Time Warner's public access channels in Manhattan. This case involves a complaint against MNN regarding its management of the public access channels.

B

. . . DeeDee Halleck and Jesus Papoleto Melendez produced public access programming in Manhattan. They made a film about MNN's alleged neglect of the East Harlem community. Halleck submitted the film to MNN for airing on MNN's public access channels, and MNN later televised the film. Afterwards, MNN fielded multiple complaints about the film's content. In response, MNN temporarily suspended Halleck from using the public access channels.

Halleck and Melendez soon became embroiled in another dispute with MNN staff. In the wake of that dispute, MNN ultimately suspended Halleck and Melendez from all MNN services and facilities.

283

Halleck and Melendez then sued MNN, among other parties, in Federal District Court. The two producers claimed that MNN violated their First Amendment free-speech rights when MNN restricted their access to the public access channels because of the content of their film. . . . We granted certiorari to resolve disagreement among the Courts of Appeals on the question whether private operators of public access cable channels are state actors subject to the First Amendment.

II

Ratified in 1791, the First Amendment provides in relevant part that "Congress shall make no law . . . abridging the freedom of speech." Ratified in 1868, the Fourteenth Amendment makes the First Amendment's Free Speech Clause applicable against the States: "No State shall make or enforce any law which shall abridge the privileges or immunities of citizens of the United States; nor shall any State deprive any person of life, liberty, or property, without due process of law. . . ." § 1. The text and original meaning of those Amendments, as well as this Court's longstanding precedents, establish that the Free Speech Clause prohibits only governmental abridgment of speech. The Free Speech Clause does not prohibit private abridgment of speech.

In accord with the text and structure of the Constitution, this Court's state-action doctrine distinguishes the government from individuals and private entities. By enforcing that constitutional boundary between the governmental and the private, the state-action doctrine protects a robust sphere of individual liberty.

Here, the producers claim that MNN, a private entity, restricted their access to MNN's public access channels because of the content of the producers' film. The producers have advanced a First Amendment claim against MNN. The threshold problem with that First Amendment claim is a fundamental one: MNN is a private entity.

Relying on this Court's state-action precedents, the producers assert that MNN is nonetheless a state actor subject to First

284

Amendment constraints on its editorial discretion. Under this Court's cases, a private entity can qualify as a state actor in a few limited circumstances — including, for example, (i) when the private entity performs a traditional, exclusive public function, see, e.g., Jackson, 419 U.S. at 352-354, 95 S. Ct. 449; (ii) when the government compels the private entity to take a particular action, see, e.g., Blum v. Yaretsky, 457 U.S. 991, 1004-1005, 102 S. Ct. 2777, 73 L. Ed. 2d 534 (1982); or (iii) when the government acts jointly with the private entity, see, e.g., Lugar v. Edmondson Oil Co., 457 U.S. 922, 941-942, 102 S. Ct. 2744, 73 L. Ed. 2d 482 (1982).

The producers' primary argument here falls into the first category: The producers contend that MNN exercises a traditional, exclusive public function when it operates the public access channels on Time Warner's cable system in Manhattan. We disagree.

A

Under the Court's cases, a private entity may qualify as a state actor when it exercises "powers traditionally exclusively reserved to the State." It is not enough that the federal, state, or local government exercised the function in the past, or still does. And it is not enough that the function serves the public good or the public interest in some way. Rather, to qualify as a traditional, exclusive public function within the meaning of our state-action precedents, the government must have traditionally and exclusively performed the function.

The Court has stressed that "very few" functions fall into that category. Under the Court's cases, those functions include, for example, running elections and operating a company town. The Court has ruled that a variety of functions do not fall into that category, including, for example: running sports associations and leagues, administering insurance payments, operating nursing homes, providing special education, representing indigent criminal defendants, resolving private disputes, and supplying electricity.

The relevant function in this case is operation of public access channels on a cable system. That function has not traditionally and exclusively been performed by government. Since the 1970s, when public access channels became a regular feature on cable systems, a variety of private and public actors have operated public access channels, including: private cable operators; private nonprofit organizations; municipalities; and other public and private community organizations such as churches, schools, and libraries.

The history of public access channels in Manhattan further illustrates the point. In 1971, public access channels first started operating in Manhattan. See D. Brenner, M. Price, & M. Meyerson, Cable Television and Other Nonbroadcast Video § 6:29, pp. 6-47 (2018). Those early Manhattan public access channels were operated in large *1930 part by private cable operators, with some help from private nonprofit organizations. See G. Gillespie, Public Access Cable Television in the United States and Canada 37-38 (1975); Janes, History and Structure of Public Access Television, 39 J. Film & Video, No. 3, pp. 15-17 (1987). Those private cable operators continued to operate the public access channels until the early 1990s, when MNN (also a private entity) began to operate the public access channels.

In short, operating public access channels on a cable system is not a traditional, exclusive public function within the meaning of this Court's cases.

B

To avoid that conclusion, the producers widen the lens and contend that the relevant function here is not simply the operation of public access channels on a cable system, but rather is more generally the operation of a public forum for speech. And according to the producers, operation of a public forum for speech is a traditional, exclusive public function.

That analysis mistakenly ignores the threshold state-action question. When the government provides a forum for speech (known as a public forum), the government may be constrained by the First Amendment, meaning that the government ordinarily may not exclude speech or speakers from the forum on the basis

286

of viewpoint, or sometimes even on the basis of content. See, e.g., Southeastern Promotions, Ltd. v. Conrad, 420 U.S. 546, 547, 555, 95 S. Ct. 1239, 43 L. Ed. 2d 448 (1975) (private theater leased to the city); Police Dept. of Chicago v. Mosley, 408 U.S. 92, 93, 96, 92 S. Ct. 2286, 33 L. Ed. 2d 212 (1972) (sidewalks); Hague v. Committee for Industrial Organization, 307 U.S. 496, 515-516, 59 S. Ct. 954, 83 L. Ed. 1423 (1939) (streets and parks).

By contrast, when a private entity provides a forum for speech, the private entity is not ordinarily constrained by the First Amendment because the private entity is not a state actor. The private entity may thus exercise editorial discretion over the speech and speakers in the forum. This Court so ruled in its 1976 decision in Hudgens v. NLRB. There, the Court held that a shopping center owner is not a state actor subject to First Amendment requirements such as the public forum doctrine. 424 U.S. at 520-521, 96 S. Ct. 1029; see also Lloyd Corp. v. Tanner, 407 U.S. 551, 569-570, 92 S. Ct. 2219, 33 L. Ed. 2d 131 (1972); Central Hardware Co. v. NLRB, 407 U.S. 539, 547, 92 S. Ct. 2238, 33 L. Ed. 2d 122 (1972); Alliance for Community Media, 56 F. 3d at 121-123.

The Hudgens decision reflects a commonsense principle: Providing some kind of forum for speech is not an activity that only governmental entities have traditionally performed. Therefore, a private entity who provides a forum for speech is not transformed by that fact alone into a state actor. After all, private property owners and private lessees often open their property for speech. Grocery stores put up community bulletin boards. Comedy clubs host open mic nights. As Judge Jacobs persuasively explained, it "is not at all a near-exclusive function of the state to provide the forums for public expression, politics, information, or entertainment." 882 F.3d at 311 (opinion concurring in part and dissenting in part).

In short, merely hosting speech by others is not a traditional, exclusive public function and does not alone transform private entities into state actors subject to First Amendment constraints.

If the rule were otherwise, all private property owners and private lessees who open their property for speech would be subject to First Amendment constraints and would lose the ability to exercise what they deem to be appropriate editorial discretion within that open forum. Private property owners and private lessees would face the unappetizing choice of allowing all comers or closing the platform altogether. . . . The Constitution does not disable private property owners and private lessees from exercising editorial discretion over speech and speakers on their property.

C

Next, the producers retort that this case differs from Hudgens because New York City has designated MNN to operate the public access channels on Time Warner's cable system, and because New York State heavily regulates MNN with respect to the public access channels. Under this Court's cases, however, those facts do not establish that MNN is a state actor.

New York City's designation of MNN to operate the public access channels is analogous to a government license, a government contract, or a government-granted monopoly. But as the Court has long held, the fact that the government licenses, contracts with, or grants a monopoly to a private entity does not convert the private entity into a state actor—unless the private entity is performing a traditional, exclusive public function. The same principle applies if the government funds or subsidizes a private entity.

Numerous private entities in America obtain government licenses, government contracts, or government-granted monopolies. If those facts sufficed to transform a private entity into a state actor, a large swath of private entities in America would suddenly be turned into state actors and be subject to a variety of constitutional constraints on their activities. As this Court's many state-action cases amply demonstrate, that is not the law. Here, therefore, the City's designation of MNN to operate the public access channels on Time Warner's cable system does not make MNN a state actor.

So, too, New York State's extensive regulation of MNN's operation of the public access channels does not make MNN a state actor. Under the State's regulations, air time on the public access channels must be free, and programming must be aired on a first-come, first-served basis. Those regulations restrict MNN's editorial discretion and in effect require MNN to operate almost like a common carrier. But under this Court's cases, those restrictions do not render MNN a state actor.

In Jackson v. Metropolitan Edison Co., the leading case on point, the Court stated that the "fact that a business is subject to state regulation does not by itself convert its action into that of the State." In that case, the Court held that "a heavily regulated, privately owned utility, enjoying at least a partial monopoly in the providing of electrical service within its territory," was not a state actor. The Court explained that the "mere existence" of a "regulatory scheme"—even if "extensive and detailed"—did not render the utility a state actor. Nor did it matter whether the State had authorized the utility to provide electric service to the community, or whether the utility was the only entity providing electric service to much of that community.

This case closely parallels Jackson. Like the electric utility in Jackson, MNN is "a heavily regulated, privately owned" entity. As in Jackson, the regulations do not transform the regulated private entity into a state actor.

Put simply, being regulated by the State does not make one a state actor As the Court's cases have explained, the "being heavily regulated makes you a state actor" theory of state action is entirely circular and would significantly endanger individual liberty and private enterprise. The theory would be especially problematic in the speech context, because it could eviscerate certain private entities' rights to exercise editorial control over speech and speakers on their properties or platforms. . . .

In sum, we conclude that MNN is not subject to First Amendment constraints on how it exercises its editorial discretion with respect to the public access channels. To be sure, MNN is subject to state-law constraints on its editorial discretion (assuming those state laws do not violate a federal statute or the Constitution). If MNN violates those state laws, or violates any applicable contracts, MNN could perhaps face state-law sanctions or liability of some kind. We of course take no position on any potential state-law questions. We simply conclude that MNN, as a private actor, is not subject to First Amendment constraints on how it exercises editorial discretion over the speech and speakers on its public access channels.

III

Perhaps recognizing the problem with their argument that MNN is a state actor under ordinary state-action principles applicable to private entities and private property, the producers alternatively contend that the public access channels are actually the property of New York City, not the property of Time Warner or MNN. On this theory, the producers say (and the dissent agrees) that MNN is in essence simply managing government property on behalf of New York City.

The short answer to that argument is that the public access channels are not the property of New York City. Nothing in the record here suggests that a government (federal, state, or city) owns or leases either the cable system or the public access channels at issue here. Both Time Warner and MNN are private entities. Time Warner is the cable operator, and it owns its cable network, which contains the public access channels. MNN operates those public access channels with its own facilities and equipment. The City does not own or lease the public access channels, and the City does not possess a formal easement or other property interest in those channels. The franchise agreements between the City and Time Warner do not say that the City has any property interest in the public access channels. On the contrary, the franchise agreements expressly place the public access channels "under the jurisdiction" of MNN. . . .

It does not matter that a provision in the franchise agreements between the City and Time Warner allowed the City to designate a private entity to operate the public access channels on Time Warner's cable system. Time Warner still owns the cable system. And MNN still operates the public access channels. To reiterate, nothing in the franchise agreements suggests that the City possesses any property interest in Time Warner's cable system, or in the public access channels on that system.

It is true that the City has allowed the cable operator, Time Warner, to lay cable along public rights-of-way in the City. But Time Warner's access to public rights-of-way does not alter the state-action analysis. For Time Warner, as for other cable operators, access to public rights-of-way is essential to lay cable and construct a physical cable infrastructure. But the same is true for utility providers, such as the electric utility in Jackson. Put simply, a private entity's permission from government to use public rights-of-way does not render that private entity a state actor.

Having said all that, our point here should not be read too broadly. Under the laws in certain States, including New York, a local government may decide to itself operate the public access channels on a local cable system (as many local governments in New York State and around the country already do), or could take appropriate steps to obtain a property interest in the public access channels. Depending on the circumstances, the First Amendment might then constrain the local government's operation of the public access channels. We decide only the case before us in light of the record before us.

* * *

It is sometimes said that the bigger the government, the smaller the individual. Consistent with the text of the Constitution, the state-action doctrine enforces a critical boundary between the government and the individual, and thereby protects a robust sphere of individual liberty. Expanding the state-action doctrine beyond its traditional boundaries would expand governmental control while restricting individual liberty and private enterprise. We decline to do so in this case.

MNN is a private entity that operates public access channels on a cable system. Operating public access channels on a cable system is not a traditional, exclusive public function. A private entity such as MNN who opens its property for speech by others is not transformed by that fact alone into a state actor. Under the text of the Constitution and our precedents, MNN is not a state actor subject to the First Amendment. We reverse in relevant part the judgment of the Second Circuit, and we remand the case for further proceedings consistent with this opinion.

It is so ordered.

JUSTICE SOTOMAYOR, with whom JUSTICE GINSBURG, JUSTICE BREYER, and JUSTICE KAGAN join, dissenting.

The Court tells a very reasonable story about a case that is not before us. I write to address the one that is.

This is a case about an organization appointed by the government to administer a constitutional public forum. (It is not, as the Court suggests, about a private property owner that simply opened up its property to others.) New York City (the City) secured a property interest in public-access television channels when it granted a cable franchise to a cable company. State regulations require those public-access channels to be made open to the public on terms that render them a public forum. The City contracted out the administration of that forum to a private organization, petitioner Manhattan Community Access Corporation (MNN). By accepting that agency relationship, MNN stepped into the City's shoes and thus qualifies as a state actor, subject to the First Amendment like any other. . . .

Years ago, New York City (no longer a party to this suit) and Time Warner Entertainment Company (never a party to this suit) entered into a cable-franchise agreement. App. 22. Time Warner received a cable franchise; the City received public-access channels. The agreement also provided that the public-access channels would be operated by an independent, nonprofit corporation chosen by the Manhattan borough president. But the City, as the practice of other New York municipalities confirms, could have instead chosen to run the channels itself.

MNN is the independent nonprofit that the borough president appointed to run the channels; indeed, MNN appears to have been incorporated in 1991 for that precise purpose, with seven initial board members selected by the borough president (though only two thus selected today). The City arranged for MNN to receive startup capital from Time Warner and to be funded through franchise fees from Time Warner and other Manhattan cable franchisees. As the borough president announced upon MNN's formation in 1991, MNN's "central charge is to administer and manage all the public access channels of the cable television systems in Manhattan."

. . . The channels are clearly a public forum: The City has a property interest in them, and New York regulations require that access to those channels be kept open to all. And because the City (1) had a duty to provide that public forum once it granted a cable franchise and (2) had a duty to abide by the First Amendment once it provided that forum, those obligations did not evaporate when the City delegated the administration of that forum to a private entity. Just as the City would have been subject to the First Amendment had it chosen to run the forum itself, MNN assumed the same responsibility when it accepted the delegation. . . .

This Court has not defined precisely what kind of governmental property interest (if any) is necessary for a public forum to exist. I assume for the sake of argument in this case that public-forum analysis is inappropriate where the government lacks a "significant property interest consistent with the communicative purpose of the forum."

Such an interest is present here. As described above, New York State required the City to obtain public-access channels from Time Warner in exchange for awarding a cable franchise. See supra, at 1934-1935. The exclusive right to use these channels (and, as necessary, Time Warner's infrastructure) qualifies as a property interest, akin at the very least to an easement. . . .

As noted above, there is no disputing that Time Warner owns the wires themselves. See Turner, 512 U.S. at 628, 114 S. Ct. 2445. If the wires were a road, it would be easy to define the public's right to walk on it as an easement. See, e.g., In re India Street, 29 N.Y.2d 97, 100-103, 324 N.Y.S.2d 1, 272 N.E.2d 518,

518-520 (1971). Similarly, if the wires were a theater, there would be no question that a government's long-term lease to use it would be sufficient for public-forum purposes. Southeastern Promotions, 420 U.S. at 547, 555, 95 S. Ct. 1239. But some may find this case more complicated because the wires are not a road or a theater that one can physically occupy; they are a conduit for transmitting signals that appear as television channels. In other words, the question is how to understand the right to place content on those channels using those wires.

The right to convey expressive content using someone else's physical infrastructure is not new. To give another low-tech example, imagine that one company owns a billboard and another rents space on that billboard. The renter can have a property interest in placing content on the billboard for the lease term even though it does not own the billboard itself.

The same principle should operate in this higher tech realm. Just as if the channels were a billboard, the City obtained rights for exclusive use of the channels by the public for the foreseeable future; no one is free to take the channels away, short of a contract renegotiation. The City also obtained the right to administer, or delegate the administration of, the channels. The channels are more intangible than a billboard, but no one believes that a right must be tangible to qualify as a property interest. And it is hardly unprecedented for a government to receive a right to transmit something over a private entity's infrastructure in exchange for conferring something of value on that private entity; examples go back at least as far as the 1800s. . . .

With the question of a governmental property interest resolved, it should become clear that the public-access channels are a public forum. Outside of classic examples like sidewalks and parks, a public forum exists only where the government has deliberately opened up the setting for speech by at least a subset of the public. "Accordingly, the Court has looked to the policy and practice of the government," as well as the nature of the property itself, "to ascertain whether it intended to designate a place not traditionally open to assembly and debate as a public forum." For example, a state college might make its facilities open to student groups, or a municipality might open up an auditorium for certain public meetings.

The requisite governmental intent is manifest here. As noted above, New York State regulations require that the channels be made available to the public "on a first-come, first-served, non-discriminatory basis." 16 N.Y. Codes, Rules & Regs. § 895.4(c) (4); see also §§ 895.4(c)(8)-(9). The State, in other words, mandates that the doors be wide open for public expression. MNN's contract with Time Warner follows suit. App. 23. And that is essentially how MNN itself describes things. See Tr. of Oral Arg. 9 ("We do not prescreen videos. We—they come into the door. We put them on the air"). These regulations "evidenc[e] a clear intent to create a public forum." .

If New York's public-access channels are a public forum, it follows that New York cannot evade the First Amendment by contracting out administration of that forum to a private agent. When MNN took on the responsibility of administering the *1940 forum, it stood in the City's shoes and became a state actor . . .

Not all acts of governmental delegation necessarily trigger constitutional obligations, but this one did. New York State regulations required the City to secure public-access channels if it awarded a cable franchise. 16 N.Y. Codes, Rules & Regs. § 895.4(b)(1). The City did award a cable franchise. The State's regulations then required the City to make the channels it obtained available on a "first-come, first-served, nondiscriminatory basis." *1941 § 895.4(c)(4). That made the channels a public forum. See supra, at 1938-1939. Opening a public forum, in turn, entailed First Amendment obligations.

The City could have done the job itself, but it instead delegated that job to a private entity, MNN. MNN could have said no, but it said yes. (Indeed, it appears to exist entirely to do this job.) By accepting the job, MNN accepted the City's responsibilities. See West, 487 U.S. at 55, 108 S. Ct. 2250. The First Amendment does not fall silent simply because a government hands off the administration of its constitutional duties to a private actor.

III

The majority acknowledges that the First Amendment could apply when a local government either (1) has a property interest in public-access channels or (2) is more directly involved in administration of those channels than the City is here. Ante, at 1933-1934. And it emphasizes that it "decide[s] only the case before us in light of the record before us." Ibid. These case-specific qualifiers sharply limit the immediate effect of the majority's decision, but that decision is still meaningfully wrong in two ways. First, the majority erroneously decides the property question against the plaintiffs as a matter of law. Second, and more fundamentally, the majority mistakes a case about the government choosing to hand off responsibility to an agent for a case about a private entity that simply enters a marketplace. . . .

This is not a case about bigger governments and smaller individuals, ante, at 1934; it is a case about principals and agents. New York City opened up a public forum on public-access channels in which it has a property interest. It asked MNN to run that public forum, and MNN accepted the job. That makes MNN subject to the First Amendment, just as if the City had decided to run the public forum itself.

While the majority emphasizes that its decision is narrow and factbound, that does not make it any less misguided. It is crucial that the Court does not continue to ignore the reality, fully recognized by our precedents, that private actors who have been delegated constitutional responsibilities like this one should be accountable to the Constitution's demands. I respectfully dissent.